THE NEAR-DEATH OF THE AUTHOR

Creativity in the Internet Age

In the modern world of networked digital media, authors must navigate many challenges. Most pressingly, the illegal downloading and streaming of copyright material on the internet deprives authors of royalties, and in some cases it has discouraged creativity or terminated careers. Exploring technology's impact on the status and idea of authorship in today's world, *The Near-Death of the Author* reveals the many obstacles facing contemporary authors.

John Potts details how the online culture of remix and creative reuse operates in a post-authorship mode, with little regard for individual authorship. The book explores how developments in algorithms and artificial intelligence (AI) have yielded novels, newspaper articles, musical works, films, and paintings without the need of human authors or artists. It also examines how these AI achievements have provoked questions regarding the authorship of new works, such as Does the author need to be human? And, more alarmingly, Is there even a need for human authors?

Providing suggestions on how contemporary authors can endure in the world of data, the book ultimately concludes that network culture has provoked the *near*-death, but not the *death*, of the author.

JOHN POTTS is a professor of media and the director of the Centre for Media History at Macquarie University.

The Near-Death of the Author

Creativity in the Internet Age

JOHN POTTS

UNIVERSITY OF TORONTO PRESS
Toronto Buffalo London

© University of Toronto Press 2023
Toronto Buffalo London
utorontopress.com

ISBN 978-1-4875-4134-7 (cloth)   ISBN 978-1-4875-4136-1 (EPUB)
ISBN 978-1-4875-4612-0 (paper)   ISBN 978-1-4875-4135-4 (PDF)

___

Library and Archives Canada Cataloguing in Publication

Title: The near-death of the author : creativity in the internet age / John Potts.
Names: Potts, John, 1959–, author.
Description: Includes bibliographical references and index.
Identifiers: Canadiana (print) 20220225508 | Canadiana (ebook) 20220225567 | ISBN 9781487541347 (cloth) | ISBN 9781487546120 (paper) | ISBN 9781487541361 (EPUB) | ISBN 9781487541354 (PDF)
Subjects: LCSH: Authorship – History. | LCSH: Creation (Literary, artistic, etc.) | LCSH: Disruptive technologies. | LCSH: Internet.
Classification: LCC PN145 .P68 2023 | DDC 808.02/09 – dc23

___

We wish to acknowledge the land on which the University of Toronto Press operates. This land is the traditional territory of the Wendat, the Anishnaabeg, the Haudenosaunee, the Métis, and the Mississaugas of the Credit First Nation.

This book has been published with the help of a grant from the Australian Research Council.

University of Toronto Press acknowledges the financial support of the Government of Canada, the Canada Council for the Arts, and the Ontario Arts Council, an agency of the Government of Ontario, for its publishing activities.

 Canada Council for the Arts   Conseil des Arts du Canada

 ONTARIO ARTS COUNCIL
CONSEIL DES ARTS DE L'ONTARIO
an Ontario government agency
un organisme du gouvernement de l'Ontario

Funded by the Government of Canada   Financé par le gouvernement du Canada

Contents

List of Figures vii

Acknowledgments ix

Introduction 3

1 "Heroes with Names": What Is the Author? 8

2 "I Don't Own It": Contemporary Complications 23

3 Who Is the Author / Who Are the Authors? 42

4 A Brief History of the Author 63

5 The Alleged Death of the Author: Post-structuralism and Postmodernism 93

6 The Author and Technology: Downloading vs. Copyright 108

7 Big Data Writing: Author as Algorithm 135

8 AI vs. the Author 146

9 "Creative Reuse": Post-authorship in Internet Culture 160

Epilogue: The Near-Death, Not the Death, of the Author 172

Notes 175

Bibliography 193

Index 205

Figures

2.1 Joseph Quilter aka WEI2, graffiti art   33
2.2 Justine Varga, *Maternal Line*, 2017, chromogenic photograph, 160.0 x 125.0 cm (frame)   40
3.1 Karen Pearlman, *I Want to Make a Film about Women* (2019), still   54
3.2 Wikipedia homepage   57
3.3 *The Noon Quilt*, edited by Teri Hoskin and Sue Thomas   61
4.1 Cuneiform script, clay tablet, from Northern Mesopotamia Media-Assyria Kingdom, second half of the second millennium BCE   69
4.2 William Shakespeare, *Hamlet* in *First Folio*, 1623   82
4.3 Illustration from the frontispiece of the 1831 edition of *Frankenstein* by Mary Shelley   89
6.1 Download progress bar   109
7.1 Ben Rubin and Mark Hansen, *Moveable Type*, 2007   137
7.2 Chris Rodley and Andrew Burrell, *Death of an Alchemist*, 2015   141
7.3 Chris Rodley and Andrew Burrell, *Death of an Alchemist* (detail)   142

Acknowledgments

I wish to thank Mark Thompson at Toronto University Press for his support of this book project. I am grateful to colleagues at Macquarie University for their specialist advice on pertinent topics: Steve Collins on copyright and copyright minimalism; Karen Pearlman on film authorship; Rita Matulionyte on AI and creativity; Jan Zwar on authors and digital disruption; Stefan Solomon on NFTs; and Joseph Quilter on graffiti art and copyright law. I also thank Gordon McMullan at King's College London for his expert advice on Shakespeare and authorship.

I am also grateful for the artists who have granted permission to reproduce their works in this book: Justine Varga, Ben Rubin and Mark Hansen, Sue Thomas, Chris Rodley and Andrew Burrell, Joseph Quilter, Karen Pearlman.

Part of the research for this book was conducted for an Australian Research Council (ARC) Linkage Grant on digitizing the archive. I acknowledge the support of the ARC in the form of this grant. I also acknowledge the support for my research provided by the Faculty of Arts, Macquarie University.

Special thanks for inspiration: Sophie and Leo.

THE NEAR-DEATH OF THE AUTHOR

Introduction

In the internet age, all that is solid melts into data. Media forms and works of art that once came in solid form – books, newspapers, magazines, music discs, films, paintings – now take immaterial form, as data. This data is infinitely malleable, easily copied, and distributed instantly across the internet – where it may be quickly downloaded or streamed. The copying and distribution of data may occur legally – ensuring that copyright holders receive recompense in the form of royalties – or illegally, in defiance of copyright law.

The author must navigate many challenges in the world of data. Most pressingly, the illegal transmission of copyright material on the internet deprives authors of royalties, and in some cases has discouraged creativity or terminated careers. But there are numerous other challenges. Electronic artworks perform dynamic or "big data" writing, in which an algorithm generates constant new text drawn from an enormous database: here there is no author at all, only an algorithm. Developments in artificial intelligence (AI) have yielded novels, newspaper articles, musical works, films, and paintings produced not by authors or artists but by AI. These AI achievements have provoked questions regarding the authorship of new works: does the author need to be human? And, more alarmingly: is there even a need for human authors?

These existential questions probe the very nature and status of authorship. Other aspects of the internet age question assumptions regarding the modern author, understood as the individual (human) creator of original works. The internet accommodates myriad instances of collective or collaborative writing, including Wikipedia: these sites and works cannot be attributed to an individual author. Remix culture, creative reuse and open source coding are founded on multiple and continuous authoring, in which the text, code or work is never completed: there is no definitive or final work, and there is no definitive author.

Anonymous or pseudonymous blogging contradicts the convention of named authorship, while the highly popular practice of fan fiction is celebrated as a form of "transformative" writing, based on the copyrighted works of established authors. All of these practices combine to confront notions of the author in the most recent chapter of the history of the author.

This book includes a history of authorship, tracing the changes in the status of the author from prehistory and ancient cultures to the present. A central factor in this history is the function of technologies to reproduce and publish authored works: first the printing press, later digital technologies and transmission via the internet. I propose that if there is a contemporary threat to the social role of the author, it derives not from the post-structuralist theory of Roland Barthes in "The Death of the Author," but from the disruptive practices associated with the internet and digital technology. To broaden the scope of authorship, in this book I discuss not only the literary author but also the filmmaker, composer, songwriter, choreographer, visual artist, designer: all creators of original works protected by copyright, all authors affected by data and the network culture.

In 1848, Karl Marx wrote of the radical social changes effected by industrial capitalism; he described the "constant revolutionising of production" unleashing "uninterrupted disturbance of all social conditions." The old social order had been swept away in the "bourgeois epoch," leaving unprecedented levels of production, but also "everlasting uncertainty and agitation." Marx's most poetic account of this radical social change was his assertion that "all that is solid melts into air, all that is holy is profaned."[1]

In the twenty-first century, post-industrial technology has effected a new generation of constant revolutionizing, uninterrupted disturbance, and everlasting uncertainty. The problems afflicting the contemporary author emerged in the mid-1990s, when the World Wide Web became the central domain for expression and communication. Digitization creates the means by which data can be transmitted and received on personal devices including smart phones, tablets, and laptops: this data includes creative works that may have taken years to complete, but which can be streamed instantly or downloaded in seconds.

Post-industrial society is a world of data, in which much communication is controlled by powerful algorithms. These algorithms – in the form of AI – even have the capacity to create texts and works of art themselves, performing the social function of authors. The realm of data is immaterial, yet it has profound material consequences. We can update Marx's poetic description for the age of post-industrial capitalism: today all that is solid melts into data. This book considers whether the author itself will melt away, or survive in altered form.

Chapter 1 charts the defining characteristics of the contemporary author. Consideration is given to the legal construction of the author as the creator of original works protected by copyright law, and to the economic aspect of the author as producer of commodities sold on the market. I describe authors as "heroes with names" because they have inherited the role of author as cultural hero established in the Romantic period; they have their names attached to their works in a way that other professional writers – ghostwriters, copywriters – do not. Chapter 2 ventures beyond legal and economic dimensions in attempting to define the contemporary author. The issue of inspiration for creative authors is considered: where does inspiration come from, and is it the factor distinguishing human authors from AI systems? A number of issues of contested authorship are discussed, introducing some of the complications besetting the contemporary author.

Chapter 3 examines the differences between the individual author – recognized by copyright law – and collaborative or collective authorship. In the internet age, online artworks are multi-authored as well as multimodal, combining the skills of designers, writers, artists, composers, coders, video artists: these works are not the product of one author. Debates within film theory concerning the authorship of films – whether the director is "auteur" of the work, or whether a collective authorship should be ascribed to all who work on the film – are extended to other collaborative works, including video games, animations, online encyclopaedias, and much online collective writing.

Chapter 4 takes the form of a brief history of authorship, observing the profound shifts in the status and social role of the author through the centuries. Significant determining factors in the history of authorship include: the collective storytelling tradition of oral societies, despite the later attribution of authorship of epic poems such as *The Iliad* to a single author – "Homer"; the functions of "scriptor" and "auctor" – precursors of the modern author – in medieval manuscript writing; the invention of the printing press in the fifteenth century, resulting in mass printing and the book as commodity; the inauguration of copyright with the Statute of Anne in 1710; the idea of the individual – rather than collective – author, protected by the law of copyright, established in the eighteenth century; the elevation of the author as "genius" and heroic creator of original works in the Romantic era; and the invention of copying technologies in the twentieth century, culminating in internet culture from the 1990s.

Chapter 5, "The Alleged Death of the Author," concerns not the technologies that have affected authorship in the twentieth and twenty-first centuries, but rather the ideas that shifted the social status of the author in that period. Literary theory, art theory, structuralism and post-structuralism forged a conceptual re-orientation of the author in the twentieth century. The nineteenth century Romantic conception of the author had centred all meaning and value derived from a text in the intention of the author; by the late 1960s, the post-structuralists Michel Foucault and Roland Barthes conceived of authorship in ways far removed from this Romantic idea. In his famous essay, "The Death of the Author," Barthes claimed the death not of all authorship but of the Romantic, God-like conception of the Author; in its place he posited a function more like the medieval scriptor: a figure with the power only to "mix writings," drawing on the "immense dictionary of culture." Barthes's essay was influential in shaping new ideas of authorship in the postmodern 1980s and 1990s, a period which coincided with the advent of digital appropriation devices, the scanner and the sampler. The artist or author was reconfigured as a processor of information; and postmodern appropriation was later remodelled in the twenty-first century as "creative reuse" of found materials.

Chapter 6 considers the intersection of authorship and the properties of digital technology. The illegal copying and transmission of copyright works – and the severe impact on authors' income – has been a highly public issue since 2000, when Napster and other peer-to-peer music file-swapping networks were sued by major record companies for breach of copyright. The illegal downloading of MP3 music files was quickly followed by the downloading of book files and the downloading – then streaming – of film and TV works. With the expectation of little or no revenue from royalties due to illegal downloading and streaming, many musicians and songwriters have abandoned recording of their music altogether, and literary authors have retired from publishing their works. This chapter examines the internet-enabled infringement of copyright as a key factor in the near-death of the author. It also considers the arguments against copyright, including the proposition that the internet has created a new digital commons, in which copyright functions as a restriction of the free flow of information and culture.

Chapter 7 addresses the world of "big data" and the possibility of authorship by algorithm. Algorithms are the invisible engines of big data and the networked society: they continually sort data, run online searches, operate electronic banking – and, increasingly, generate texts and artworks. There are already many big data artworks, dynamic texts that have no author; they are generated according to the rules of the algorithm driving the work. These big data writing works, made since the mid-1990s with the development of the internet, have moved beyond the "death of the author" to a reconstituted author-as-algorithm. This chapter explores the consequences for authorship of dynamic electronic writing. If no-one is writing these texts, can the algorithm be credited as the author? Or are they truly author-less works, spinning an infinite complexity of data combinations from the database?

Chapter 8 stages a confrontation between AI and the author. AI has made profound advances in the twenty-first century, including the production of creative works in many forms. Significantly, the quality of AI-generated works has often confounded audiences or readers, unable to distinguish between works made by AI and those created by human authors. The proliferation of AI-generated works has prompted a questioning of authorship, including the question of which creative works deserve copyright protection. Does an artwork need to be created by a human? If AI programs can generate works indistinguishable from those made by human authors, should the AI be recognised as an author? The near-death of the author is glimpsed in the autonomously produced creative works generated by AI.

Chapter 9 approaches "creative reuse" of copyright material as a significant challenge for the contemporary author. The internet has been celebrated for its "gift economy," a newly constituted public domain in which digitized works may be freely used and reused by other creative authors – the "people formerly known as the audience." Remix culture – of music and other forms – creates a multiple authorship across time, devaluing the original author as the work mutates through different remixes by different authors. A work may have no definitive version – and no definitive author – as it is continuously reused and remixed on the internet. This principle of constant modification of the original – a core element of the open source movement for software – is extended in "creative reuse" to encompass all types of digital information. A huge volume of works has been made available with the advent of digital archives, which have published – for instant access and creative reuse – previously restricted historical material. The free-wheeling use of previously copyrighted materials, however, constitutes a form of post-authorship, as authors are rarely recompensed for their creative efforts. The creative reuse of copyright works may further endanger the health of the modern author, already severely damaged by the loss of royalties and livelihood as author of original works.

The book concludes with a brief Epilogue, in which all the factors contributing to the near-death of the author are assessed, and the future of the author is considered.

Chapter One

"Heroes with Names": What Is the Author?

In his landmark 1969 essay "What Is an Author?," Michel Foucault argued that there is no universal idea of authorship; rather, each epoch has its own variant of the "author-function," shaped by specific cultural expectations and rules concerning what constitutes an author.[1] When we ask "what is the author?," therefore, we are inquiring into the constitution of the contemporary author-function; we are describing the function of the author in the twenty-first century.

The Modern Author

The contemporary author has many of the characteristics of the modern author, as detailed in numerous studies in the history of authorship. The modern author was largely shaped by a confluence of economic, legal, and technological developments in the eighteenth and nineteenth centuries. These developments were: the widespread use of the printing press, which allowed for the production and circulation at high volume of books, pamphlets, magazines, newspapers, journals and other printed forms; the sale of books and other printed formats at high volume on the market – that is, as commodities; the introduction of the law of copyright in England in 1710, which eventually came to protect the rights of authors in the copying, distribution and sale of their works; and the conception – and celebration – of the author as individual creator of original works, an idea vigorously promoted in the Romantic period of the late eighteenth and early nineteenth centuries.

Many of the historical studies of authorship emphasise the forging of the modern author, primarily in eighteenth century Europe, as a result of the coalescing of these determinant factors. For Mark Rose, in his book *Authors and Owners*, the modern author is "conceived as the originator and therefore the owner of a special kind of commodity, the work."[2] The crucial characteristic of the modern author for Rose is "proprietorship": the author is considered in law and economic theory to be the owner of a specific commodity – the artwork, composition or book – which they have created.

Prior to the eighteenth century, authors depended for their livelihood not on the sale of their works in the market; rather, they depended on patronage, generally from the monarchy, church, or aristocracy. Wealthy patrons provided financial support for writers, artists, or composers, as well as the means of publishing or performing their works. Authors, however, had little or no proprietorship – that is, they had no rights to the works they created. William Shakespeare, for example, sold his plays to the theatre company of which he was a member in the late sixteenth and early seventeenth centuries; but he had no claims to royalties, residuals or even the integrity of the works, which could be treated in any manner by their owner – the theatre company.

Technology, ideology, economics, and law converged in the invention of the modern author. Copyright, defined by Rose as "the practice of securing marketable rights in texts that are created as commodities,"[3] met the demands of the printing industry, the market economy of the eighteenth century, and the "individualization of authorship." The emphasis on the individual creator of works emerged in the European Renaissance, and was consolidated in the eighteenth-century liberal theory of "possessive individualism," focused on the individual's right to property – including intellectual property.[4]

In his political economic study of the history of copyright, Ronald Bettig observes that "intellectual property rights are both economic and statutory in nature." Bettig also notes that the printing press was "among the first inventions to be exploited by capitalists."[5] Once a market for the sale of these new commodities – printed books – had developed, the author's right to control and benefit from the copying and sale of books was eventually established – late in the eighteenth century – in the form of copyright. Copyright – or "the exclusive right to exploit a copyrighted work" – was intended to provide motivation or incentive for creative practitioners to create new works. Its other practical aim, as Bettig notes, was to provide a source of income – in the form of royalties for works sold on the market – to authors, artists, and other creators of copyrighted works.[6] Copyright, therefore, is both a legal and economic construction of authorship.

Agere/augere/auieo/autentim/auctoritas/auctor/author

How do we define the author? The etymology of the English word "author" is notoriously elusive, as attested by scholars of authorship – including Andrew Bennett and Seán Burke – and scholars of medieval authorship, including A.J. Minnis. Various candidates for the Latin root word of "author" have been nominated: *agere*, "to act or perform"; *augere*, "to grow"; *auieo*, "to tie"; *autentim*, Greek for "authority"; *auctoritas*, Latin for "authority." In the European medieval period, the "auctor" was a writer invested with a certain authority to guarantee the validity of a written argument or manuscript. But the medieval author-function was "entirely remote" from that of the modern author, as Burke observes, since the auctor was not expected to demonstrate autonomy or originality.[7] Writers – frequently scribes working within monasteries – derived their authority from their faithfulness to religious tradition and texts; ultimately their authority issued from the supreme *auctoritas* of God. The medieval *auctor* worked within the scriptural canon and tradition, and in many instances worked anonymously.

However, Bennett records that by the end of the fourteenth century, "auctor" had assumed the meaning of one who "originates or gives existence to anything"; this shift in meaning coincided with the widespread popularity of original works by the English poets Chaucer, Langland, and Gower – who were named as *auctores* of their works. The word *auctor* gradually transformed into *aucthour*, then *authour* and *author*. Bennett suggests that the development of the modern author in the eighteenth century is charted by the array of words that entered the English language in that century: "authorship" (1710); "authorless" (1713); "authoring" (1742); "authorial" (1796).[8]

Law and Economy

In his essay "What Is an Author?," Foucault is mainly concerned with the modern author-function; and while his intellectual history of the author is vague concerning a timeline, he does mention the late eighteenth century as a significant turning-point for the modern author. While Foucault's analysis for the most part operates on the general level of discursive systems and rules, he refers to specific "legal and institutional systems" circumscribing the modern author-function. In particular, he nominates the "system of ownership and strict copyright rules," established at the end of the eighteenth and beginning of the nineteenth centuries, as the point at which the author "was accepted into the social order of property which governs our culture."[9] However, Foucault does not develop this aspect of his analysis.

For Foucault, the author is a "function of discourse," determined by the discursive rules operating in specific historical periods. In his 1986 deliberation on Foucault's essay, Alexander Nehamas proposes that the author was historically determined at a certain point as an "agent" of texts, a "plausible historical variant of the writer." Following Foucault, Nehamas finds that the modern author was construed as a cultural agent only after the Renaissance, resulting in a "historical agent causally and legally responsible for the text."[10]

Foucault suggests that the modern author emerged as a "principle of unity in writing" that could impose a wholeness on a work, even justifying unevenness of production.[11] This idea – that the notion of "author" is a concept that performs a cultural role, ensuring the coherence of works – has been developed by later theorists of authorship. Aaron Meskin, in exploring the difficult issue of film authorship, describes the author as "a causal-explanatory notion." A work such as a film can be assigned an "implied author," with implied authorial intention and focus, even though that work has been created by multiple contributors to its production. Similarly, Geoffrey Nowell-Smith has termed the author a "fiction," whose "notional coherence provides the means for us to grasp the text in the moments of its production before us."[12]

Foucault's essay has been extremely influential in later scholarship of the author, both in historical studies of authorship and in attempts to analyse or define the idea of "author." But later theorists have also levelled critiques at Foucault's brief foray into authorship theory. In her 1987 essay "What Was an Author?," Molly Nesbit found fault with Foucault for his lack of attention to two crucial factors: the law and the economy. Nesbit declares it "odd" that Foucault fails to examine the French law of *droits d'auteur* – author's rights – enacted in 1793. She also remarks that while Foucault is concerned with the "circulation and operation of discourses," he fails to situate this circulation within a market economy – the economic system that "defined the author in the first place." Nesbit adds that this omission is not surprising, as "the economy is Foucault's blind spot."[13]

Another blind spot in Foucault's intellectual history – including his history of authorship – is individual agency. Foucault's theoretical method is post-humanist as well as post-structuralist; his histories favour discursive systems – organizations of knowledge – over human agency. At the beginning of "What Is an Author?," Foucault even chastises himself for employing the names of authors "in a naïve and crude fashion" in his earlier book *The Order of Things* (the book which ends with a famous image of man "erased, like a face drawn in sand at the edge of the sea").[14] Foucault is more comfortable in the "What Is an Author?" essay construing the author as a "function of discourse."

But Foucault's emphasis on abstractions – named "discourse" or "power-knowledge" – creates a form of discursive determinism in his historical analyses, generating the impression that history is shaped by an abstract entity called discourse. "Post-Foucauldian" intellectual history has re-instated individual agents – and authors – in considerations of cultural and intellectual history. Ian Maclean has criticised Foucault's discursive analysis as resembling "a laboratory without a scientist in it," while Mark Bevir has argued that history can include "a space for conscious and rational human agency," the ability of individual authors "to act creatively in any given social context."[15]

Nesbit maintains that because of Foucault's focus on discursive systems, his version of the author exists "in a disembodied, non reflecting, dispersed state, in knowledge, not in the world." She considers it "odd" that Foucault neglects the 1793 French *droits d'auteur* act, because this French copyright law was a statutory discourse actively circumscribing – even defining – authorship. Nesbit finds that the legal definition of the author is "dry" but "plain": "the author is given rights to a cultural space over which he or she may range and work."[16] Nesbit cautions, however, about deriving much in the way of definition of the author from statutes, which usually provide only minimal description. This point is also made by Daniela Simone, in her 2019 book *Copyright and Collective Authorship*. Simone observes that the UK's Copyright Designs and Patents Act of 1988 offers only the briefest definition of "author" – as the person who creates a work. She further remarks that at the level of international copyright law, there is no definition of "author" at all. The Berne Convention – an international treaty governing copyright in member nations, established in 1886 – omits defining the author, possibly because the signatory nations in the early stages of the Convention enjoyed a consensus concerning the status of author, and did not require it to be articulated in law.[17]

Nesbit is more concerned with the "property rights" assigned to authors by the 1793 act, and how the law of author's rights determined authorship. The French copyright law stipulated that an author's work was a kind of cultural labour (as distinct from industrial labour). An author applied imagination and labour in the creation of a work; this cultural labour took place in particular media forms certified within the act: writing, music composition, painting, drawing, and engraving. (These provisions, that a work must take material form, and that it must involve a certain skill or labour on the part of the author, were included in most subsequent national copyright laws.)

Whereas Foucault focused on the narrow sense of author as writer, copyright law in France – from 1793 onwards – encompassed other forms of media and creative expression. Nesbit notes that the media and form of works afforded copyright protection expanded in the twentieth century, as copyright law caught up (eventually) with new technologies of media. A revision of the French copyright law in 1957 extended the field of authored works warranting copyright protection to photography and cinema, dance, and pantomime, while another revision in 1985 encompassed audio-visual works and computer software. Nesbit recognises this extended field of authorship beyond that of literary texts; I use this expanded definition of the author – expressed in a range of media and forms – in this book.

The studies in the political economy of the construction of authorship – by Bettig, Rose, Nesbit, Lyman Ray Patterson, Benjamin Kaplan, Martha Woodmansee, and others[18] – emphasise the economic as well as legal dimension of the author: authors produced commodities, while copyright was a new means of generating wealth. As a result of these considerations, we may propose a definition of the modern author as: a legal/economic entity whose original works are protected by copyright.

The author is construed as an individual creator in copyright law – originating in the eighteenth century – despite the reality that much writing and creativity is a collaborative or corporate activity. Masses of professional writing – reports, advertising, public relations, marketing, public information – are performed on a collective or corporate basis; but most of this writing is not considered to be authored in the manner of books, compositions or artworks created by individuals. The classification of author is distinguished from those other professional writers who do not have a by-line or "name," and whose works are not protected by copyright. Originality is the other important factor, again established as an aesthetic and legal orthodoxy in the eighteenth century. A work is protected by copyright only if it can be deemed an original creation – that is, different from other works.

If the modern author was born in the congruence of commodification and the market for printed books, this does not mean that the author is a feature only of capitalist societies. Communist China, for example, is a member of the Berne Convention and Universal Copyright Convention, and has had a national copyright law since 1991. The works of an author or artist, however, may suffer severe censorship – or suppression – in an authoritarian, single-party state.

In countries not signed to the Berne Convention and with little or no national copyright law, the modern author as defined above cannot function. The author-function in such contexts is closer to that of the European author pre-copyright: dependent on patronage for a livelihood and the means to publish works. In authoritarian states where there is no – or inadequate – copyright law, writers, artists, film-makers, or composers must receive commissions – and grants – from the state in order to create works. This system of state patronage functions as a form of censorship and political control of creative expression – as did the royal patronage, in the form of "privileges," functioning in Europe prior to the advent of copyright.

The Contemporary Author

The modern author, then, was established as a legal, economic, and aesthetic entity by the end of the eighteenth century. But in the twenty-first century, the contemporary author differs in several significant ways from the modern author – and the determining factors are once again technological, economic, and legal. The major difference is a weakening of the proprietorship which Mark Rose considers the essential characteristic of the modern author. In the internet age, authors have lost much of the exclusive right to exploit their works. Copyright law – designed to protect authors' rights of ownership – has been defied in billions of acts of illegal downloading and streaming.

One of the founding principles of the internet was the social benefit of connectivity, supported by the free and unrestricted flow of information. But the "Information wants to be free" rallying cry of electronic civil libertarians in the 1990s later became the belief that information should be free of charge. Many internet users from the late 1990s onwards refused to acknowledge authors' ownership of the songs, texts, images, TV programs or films distributed across the internet; or at least, they refused to acknowledge the authors' right to be financially recompensed for the copying and distribution of their works.

Indeed, in the internet age the concept of ownership passed from authors to users: internet users often expressed a conviction of entitlement, that everything on the web should be freely available – for free – to users. This freely available information included news and also pop music, films, literary works, and the latest TV series. The internet was conceptualized as the base of a "digital commons" or electronic public domain; authorship of individual works within this new commons was deemed irrelevant, as the greater good was served by the free use and creative reuse of works available on the web. Copyright has been decried – by internet libertarians – as an obstacle to creative reuse of found materials; for its detractors in the digital age, the enforcement of copyright functions as a form of censorship, a brake on creative expression.[19]

The "gift economy," another term applied to the digital commons, entailed an opposition to the proprietorship of the modern author. According to the principles of the gift economy, works in the digital commons should be freely offered to the community as gifts, to be re-worked by other creators, then re-gifted back into the digital economy.[20] Authors' rights suffer in the gift economy, as does the very concept of authors as owners of their works. The financial consequences for authors – including the jeopardizing of careers as artists or authors – have been well documented, and are examined in detail in chapter 6, "Downloading Versus Copyright."

The writer and theorist Mark Amerika observed in 2000 that the internet had "radically refigured the writer into a kind of Internet artist." By this he meant that electronic writing allowed new possibilities for text, including hypertext: this new "hypertextual consciousness" had as its motto "I link therefore I am."[21] Amerika also proposed that writers could contribute to new forms of digital works that "defy categorization." A writer may find creative outlet in internet-based multimodal works, incorporating not only text but sound, music, images, moving images, animation, art and design. This artistry may embrace collaborative or collective authorship of multimodal works; it may involve remix culture, or the creative reuse of other authors' works. Amerika remarked in 2000 that internet-based writer-artists were "reinventing writerly practice – particularly our accepted notions of 'authorship,' 'text' and 'publishing.'"[22] This form of creative activity subverts the ideas of individual authorship, ownership, and originality implicit in the concept of the modern author. The consequences for the contemporary author of the "creative reuse" of copyright works – in a "post-authorship" culture – are explored in chapter 9.

Heroes with Names

In his 1993 song "Big Time Operators," the singer-songwriter Van Morrison sings: "They were glorified by the media, they were heroes who had names."[23] Van Morrison in this song denounces certain music industry executives, but his description of these individuals as "heroes with names" serves as a succinct characterization of the modern author. The author from the eighteenth century to the twenty-first has been celebrated as a cultural hero; the author is named and celebrated as the creator of original works.

In chapter 4, I delineate the historical development of the author as a type of cultural hero, an idea most vividly asserted in the early nineteenth century Romantic period. The poet Percy Bysshe Shelley's assertion in 1821 that "Poets are the unacknowledged legislators of the World" is simply the most well-known claim for a heroic status for the author, a figure of cultural prestige and authority.

In the contemporary context, "heroes with names" refers to authors female and male. Feminist literary theorists have demonstrated, however, that the author developed historically as a gendered construct. Sandra Gilbert and Susan Gubar, in their 1979 book *The Madwoman in the Attic*, observed that one of the early meanings of "author" was "begetter": the author was deemed to "father" or beget his texts, at a time when authors were exclusively male.[24] Emerging literary canons of almost entirely male authors further revealed the patriarchal character of authorship. The idea of the hero, including the cultural hero, was also an intrinsically gendered concept, as advanced by the historian Thomas Carlyle in his 1841 book *On Heroes, Hero-Worship and the Heroic in History*. Carlyle voiced the Great Man theory of leadership when he claimed that the "history of the world is but the biography of great men."[25] In the early nineteenth century, when the Romantic idea of the great author as "genius" and cultural hero was entrenched, authors, artists and composers were almost exclusively male.

Decades of feminist literary theory, curation and criticism have ensured that literary and art canons have expanded to include many more female authors and artists than were included in the nineteenth century. The contemporary understanding of "author" incorporates female and male practitioners; nevertheless, contemporary culture has inherited the Romantic veneration of the author or artist. This notion characterises the author as a figure to be revered, yet a figure somehow set apart from the rest of society by virtue of their talent and vision. Here are the reflections in 2021 of the photographer Henry Diltz on the most celebrated singer-songwriters, including Joni Mitchell and Neil Young: "there's a reason these people are loved around the world and it's simply that they are interesting people. They are a little bit different to us, they are special … They have a certain kind of freedom from their lifestyles and that gives them time to sit and think and to reflect … They are a cut above the average person."[26] The author – that individual "a cut above" the average person – has a name; the author is admired as a creator, and is highly visible within the culture. This is in contrast to the countless creators, storytellers, poets, and artists of prehistory, who created anonymously in collaboration with others to produce epic narratives and works of art. It is also in contrast to the vast amounts of professional writing generated in contemporary culture, in the form of reports, information, advertising, and marketing. This writing is also collaborative and anonymous; it may saturate contemporary media culture, but its authors are not individuated and they remain unknown: they do not have names.

The esteemed – and rewarded – individual authors are "heroes with names." The author's name is the signifier of authorship – the "by-line" which states that the work has been created by the named author. The author's name may be a pseudonym or pen name – Mark Twain, George Eliot, Elena Ferrante – but this pseudonym *is* the author's name; it allows prospective readers or consumers of the work to identify a particular work as the creation of a particular author. An exception to the identification of a work by the author's name is the (relatively rare) work by "Anonymous"; but anonymous publications – especially political exposés – usually incite a media frenzy to track down and reveal the true name of the author.

The most successful authors even transcend their name to become a "brand name" – such as Stephen King or Alfred Hitchcock. At this level, the author's name functions like a commercial brand name, attached to a cultural product such as a film or novel, designating certain qualities and characteristics of the work. The work can be more easily marketed and promoted when its author has acceded to the status of "brand name," as readers or audiences readily know what to expect from this particular brand.

The author's name is also the signature on a contract that empowers the publisher to produce the work and sell copies on behalf of the author. Authors assign their copyright in the work to publishers; in return the publisher pays the author a royalty – or percentage – of every copy of the work sold. This contractual agreement – by which the author's copyright is protected and exploited by the publisher, allowing the author a financial benefit in the form of royalties – is what distinguishes the author from other professional writers or creators. The author is a named cultural producer who receives ongoing financial reward from the exploitation of copyrighted works.

Other writers – non-authors – do not receive royalties, and are often not named as creators. Foucault made this point in "What Is an Author?," when he observed that "the name of an author is a variable that accompanies only certain texts to the exclusion of others." Foucault offered examples of writing that do not have authorship attached: "a private letter may have a signatory, but it does not have an author; a contract can have an underwriter, but not an author; and, similarly, an anonymous poster attached to a wall may have a writer, but he cannot be an author."[27] Professional writers/creators who cannot be termed authors include: ghostwriters, part-writers, report writers, advertising copywriters, marketing and public relations writers, public information designers and writers. These creators may be full-time professional writers with prolific outputs – but they do not have a name; they are not recognised as authors.

Instead of royalties, non-authors are generally paid a flat fee for their work, or their financial remuneration is in the form of a salary. This means that they are not entitled to any benefit from ongoing sales of the work, even if that work proves enormously successful over a long time-span. The non-author is also invisible to the public, with no name attached to the work, as is the case with the aptly named "ghostwriter." A ghostwriter is a professional writer, generally operating on a freelance basis, who writes all or part of works credited to another writer – the named "author" of the work. Ghostwriters are commonly employed to write memoirs – or so-called "autobiographies" – of politicians, public figures, or celebrities. The subject of the autobiography may lack the literary skills – or the time – to actually write their life-story; that work is undertaken instead by the ghostwriter, who may confer with the book's subject in interviews in order to gather material to write the memoir.

Ghostwriters may be paid handsomely by publishers for their work, especially if the subject of the memoir is a high-profile public figure whose "autobiography" is likely to be a best-seller. But this payment is a one-off fee only, without the ongoing financial reward of royalties. And the ghostwriter must be content with invisibility, as the authorship of the memoir will be attributed to the celebrity – who in many cases will not have written a single word of the autobiography. Ghostwriters will never be invited to sign copies of the books they have written at launches or literary events: their signature has no value, because they have no name attached to the work as author. The figure whose name appears on the front cover of the book, however, *will* be asked to sign copies of the work at launches or literary events: the named author's signature adds value to the book, even if that signature is the only piece of writing achieved by the "author" within the work.

Despite the invisibility and lack of public recognition for ghostwriters as authors, ghost-writing proliferates in contemporary culture. Novels have been ghost-written by anonymous writers, paid to write in the style of a named author, while many online blogs and social media posts are ghost-written on behalf of celebrities and public figures. In some cases, the ghostwriter of a book may be permitted a small acknowledgment by the publisher – as in the front cover designation of a memoir, stating that the work is "as told to." The ghostwriter may even be granted an actual by-line – in much smaller font – beneath the by-line of the brand-name author, designating that the ghostwriter is part-writer of the work (in most cases that part will in fact be a majority part). In such instances, the ghostwriter may even be rewarded with a small royalty for ongoing sales of the work. For a great many ghost-written works, however, ghostwriters receive no by-line, no royalty, and no public recognition. They have no name connected with their works, and are not classified as authors.

Author as Factory

Whole genres of popular fiction – romance, thriller, young adult fiction – are set up in part by the publishing industry as veritable writing factories. Writers are hired to complete a manuscript – based on a story treatment or narrative formula provided by the publisher – and with strict guidelines regarding literary style, narrative conventions, manuscript length and deadline for delivery of the work. In some instances, the professional writer may be credited as author or co-author of the work they have written; in others, credit for authorship is assigned to the named author contracted to the publisher – especially if that author is eminent enough to be considered a "brand name" attached to a series of books.

James Patterson – who became in the early twenty-first century the best-selling living author in the world – also became in that time the publishing industry's greatest brand name. An industry of book production – in popular genres including thriller, romance, young adult, children's fiction, and science fiction – has generated millions of sales of books under the name "James Patterson." Patterson was so prolific in the first two decades of the twenty-first century that he had published well in excess of one hundred novels by 2014; and it has been estimated that between 2006 and 2010, one in every 17 novels sold in the US was authored by Patterson. The Patterson publishing output is staggering: in 2012 and 2013 he published 13 books in each year.[28]

But "published" and "authored by Patterson" have been contested phrases. No single writer could possibly publish 13 books in one year. Patterson readily admits that he hires writing collaborators, and that many of these books have been written or co-written by other professional writers, under the Patterson name-signifier. In 2017, the digital humanities scholars Simon Fuller and James O'Sullivan published an article in which they claimed to show – using stylometric analysis of "Patterson" books – that the great majority of text in these books was written not by Patterson but by his collaborators. The intention of Fuller and O'Sullivan was not to expose or shame Patterson for falsely attributed authorship; they acknowledge that Patterson has publicly declared his collaborative model of writing. Their aims rather were to situate Patterson's industrial mode of authorship within the economic realities of the publishing industry, and to problematize the concept of the author in contemporary culture.

Fuller and O'Sullivan reveal that Patterson oversees a publishing empire in which he exercises control over the writing and marketing of the books published under his name. But the vast majority of that writing is performed by others. Patterson organizes a team of writers, assigned to particular genres or series within the Patterson publishing business; he pays those writers a flat rate with bonuses but no royalties.[29] Patterson's role in the writing process is managerial: he writes the outline of a book, assigns the writing to one of his collaborators, then edits the text where needed to ensure quality control, before putting his name on the front cover to designate his authorship of the book.

In some instances, the collaborator is also given a by-line – often in much smaller font size – beneath Patterson's name. But this by-line on the front cover – even if in large font – does not necessarily signify co-authorship of the book. The children's book *Dog Diaries*, for example, published in 2018, has a dual by-line on the front cover: "by Steven Butler and James Patterson." However, the copyright page stipulates that copyright in the work is held by James Patterson only, and that "James Patterson has asserted his right to be identified as the Author of the work" in accordance with the copyright act of the country of publication.[30] Patterson's name is a selling-point for the book; he asserts authorship of all the books published under his name. The James Patterson name as author is in fact a brand name indicating a certain quality of product; as he declares, "my name on the cover is the assurance of a good read."[31]

Patterson has been criticized for operating a writing factory and for the poor literary quality of his works; fellow brand name author Stephen King has publicly disparaged Patterson as "a terrible writer."[32] But Patterson has ready answers for his critics. He observes that the genre of popular fiction is not known for its literary qualities; rather, a successful popular novel – a "page-turner" – is founded on its plot. Patterson the marketer identifies the centrality of plot in Patterson "brand" novels: "above all my brand stands for story. I became successful when I stopped writing sentences and started writing stories. Editors think it's about style. It's not. It's all story."[33] Patterson's factory system of hired collaborators works within the limited literary ambitions of popular fiction. Patterson's contribution is to provide the plot – in the form of a treatment outlining plot developments – and guidelines for the book's format. This format involves short chapters allowing for easy reading and swift narrative development. The hired collaborators write the great majority of the text according to these guidelines: the result is an industry of entertaining, highly popular "commuter fiction," designed to be read on buses, trains, and planes (or – in audio-book format – cars and trucks.)

Patterson has also defended his collaborative process, pointing to its successful – and uncriticized – application to other cultural forms, including cinema, television, newspapers, even medieval cathedrals.[34] Fuller and O'Sullivan identify precedents for the author-as-factory approach in nineteenth century literature, suggesting that beneath the public image of the solitary writer, collaborative networks have generated popular literary works well before James Patterson made his fortune.

Walter Benjamin's study of mid-nineteenth century French literature emphasized the "industrialising" of the commercial form of the novel, in the collaborative writing practised by authors Sue, Scribe, Dumas and others.[35] The foremost exponent of an industrialized "division of labour" approach to writing was Alexandre Dumas, celebrated author of enormously popular novels such as *The Three Musketeers* and *The Count of Monte Cristo*. Dumas signed simultaneous contracts to serialize numerous novels in different journals (serialization was a common practice in the mid-nineteenth century), then delegated the actual writing to others in order to meet the publishing demand.

Dumas was criticised by his contemporaries for running "a factory of novels." Benjamin cites one caricature: "It was said that Dumas employed a whole army of poor writers in his cellars," while Dumas drank champagne with actresses.[36] At times the resentment felt by the cellar-dwelling ghostwriters erupted into public indignation: one critic named Dumas' collaborators, then denounced the named author: "he dares, monster that he is, to sign his name alone." One of the major collaborators sued for a higher rate of pay and recognition as co-author; Dumas offered a pay raise but not a by-line. Dumas' defence of his factory practice, in which the toilers remained publicly invisible, was that he had created a publishing industry with employment for over eight thousand people, in a 20-year period in which he published 400 novels and 35 plays.[37] That staff included proofreaders, typesetters, machinists and writers – but the name as author was reserved for Dumas.

James Patterson has similarly pointed to the professional opportunities available in his writing factory. Patterson appears to have a more satisfied workforce than did Dumas; this is perhaps due to the generous rate of pay for his writers. Another factor is that the practice of writing for Patterson provides experience in publishing, which has allowed collaborators to later launch solo – and named – writing careers. Patterson boasted in 2012 of his workforce that "nobody quits" and "nobody asks for a raise."[38]

It may also be remarked that the writing factories organised by Dumas and Patterson, with prolific output attributed to the single named author, are literary versions – in the nineteenth and twenty-first centuries – of the art studios overseen by major visual artists in the Renaissance. A Renaissance artist could be commissioned to complete several large-scale projects at the same time; much of this work was performed by studio assistants under the supervision of the master artist, whose name was attached to the completed work. Art historians have described the workings of this studio system, in which a large commission "required considerable skill in organising group activity" within the studio. As a result, it has been observed that "the practice of the arts in the Renaissance was both public and collaborative,"[39] even though the great Renaissance works have been ascribed to individual artists, famous names such as Michelangelo, Raphael, and Leonardo.

Given the undoubted commercial success of the Patterson method, and its elevation of Patterson to the status of the world's best-selling author, Fuller and O'Sullivan ask the question: "What does this mean for our constructions of 'the author'"?[40] "Author" is placed in inverted commas in this question, because the mode of authorship practised by Patterson deviates from the conception of the modern author as celebrated since at least the eighteenth century.

Patterson is not an individual creator of his works; his sole act of original creation is usually the writing of a treatment outlining the plot of a novel, which is then written by others. Fuller and O'Sullivan find that the name "James Patterson" on the front cover of a book functions as a "stamp of quality," rather than as an indication that Patterson actually wrote the book. It means that the book has been "approved" by Patterson, as worthy of being published under his name. "Author" in Patterson's case means: cultural producer comprising "creator, brand, and corporation." He is "as much a trademark as he is a writer. His name is a stamp of approval."[41] Within a twenty-first century publishing industry functioning in a market economy, Patterson successfully established his name as the market-leading brand name of his time.

Chapter Two

"I Don't Own It": Contemporary Complications

In the previous chapter, I focused on the technological, economic, and legal factors determining the construction of the author as a concept. But the author is more than a legal/economic construct; the author is not simply shaped by the properties of technology. In this chapter, I discuss other defining characteristics of the author: the author's inspiration, and the unconscious as contributor to authorship of works. I consider these characteristics in the context of the contemporary author, outlining the ways in which the contemporary version of the author differs from the modern author. I conclude the chapter with discussion of diverse complications for the contemporary author; these complications of authorship and ownership further disturb the idea of the author in the twenty-first century.

The Author's Inspiration

Part of the heroic status of creative authors and artists derives from the mysterious idea of inspiration. Authors and artists are admired for their talent in creating original works; this talent is thought to flow from an inspiration that is granted to the rare few. But inspiration remains ineffable: where does it come from? Songwriters, poets, and novelists often remark that the work "came from somewhere else" or "wrote itself." Inspiration is at times considered a mystical force, resulting in art works whose creative process is little understood even by the author or artist. Authors may assert that in certain instances they function as a "vessel" or "medium" for a power of creative inspiration. Even the word "inspiration" connects the visions of a creative author to the spiritualist, shamanic or religious traditions of earlier cultures: "inspiration" derives from the Latin *inspirare*, "to breathe in," as if "prompted by or emanating from a supernatural source."[1]

There are many instances of authors and artists professing bewilderment at the creative process, when whole works of art seem to have created themselves. The songwriter John Lennon described the inspiration behind his song "Across the Universe," released by the Beatles in 1970: "I was lying next to my first wife in bed and I was thinking ... She'd gone to sleep and I kept hearing, 'Words are flowing out like endless streams' ... I went downstairs and it turned into a sort of cosmic song ... The words are purely inspirational and were given to me – except for maybe one or two where I had to resolve a line or something like that. I don't own it; it came through like that."[2] Lennon the songwriter is moved to disclaim his ownership of this song – "I don't own it" – even though copyright law firmly establishes him as its creator and owner (or rather the songwriting team of Lennon-McCartney is credited, based on an agreement by the two songwriters that any joint or solo composition during the life of the Beatles would be published as a Lennon-McCartney work).

The songwriter John Fogerty described the genesis of his song "Ramble Tamble," released by Creedence Clearwater Revival in 1970, in similar terms, as if the song were transmitted to him from another sphere: "This was one of those amazing times where you realise there's some heavenly radio antennae that comes from God or from the whole universe, which is God – it's not coming from you."[3] A more recent expression of a similar experience of inspiration was made by the singer-songwriter Aoife Nessa Frances in 2020: "I really love letting words come to me. There's always this beautiful moment of inception when words sort of happen and afterwards, I don't necessarily feel that I wrote the song myself. It comes from this other place."[4] The singer-songwriter Kurt Vile released a song in 2013 – "Goldtone" – devoted to the condition of creative inspiration. In this song Vile makes no recourse to the mystical or religious vocabulary used by other creative artists to describe inspiration; instead he likens inspiration to a state of intoxication: "Sometimes when I get in my zone, you'd think I was stoned. But I never, as they say, touch the stuff."[5] Contemporary neuro-science, with its ability to monitor neural activity in different cognitive states, has provided an empirical basis for this "zone" of heightened creativity, also known as the "alpha state." The inspirational "zone" of consciousness generally occurs when brainwave activity slows to below 14 Hertz (cycles per second), enabling a condition of mind more receptive and open to inter-connectedness – more creative – than the normal functioning state of consciousness. But few creative authors or artists would conceptualise their creative "zones" in such scientific terms; and when intense moments of inspiration occur, delivering whole works as if from another plane, this creativity is usually described in otherworldly terms, as in the songwriters' statements above.

This mysterious dimension to the experience of inspiration connects contemporary artists to prehistory, to a tradition as old as the history of creative expression in the earliest human societies. Hunter-gatherer societies were intensely animistic; that is, they experienced their world as animated and infused by spiritual presences. They believed that the natural world had been made by spirit-creators or spirit-ancestors, whose presence permeated the landscape; mythical narratives connected the past with the present, while visual art portrayed the "bipresence" of the spiritual and the worldly in the land.[6] The traditional art of Aboriginal Australia, for example, created spiritual maps of the territory occupied and traversed by each people: these painted maps depicted the paths of spirit-ancestors, their location in the land, and portals between the earthly and spiritual planes.

In hunter-gatherer societies, certain specialist individuals – shamans – were believed to have the power to venture to the spirit world, for the benefit of the social group. Shamans were thought to access the spiritual plane while in a trance, which was induced by hallucinogenic substances, by rhythmic music, or by physical deprivation. Shamans were practitioners of magic, in that they were believed to have the ability to affect the natural world – through healing, or ensuring the plenty of animals, plants and rainfall – for the well-being of their community. In some cultures, shamans expressed their knowledge of spirit-ancestors and spirit-animals through storytelling and visual depiction of the spirit-world. Shamanism – humanity's first form of religion, also a magical and creative practice – has persisted into the contemporary world, at least as an idea of transcendence through ritual. The artist Joseph Beuys identified as a modern shaman in the late twentieth century, while the performance artists Marina Abramović and Mike Parr use aspects of shamanic tradition – physical deprivation, endurance, purification – in quests for some form of transcendence in performance.

Something of the shaman's role as spiritual practitioner endured – in transformed states – once human societies became settled and founded on agriculture, and once shamans were replaced by priests as the administrators of new religions. Prophets were believed to speak for the gods, or God, in ecstatic or inspired speech; some were thought to possess healing powers. Oracles were thought to transmit the word of the gods when the Sybil or medium was in a trance state, induced by hallucinogenic substances. Poets and bards – storytellers in a great oral tradition – were believed to be inspired in their songs or verses by divine sources. The earliest surviving examples of writing – clay tablets inscribed with cuneiform script in ancient Mesopotamia – include magic spells and incantations, often with the inscription "The incantation is not mine," meaning that it has come from the gods.[7]

The ancient Greeks externalised inspiration in the form of the Muses, who were thought to inspire poets and other creative practitioners. In his dialogue *Ion*, written in the fourth century BCE, Plato explicitly locates poets' inspiration in external sources: the Muse or "Bacchic transport." For Plato, the Muse "makes men inspired" so that the good epic poets "have their excellence, not from art, but are inspired, possessed, and thus they utter all these admirable poems." Lyric poets may be "possessed" by the spirit of Bacchus (or Dionysus), so that the poets when in a state of inspiration are as if intoxicated, "not in their senses," or "beside themselves"[8] (the word *ecstasy* literally means "standing outside" of oneself).

Plato reduces the status of poets to that of vessels or "ministers" of divine utterances: in this respect the poets perform a similar function to that of prophets, soothsayers and "godly seers" – that is, they transmit the word of the gods. Plato accords poets only a provisional authorship status (by comparison with philosophers, who are fully in control of their minds and are therefore authors of their own thoughts). Plato states that the deity uses poets as "ministers" so that listeners may know it is not the poets "who utter these precious revelations while their mind is not within them, but that it is the god himself who speaks." Plato is even dismissive of the poets as authors because they lack autonomy and control of their minds; poets are "nothing but interpreters of the gods, each one possessed by the divinity to whom he is in bondage."[9]

In the early Christian era, inspiration was believed to derive directly from the Holy Spirit. The apostle Paul, in his letters from around 50 CE, invented the word "charisma" – meaning "spiritual gift" – to describe the abilities bestowed on members of the community from the Spirit; the highest of these gifts was held to be prophecy or inspired speech.[10] Paul's sense of charisma as a spiritual gift persists in some form in the present: we still speak of a charismatic or extremely talented individual as being "gifted." The *auctor* of medieval Europe worked strictly within the Christian tradition, in which inspiration flowed from the Holy Spirit, and the ultimate authority (and author) was God.

In the eighteenth and nineteenth centuries, the long process of secularization in European thought resulted in a conception of inspiration shorn of religious context, but maintaining some of the ancient mystical-spiritual connotations. This is vividly expressed in the Romantic poet Samuel Taylor Coleridge's visionary poem *Kubla Khan*, published in 1816. The poet longs to revive the intensity of a former vision; if he were to be successful, then:

all should cry, Beware! Beware!
His flashing eyes, his floating hair!
Weave a circle round him thrice,
And close your eyes with holy dread,
For he on honey-dew hath fed,
And drunk the milk of Paradise.[11]

The inspired figure in this poem exhibits the other-worldly qualities previously attributed to shamans, prophets, oracles, and seers; this is the charge of inspiration and intoxication that Coleridge – along with others in the Romantic period – celebrated as the source of creativity itself.

The contemporary world has inherited this secular-but-spiritual idea of inspiration from the Romantics; the song-writers quoted above all make use of this idea in attempting to describe their own inspiration. However, there are other ways of describing the creative process – and authors and theorists have accounted for creative arts practice without recourse to a mystical idea of inspiration. Many authors and artists prefer to emphasise the importance of craft and technique in creating a work. Contemporary writing courses – including song-writing courses – teach craft and skills rather than inspiration.

The twentieth century provided a plethora of theoretical models for describing the creative arts in materialist – or mechanistic – terms. The Russian Formalists, structuralists and post-structuralists all focused on the structures of language and narrative, demonstrating how culture or language itself generates new texts and works. In Modernist art, the Italian Futurists sought to imbue art works with the properties of machines, while the Russian Constructivists conceived of the artist as an "engineer," working like a technician to benefit the people. In Pop Art, Andy Warhol called his studio a "Factory" and sought to emulate the techniques of mass production in his art. Roland Barthes's theory of the author helped develop the concept of the contemporary artist or author as a processor of information, rummaging in the "immense dictionary" of culture – or, in the internet age, in the vast database of contemporary culture.

Materialist theoretical accounts of creativity focus not on the spiritual base of inspiration but on the social formations necessary for creative practice to occur. The sociologist Pierre Bourdieu situated "the rules of art" strictly within the "field of cultural production," while the psychologist Mihaly Csikszentmihalyi developed a "systems model of creativity," in which the author is located within a structured social system.[12] All these theoretical models and ideas combine in a multifaceted conception of the contemporary author.

And yet, the older idea of inspiration resides there too. Indeed, inspiration and the unfathomable mysteries of the creative process are often invoked when debates over AI and authorship are staged. It is well documented that AI systems have generated many works of art in diverse media forms; it has been proposed that there is no essential difference between an AI-generated work and a work created by a human author. The defenders of the human author in this debate may point to inspiration and creativity as the distinguishing characteristics of human authorship. An AI system processes and recombines information in the database to produce a new work; if a human author can be said to achieve more than this, it is often through reference to the creative process and the mystery of inspiration (this issue is further explored in chapter 8).

"Scrambled Eggs": The Unconscious as Author

Inspiration can strike – in the form of dreams – when the author is asleep and making no conscious input. In such cases, attribution of authorship is made to that individual even when the work was properly generated by the unconscious. Two famous instances are the song "Yesterday," whose melody came to Paul McCartney in a dream, and the poem *Kubla Khan*, which manifest to Samuel Taylor Coleridge in an opium-fuelled dream.

In the Beatles' *Anthology* documentary series and book, McCartney describes the genesis in 1965 of the song "Yesterday," perhaps the Beatles' best-known song and one of the most-recorded pop songs in history, with at least 2,200 cover versions:

> I woke up one morning with a tune in my head and I thought, "Hey, I don't know this tune – *or do I?*" It was like a jazz melody ... I made sure I remembered it and then hawked it round to all my friends, asking what it was: "Do you know this? It's a good little tune, but I couldn't have written it because I dreamt it." ... It didn't have any words at first so I blocked it out with "scrambled eggs." "Scrambled eggs, oh my baby, how I love your legs – diddle diddle – I believe in scrambled eggs." ... I liked the tune and I thought I'd like to take some time over the words, get something that fitted like "scrambled eggs." And then, one day, I had the idea of "Yesterday."[13]

It is instructive that McCartney himself did not believe that he wrote this song, "because I dreamt it." He had no conscious role in creating the melody – the most important component of any pop song – and for some time his sole conscious contribution to the song was the place-holding lyric "scrambled eggs." And yet for publishing and copyright purposes, McCartney and John Lennon were credited as composers of the song.

Why does McCartney the songwriter receive credit – and enormous royalties – for this song when the melody was created by his unconscious, while he was asleep? "Yesterday" is only one example of a published work that appeared to its author – in whole or in part – in a dream. There are many songs, poems, art works, stories, films, and other forms of creative expression that manifest in dreams or hallucinatory states. In most cases, the credited author has not attempted to conceal the origin of the work in a dream; indeed, many have been pleased to acknowledge the oneiric genesis of the work.

Why then do we accept dreams and the unconscious as part of the author-function? The answer can be conveyed in one word, or rather one name: Freud. In his book *The Interpretation of Dreams*, published in 1900, Sigmund Freud declared that the "interpretation of dreams is the royal road to a knowledge of the unconscious activities of the mind."[14] In this book, Freud's most influential work, the interpretation of dreams is situated in the context of Freud's theory of the unconscious. For Freud, the unconscious is the depository of the individual's "primary" desires, most of which are repressed by a secondary conscious process, due to the primary drives' socially unacceptable nature. Freud regarded dreams as the expression of those primary desires, using dream-material including memories from the previous day and stretching back to the earliest childhood memories. Dreams for Freud were fundamentally forms of wish-fulfilment; anxiety dreams or nightmares reflected the distortion of the primary desires by the psychic mechanism of repression.

Freud's concept of the unconscious – articulated in his psychoanalytical theory and within his practice of psychoanalysis – exerted an enormous influence on Western thought in the first half of the twentieth century. Artists and writers were particularly inspired by his revelations of the workings of the unconscious mind; the Freudian concept of the unconscious was accepted as a twentieth century secular explanation of the source of creativity itself, replacing earlier spiritual or religious beliefs. Freud himself was aware of this: he observed in *The Interpretation of Dreams* that for ancient cultures, dreams were considered "revelations from gods and daemons," including visions of the future sent from supernatural sources;[15] Freud's theory was proposed as a modern "scientific" replacement for those ancient beliefs.

In other publications, Freud extended his idea of dreams as wish-fulfilment to the creative process for artists and authors, attempting to explain "from what sources that strange being, the creative writer, draws his material."[16] In his essay "Creative Writers and Day-Dreaming,"

Freud proposed that creative writing is inspired by the same process as day-dreaming – which, like night dreams, involves wish-fulfilment and fantasy.

The connection between the unconscious, dreams and creativity was explored in numerous Modernist works of art and literature in the early twentieth century. The Surrealist movement was directly inspired by Freud's theorizing, especially *The Interpretation of Dreams*. Painters including Salvador Dali and Max Ernst sought to represent dream imagery in their works, while André Breton wrote in the *Surrealist Manifesto* of 1924 that the movement's aim was to "resolve the previously contradictory conditions of dream and reality." Breton further defined surrealism as "pure psychic automatism," based on "the omnipotence of dream."[17] Surrealist writers and artists experimented with a form of automatic writing, meant to free unconscious inspiration from rational constraints. Automatic writing was inspired by the technique of "free association" used in Freudian psychoanalysis, in which unconscious desires were thought to emerge through immediate, unfiltered, "automatic" thought. Many other authors and artists seek inspiration from the hypnagogic state – the threshold between wakefulness (consciousness) and sleep (the unconscious) – in the hope that unconscious imagery or connections may emerge into the waking mind.

The Modernist novelists James Joyce, Virginia Woolf, and William Faulkner all attempted to convey the workings of the unconscious through literary techniques including "the stream of consciousness." The ultimate realization of this approach came in Joyce's 1939 novel *Finnegans Wake*, a massive work which reads like the transcription of a long, elaborate night dream. *Finnegans Wake* exhibits the techniques – in literary form – of condensation and displacement of dream material, which Freud claimed were the basic methods of "dream-work."

The influence of Freudian theory declined drastically in the second half of the twentieth century, due to growing dissatisfaction with the method of Freudian psychoanalysis, and to critiques of Freud's theoretical apparatus, including his notion of the Oedipus complex. Freudian psychoanalytical theory was criticised as lacking empirical basis and therefore functioning as a pseudo-science.[18] But elements of Freudian theory remain as foundations of contemporary thought, including his concept of the unconscious as a depository of desires and memories – and a source of creative inspiration. Paul McCartney expresses something of this concept when musing on how the melody for "Yesterday" could have appeared in a dream: "my dad used to know a lot of old jazz tunes, I thought maybe I'd just remembered it from the past."[19] The unconscious in this instance is a storehouse of old melodies, remembered from childhood; the dream-work in this case is to compose a new melody from this depository of tunes.

But what of authors pre-1900, that is, before the Freudian concept of the unconscious? Were authors and artists less likely to acknowledge inspiration for a work from a dream? The answer is: certainly not; and the evidence is the short introductory text written by Samuel Taylor Coleridge to accompany publication of his poem *Kubla Khan*. Coleridge sub-titled this poem "A Vision in a Dream. A Fragment"; and the short preface outlines these aspects of the work.

Coleridge explains that the poem was written in 1797; he further describes its genesis in a dream after he had taken "an anodyne" medicine and fallen asleep. Coleridge declares that while dreaming he "could not have composed less than from two to three hundred lines; if that indeed can be called composition in which all the images rose up before him as *things*, with a parallel production of the correspondent expressions, without any sensation or consciousness of effort."[20] Having stated that the poem derives directly from "a vision in a dream," Coleridge then describes why the published poem remains only a "fragment." After awaking from the dream, the poet had "a distinct recollection of the whole" of the poem, and proceeded to transcribe it. Unfortunately, while in the process of writing down the lines, he was "called out by a person on business from Porlock, and detained by him above an hour"; on attempting to resume the transcription, Coleridge found, to his "mortification," that the rest of the lines "had passed away."[21]

Kubla Khan is one of the most well-known poems in the English language; and Coleridge's account of the loss of the greater part of it – vanished along with the "vision in a dream" – is one of the great hard-luck stories in literary history, with the interrupting "person on business from Porlock" playing the role of villain in this minor tragedy. Literary historians and critics have been sceptical of Coleridge's account, however, suggesting that the visitor from Porlock never existed. Coleridge biographer William Christie notes that an earlier version of the preface, in another manuscript, makes no mention of the business-man caller at all; and this earlier draft also states that the poem was "composed in a sort of Reverie brought on by two grains of Opium." Christie finds it likely that the poem appeared to Coleridge while in an opium trance; and that the rest of the work eluded him as he exited the hallucinatory state.

Christie also records that Coleridge himself was confused or troubled by this poem, which he called a "psychological curiosity," and that he did not publish it until 1816 – nineteen years after it was written.[22] Coleridge seemed reluctant to credit himself as author of the poem by publishing it; it may be that for him it wasn't a complete poem at all, but rather a "fragment" of a vision emanating from a perplexing psychological zone (which, a century later, would be termed "the unconscious"). But Coleridge had no reservations in publicizing the source of his inspiration in a dream (or hallucinatory state); like other poets and artists of the Romantic generation (and those of earlier generations) he celebrated the creative force and its mysterious, irrational energy as manifest in dreams.

In the twenty-first century, neuro-science has largely usurped psychology's role as chief investigator of the workings of the brain (mind). Freud's model of the unconscious, however, remains a presence in contemporary thought; and the culture makes reference to it with terms like the "Freudian slip," which is thought to betray the true desires of the unconscious mind. Certainly, post-Freud, the unconscious of a creative author is considered an integral part of that author's mind, which is why a song or poem appearing to an author in a dream will always be credited to the individual concerned.

In the age of high-speed computers and vast databases, another image of conscious and unconscious thought has emerged: one composed of data. The 2007 electronic artwork *Moveable Type* (discussed in detail in chapter 7 as a "big data" artwork without an apparent author) makes oblique reference to the unconscious, even to those novels of James Joyce exploring the conscious and unconscious mind. In the daytime, *Moveable Type* generates text drawn from that day's *New York Times* online; at night, the artwork draws its text from the archival database of the newspaper, dating back to 1851. A newspaper review of this work in 2007 noted that at night, the algorithm powering the work is "dreaming," as it rummages through the archival database "*Finnegan's Wake*-style."[23]

"Who Made This?": Contemporary Complications

To conclude this chapter, I present a number of recent examples of contemporary culture, all of which complicate the notion of authorship. The complication may arise from the status of specific authors as creators of works, or it may focus on the status of a work itself. Questions arise: who made this work? Who owns it? Who is the author?

The Unlawful Author?

The first example is graffiti art, a contemporary form of calligraphy – writing as art – applied to urban surfaces including building walls and train carriages. Graffiti art claimed international attention in the 1970s, when graffiti artists in New York decorated subway carriages with their designs, which normally included a signature by the artist

"I Don't Own It": Contemporary Complications   33

Figure 2.1 Joseph Quilter aka WEI2, graffiti art

(using a pseudonym). In the early 1980s, graffiti art spread around the world as a part of hip-hop culture, which also comprised rap music and break dancing. Graffiti art was a form of outsider art made by the socially marginalized – especially as the practice was declared illegal in New York City and in many other cities of the world. New York City authorities – and property owners – condemned graffiti as a form of vandalism; the city's response to the rapid spread of graffiti writing was to criminalize the practice and to remove it from public property by "cleaning" city walls and subway carriages.

The question is, then: can a graffiti artist be considered an author? If we define "author" as "a legal/economic entity whose original works are protected by copyright," we must answer this question in the negative. Graffiti art on public property is in most cases illegal, so it has been widely assumed that the artist can have no legal right (copyright) as owner of the work. In addition, the graffiti art work does not form a commodity: it is not for sale on the market, so that copyright is not involved in the distribution and sale of the work. The legal status of the graffiti artist as author is questionable, when their creative practice is defined as illegal.

But this has not deterred the international practice of graffiti art in cities around the world; its many practitioners revel in their status as subversive outsider artists. They do not seek commodification of their work, and they do not require recognition by the state of their authorship status. The city surfaces are their public exhibition spaces, and recognition comes from their peers and appreciative members of the public. Their role as exponents of underground art is confirmed by their illegal status; there have been many international instances of graffiti artists being fined or even imprisoned for pursuing their practice. The most notorious of these was the sentence imposed on a graffiti artist in Singapore in 1993: four months in prison, a fine of $3,500 US, and a public caning.

However, the legal status of graffiti street art regarding copyright has been contested. In her 2016 book *Copyright Beyond the Law*, Marta Iljadica argues that street art should be protected by copyright. Iljadica points out that a work of graffiti street art satisfies the requirements for a work to be copyrighted, including that the work is original; and that it is fixed and in material form. Iljadica's argument has been vindicated in the very few instances when a graffiti artist has sued for infringement of copyright of a street art work.

In 2015, the street artist Rime sued fashion design house Moschino on the grounds that Moschino appropriated, without permission, designs in a mural called "Vandal Eyes," painted by Rime on a building wall in Detroit. Lawyers for Rime claimed copyright infringement for misappropriation of his artwork on Moschino items of clothing. The court dismissed arguments by the defence that a work of graffiti art does not qualify for copyright protection due to its illegal nature. A settlement was eventually reached in this case; the online publication *Street Art and Law* drew two conclusions from the case: first, street art meets the requirements for copyright protection as a fixed and tangible form of expression; and secondly, the illicit nature of the work (or more correctly the illicit process by which the work was created) does not affect copyright in the work.[24]

Yet cases such as this are extremely rare. Iljadica offers reasons for this: graffiti writers may endanger themselves by revealing their real name – and identifying their works – in court, as they could then be liable for "prosecution for criminal damage." Copyright is "irrelevant" for the great majority of graffiti artists, who do not "avail themselves of copyright protection." Iljadica concludes that graffiti creativity "flourishes without reference or recourse to copyright."[25]

There is an exception to this non-copyrighted protection condition of graffiti writing: this occurs when graffiti art is displayed not on city walls but on the walls of an art gallery. This happened early in the life of hip-hop graffiti: an exhibition of graffiti art by Fab 5 Freddy and Lee Quinones was staged in Rome in 1979. When graffiti art covers canvas or other art mediums, and is exhibited, for sale, in a gallery, it accedes to the status of commodity – and its creator is legally construed as the author of the work. This practice – while financially benefitting artists and legitimizing their practice as a form of art – also injects a tension into the subculture. If graffiti art originated as street-level underground expression – functioning outside the circuits of commodification and the law – then exhibiting within galleries and museums may be condemned as "selling out" or betraying the aims of the subculture.

This tension has been played out in the careers of high-profile "street artists," including the highest-profile of them all, Banksy. The pseudonymous English street artist conceals his real name because he acknowledges that much of his art is illegal; in many instances his works have been condemned as vandalism by city councils, and removed. Banksy began as a graffiti artist in the British city of Bristol, before adopting the stencilling technique, for quick applications to public spaces, with great success. His images often convey a subversive political message, befitting his conviction that graffiti art is a voice for the underclass against the powerful and the wealthy.

Despite the illegal nature of his stencilled street art works, Banksy has been able to earn revenue from his art, in the form of the sale of photographs or reproductions of his street graffiti, and other commissions or art projects. In this, he has functioned as an author in the art market, in the manner pioneered by conceptual artists in the 1960s, whose works were non-objects – such as performances or events. Richard Long, whose art works beginning in the 1960s were walks, is an example of a successful artist who transformed the non-object/non-commodity at the centre of his practice into documentations or mementoes from his walks, which could be offered for sale in galleries.

At one point in his career, however, Banksy decided no longer to sell reproductions of his street works, perhaps recoiling from their commodification. In recent years, the public stencil works have been sold, but only once the stencilled wall is itself removed from its urban location. Banksy's ambivalence to his functioning in the art market – as an underground artist – was best expressed in 2018, when his framed work *Balloon Girl* was sold at auction by Sotheby's in London for over one million pounds. At the point of the sale, an alarm sounded from inside the work's picture frame, and the canvas was partially shredded by a shredder concealed inside the frame. Sotheby's later confirmed that the self-destruction of the work was a prank by the artist[26] (although the sale of the work was also confirmed). Banksy made his name – and fame – as a marginalized, subversive street artist; it was important for his credibility that his art work should self-destruct in the auction house, one of the symbols of the art market itself.

Author by Erasure

At the 2018 Sydney Festival, a collaborative (multi-authored) work entitled *Tree of Codes* was staged. The text on which this stage work was based was the novel *Tree of Codes* by Jonathan Safran Foer. But that by-line was the source of confusion and some controversy, as the novel *Tree of Codes* was a cut-up by Foer of the short story collection *The Street of Crocodiles* by the Polish author Bruno Schulz, originally published in 1934. The title *Street of Crocodiles* becomes *Tree of Codes* with the removal of seven letters; each of the 134 pages of *Tree of Codes* has been similarly cut up or edited by Foer, using the text of *The Street of Crocodiles* as source material. Foer calls his work *Tree of Codes* a "die-cut book by erasure."[27]

From the perspective of authorship, we may ask: who is the real author of *Tree of Codes*? It could be argued that Schulz is the author (in translation), since he wrote every word in the text *Tree of Codes*. Schulz's contribution to the text includes many complete sentences and phrases, left intact by Foer's cut-up technique. Yet Foer is adamant on the question of *Tree of Codes*' authorship: "This book is mine," he has stated.[28]

There are precedents for creating works by erasure, the most well-known of which is a visual art work. In 1953, the American artist Robert Rauschenberg obtained a drawing in crayon, ink, pencil, and charcoal from the artist Willem de Kooning, at the time one of the leading American artists. Rauschenberg then took two months to remove almost all of the drawing, using a number of different erasers. To complete the work, Rauschenberg asked the artist Jasper Johns to inscribe a caption on the frame, reading: "Erased de Kooning Drawing, Robert Rauschenberg, 1953." In this case, the source material of the work – de Kooning's drawing – was almost entirely erased by Rauschenberg, who felt justified in asserting authorship of the resulting art work. Although Rauschenberg added nothing to the source material, his erasure of that work was his creative contribution, reducing the original drawing to almost nothing.

Rauschenberg had earlier reduced his own paintings to almost nothing, in the form of all-white monochrome paintings in 1951. On seeing these monochromes, the composer John Cage realized that music, by comparison with these conceptual art works, "was lagging," and created his famous (or infamous) composition *4' 33"*, which was first performed in 1952. A performance of *4' 33"* entails a pianist sitting at a piano for that duration and doing nothing; there is no music in this composition; music has seemingly been reduced to zero. But *4' 33"* was not the sound of nothing, of course: as music critic Alex Ross has observed of the work's first performance, the music "was the sound of the surrounding space,"[29] including the sounds of the audience. The piece *4' 33"* is an ambient composition, in that it incorporates the sounds of the environment – during performance of the work – into the score; and because that ambience is different each time the work is performed, Cage also incorporated an element of chance into the piece.

In literature, the erasure technique has been used by numerous poets and novelists in the twentieth and twenty-first centuries. In some cases, the act of erasing source material serves a political purpose, as in the erasure poetry of Jordan Abel and Billy-Ray Belcourt, which erases colonial documents to mirror the disappearance of Indigenous people from history. In *Tree of Codes*, Jonathan Safran Foer makes oblique reference to the disappearance of the Polish author Bruno Schulz, who was murdered by Nazis in 1942, while many of his manuscripts were lost. The erasure of much of the text of *Street of Crocodiles* is in this manner a poetic reflection on the tragic disappearance of the book's author.

The success of the erasure cut-up technique, however, depends more on what the writer selects – or leaves in – than on what is erased. The remaining words may only represent a small fraction of the original text, but they are selected to form a poem down each page. This edited text may create a new set of meanings, undermining the source material, or it may draw out the themes and meanings of the original work in a poetic manner. This is why Foer is justified in asserting ownership of *Tree of Codes* – "This book is mine" – even though every word in the text was written by Schulz. Foer has applied imagination, skill, and labour in creating the new book; this is the test in copyright law to determine if an author has created an original work. The book is his by the law of copyright; *Tree of Codes* is by Foer and not by Schulz. At the same time, Foer aims to foreground Schulz and *The Street of Crocodiles*, a book which, he has declared, he "loves actively"[30] and to which he has sought to pay tribute.

Someone Else Made This

In the first two decades of the twenty-first century, the Vietnamese-Danish artist Danh Vo staged a number of exhibitions – in the US, Europe and elsewhere – which managed to confound the contemporary art world (which is not easily confounded). The reason for the consternation – or controversy – was that Vo regularly filled his exhibitions with works and objects made by other artists, or non-artists. In a 2012 exhibition called *I am you and you are too* at the Guggenheim Museum in New York, Vo showed none of his own works at all, but exhibited hundreds of figurines and ceramics that had been collected by the Chinese-American artist Martin Wong, who died of AIDS in 1999. That this exhibition – meant to showcase the work of Vo, who had recently won the Hugo Boss Prize for art – instead featured works from the collection of another artist, confronted art critics and curators, even those sympathetic to Vo's concerns as an artist. The Guggenheim curator Katherine Brinson stated that the concept of this show affected her deeply as a curator: "Who was the author? Was it collaboration, or appropriation? The show criticized our concepts of authorship, in a way, but it was also a beautiful, generous gesture."[31] Media coverage of Vo's exhibitions declared that his art "challenges the idea of aesthetic authorship."[32]

Other exhibitions by Vo incorporated the work of other artists, or included objects made by non-artists. An exhibition entitled *Good Life* in Berlin in 2007 was of photos taken by the photographer (and former Rand Corporation analyst) Joseph Carrier in Vietnam. Far from feeling exploited by the appropriation of his photographs, Carrier was grateful for the exhibition, which took his images to an international audience. One of Vo's exhibitions displayed a chandelier from the Hotel Majestic in Paris, while another exhibited his father's most prized possessions: a Rolex watch, a Dupont lighter, and a US military signet ring.[33]

The question posed by the curator Katherine Brinson points to a complicated – or possibly expanded – conception of authorship practised by Vo in his art. On one level, his art practice involves appropriation of the work of other artists; appropriation was an aesthetic strategy conducted by many postmodern artists in the 1980s and 1990s. But Vo's art seems to transcend postmodern appropriation, and the term "collaboration," suggested by Brinson, may more accurately describe Vo's practice when incorporating the works of other artists.

Vo is less formed by the aesthetic strategy of appropriation than he is influenced by the idea of relational art, a theory of contemporary art articulated by the French theorist Nicholas Bourriaud in his 1998 book *Relational Aesthetics*. Relational art theory was influential in art schools and art theory in the first decade of the twenty-first century; and Rirkrit Tiravanija, an artist mentor of Vo's at the Royal Danish Academy of Fine Arts, was a noted advocate of relational aesthetics. In defining this theoretical approach, Bourriaud looked beyond individuals' art practice to the human relations and social context for the production and consumption of all art and media. The titles of Vo's exhibitions – *We the People*; *I Am You and You Are Too* – reflect this concern with relationships and collaborations in the creation of art. Vo's art practice – pushing and testing received notions of individual authorship – shifts the idea of the author towards a network of collaborators rather than one originating artist.

What Does the Author Do?

The final example discussed in this chapter concerns a controversial attribution of authorship in a photographic work. In Australia in 2017, the Olive Cotton Award for Photographic Portraiture, which carried a prize of $20,000 AUS, was won by the artist Justine Varga for her work *Maternal Line*. The prize was judged by Dr. Shaune Lakin, Senior Curator of Photography at the National Gallery of Australia. *Maternal Line* is a portrait of the artist's grandmother, made without a camera. The artist Justine Varga asked her grandmother to make marks on negative film using pens and saliva. Varga then spent several days in a darkroom creating a large 153.0 x 125.0 cm paper print from that negative, experimenting with its colour, size, and appearance before deciding on its final manifestation. This was the object that was then submitted to the portrait prize.

Shortly after the prize was awarded to Varga, the award was publicly contested. The first controversy focused on the eligibility of the work for the prize, based on the claim that it was not a photograph nor was it a portrait, in the conventional sense. Critics attacked the award, and hate mail was sent to the judge Lakin. The second, more sustained, controversy, focused on the authorship of the work: there were claims that the true author of *Maternal Line* was not Varga but her grandmother. One aggrieved photographer told the *Sydney Morning Herald* newspaper that the work fails to meet requirements for the prize because it was actually created by the grandmother. Varga was accused of exploitation as well as appropriation: "I believe there is a very real concern that Ms Varga has misappropriated her vulnerable grandmother's copyright in a work the old lady reportedly created."[34] This same critic focused on the issue of what an author actually does to merit the attribution of authorship. The mere act of reproducing a work (created by the grandmother) and calling it *Maternal Line* does not, for the critic, "constitute its creation," and "does not entitle the person making the reproduction to claim copyright of the work." That is, reproduction or appropriation of another's work does not constitute authorship.

This view received support from a Professor at the University of Sydney Law School, who told the *Sydney Morning Herald* that the artist would need to do more than simply reproduce her grandmother's work to be credited as author: "You have to contribute original expression to the artistic work to be an author." In the opinion of the Law Professor, the owner of

Figure 2.2 Justine Varga, *Maternal Line*, 2017, chromogenic photograph, 160.0 x 125.0 cm (frame). Courtesy of the artist, Hugo Michell Gallery, and Tolarno Galleries.

the work is in fact the grandmother, either solely or jointly with Varga. For Varga to claim sole authorship of the work, she would need to secure an assignment of ownership, in writing, from the grandmother; in this way the artist could be sure of owning the copyright in the work. An alternative approach, the Professor added, would be for Varga to establish that she controlled the creation of the work, through conceptual intention. But in that case, the Professor concluded, it could no longer be claimed that the expression, and the portrait, was by the grandmother.

The Professor's passing remark about the artist's "conceptual intention" held the key to a defence of the artist as author of this work, and to the upholding of the award of the prize to Varga. Australian copyright law, based on the Australian Copyright Act of 1968 and relevant case law, stipulates that to be protected by copyright, a work must be original, and an application of skill or labour. It must originate from the author and be the result of a substantial degree of skill, industry, or experience. The work exists as an ordered expression of thought in material form. At the height of the controversy over the authorship of *Maternal Line*, an Australian curator spoke publicly in defence of Varga's ownership of the work: "The artist's conceptual, intellectual and emotional intention is vital in this process." The crucial word is "conceptual": the artist conceptualizes the work and oversees its material creation. This notion of the author adds a further answer to the question, "What does the author do?" – at least in the context of conceptual artists.

The artist does not need to materially construct the art work; the work can be said to "originate from the author" in as much as it constitutes an "ordered expression" of the artist's thought. This has been the underlying premise of conceptual art since the 1960s, and of modern art from well before that – dating back to Marcel Duchamp's "ready-made" artworks of found objects (including a urinal in the scandalous 1917 work *Fountain*). The conceptual artist is the originator and author of the work, even if the artist makes no material contribution to that work. This expanded idea of the author is recognized, for the most part, by the law of copyright. In her study of copyright and collective authorship, Daniela Simone notes that copyright law generally refers to the author as "the person who conceptualises and directs the development of a work, rather than a person who follows those directions to execute it."[35]

What does an author do? In the case of *Maternal Line*, the author conceives of the work, and asks her grandmother to make the portrait, using markings and even saliva directly onto negative film. Varga, not her grandmother, conceptualized the work. The artist keeps the prize, despite the attempts of detractors to disqualify her as author.

Chapter Three

Who Is the Author / Who Are the Authors?

I have already mentioned the reality that much writing and creativity – in the past and in the present – has been collaborative in nature rather than individualized. In the contemporary world of online media and social media, more writing and creative expression than ever is not named – or authored – by individuals, and takes the form of collaboration. This chapter explores the complications arising for authorship when collaborative or collective writing is involved.

The One or the Many

In 1994 – at the dawn of internet culture – Martha Woodmansee and Peter Jaszi explored collective creativity in their book *The Construction of Authorship*. Woodmansee in particular was concerned to "recover collectivity" in the contemporary "author effect." She noted that copyright law recognizes – and protects – the individual author; but she also observed that much professional writing is not authored in that individualized sense. For Woodmansee, the concept of author as "an individual who is the sole creator of unique 'works'" does not "closely reflect contemporary writing practices"; indeed, she further remarks that "it is not clear that this notion ever coincided closely with the practice of writing."[1]

Much contemporary writing is conducted not on an individual but on a corporate or collective basis, and is frequently anonymous. Citing a study of professional writing practices, Woodmansee argued that "most of the writing that goes on today is in fact collaborative."[2] Examples of collaborative or corporate writing include: scientific papers, business plans and strategies, government reports and industry reports. Examples of corporate anonymous writing include: marketing plans, advertising campaigns, public design and information, much online writing.

Woodmansee concludes that the authorship recognized by copyright law is to some extent a distortion of the reality of professional writing. Its focus is on the individual author, which is – as Foucault observed – "a privileged moment of individualization in the history of ideas, knowledge and literature."[3] Woodmansee notes that the "last bastion of solitary origination" seems to be the arts and humanities, where writing is taught as an individual pursuit, in the Romantic tradition.[4] Woodmansee holds out the hope, however, that even the recalcitrant humanities may be cured of its individualist bias by the technology of electronic writing, where interactivity and hypertext encourage collaborative authorship.

Woodmansee and other contributors to *The Construction of Authorship* sought to re-balance authorship away from the individual and towards the collective. Collaborative authorship has long been a characteristic of much cultural production: Shakespeare's plays, for example, were collaborative productions including input from members of the theatre company as well as the playwright, while Shakespeare was also a "co-author" or collaborator on several plays.[5] Collective authorship continues in the present, most notably in the authorship of films, TV programs, video games, animations, and multimedia online works. Internet culture has intensified collaborative authorship – in everyday "threads" of email or text correspondence, in vast online projects such as Wikipedia, and in the ongoing creation and modification of open source code.

Writers Not Authors

There are many other instances of professional writers who are paid for their work, often working in teams, but are not recognized as authors. A staple of the publishing industry is the lifestyle book – home design, cooking, gardening, decorating – that is conspicuously un-authored. That is, the book has no by-line, as it is a compilation by the publisher of writing from a number of sources. Sherman Young, in his 2007 book *The Book Is Dead, Long Live the Book*, described this type of work as an "anti-book," and noted that such books have become common in the publishing industry in the twenty-first century.[6] The original writers of those pieces of part-writing collected in such a book may have been paid at one point, but they are certainly not named as co-author of the compilation book, and will receive no royalties.

The award-winning television series *Madmen*, which ran from 2007 to 2015, glamourized the world of the advertising industry in the 1960s, in particular the creative abilities of the fictional creative director Don

Draper. But even Don Draper was regularly shown working within a team of "creatives" to write advertising copy for clients; and when those campaigns were run on media, they were anonymous – as are all advertising, marketing, and public relations campaigns. The closest that an individual creative director ever comes to recognition of their authorship of a particular campaign is at an industry awards presentation, when that particular campaign may win an award. But such recognition is severely restricted, to industry insiders only; for the general public, advertising campaigns have no author. The creative team members responsible for published campaigns receive no royalties; rather, they are paid salaries to create campaigns and memorable ads: this is part of their job. And while a popular advertising campaign may enjoy high visibility on the media, including online media, for the authors of that campaign there is no visibility at all.

The sphere of public design and information operates according to the same principle. Foucault made this observation with his mention of the anonymous poster, which may have a prominent vantage spot in the city, seen by tens of thousands. But who designed that poster? Who designed the traffic signs obeyed every day by millions of drivers and pedestrians: the STOP sign, the green figure signifying "walk" at intersections? All these signs and items of public information were designed by individuals or teams of designers and writers – but their work is anonymous, and they are not regarded as authors.

This makes the celebration of authors as individual creators all the more remarkable. Contemporary culture has preserved the heroic status of individual authors – as original creators – which was bestowed upon artists, poets, novelists, and composers in the eighteenth and nineteenth centuries. We revere the achievement of the author in publishing a new book; or in releasing a new film.

Auteurs and Authors

But who is the author of a film? Is it the director, as proposed by the "auteur theory" originating in the 1950s? Is it the scriptwriter or writers, without whom there would be no film? Is it the producer, production team, film company or studio, who have overseen the complete production of the film? Or is it a form of collective authorship, to which every craftsperson working on the film has contributed, in a mode of distributed authorship?

At the Academy Awards ceremonies for cinema, the "Best Picture" award – the evening's major prize – is presented to the producers of the film. This indicates that for the Academy of Motion Picture Arts &

Sciences, at least, authorship of the film is ultimately attributed to its producers. However, films are commonly described with reference not to their producers but their directors: we speak of the new Martin Scorsese or Jane Campion film, or of the great films of Orson Welles or Alfred Hitchcock – without mention of the films' producers.

The issue of film authorship is a vexed one, stemming from the claim of "auteur theory" in the 1950s that the true author of a film is the director, who imprints a singular and original vision on the work; this assertion has been forcibly contested by film critics and theorists since the 1960s. The auteur theory of film authorship emerged from the pages of the French Journal *Cahiers du Cinema* in the 1950s; writers for this journal included the critic and film theorist André Bazin, and the critics François Truffaut and Jean-Luc Godard (both of whom became leading figures of the French New Wave – as directors – in the late 1950s and early 1960s).

Auteur theory was first proposed in an essay by Truffaut called "A Certain Tendency in French Cinema," in which Truffaut criticized the staid "tradition of quality" in French cinema. Truffaut contrasted this conventional, worthy type of film-making with the striking visual and narrative style of certain directors, including Robert Bresson, Jean Renoir, Jean Cocteau, and Jacques Tati. Truffaut and his colleagues at *Cahiers du Cinéma* also celebrated the films of certain Hollywood directors – including Howard Hawkes, Orson Welles, John Ford, and Alfred Hitchcock – that achieved a distinctive style despite the restrictions of the Hollywood studio system, and despite ranging across diverse film genres.

For Truffaut, these directors were true "auteurs" or authors of their films because they were able to impose a distinctive style or vision on all their works. Auteur theory was promoted in the English-speaking world in the 1960s by the film critic Andrew Sarris, who proposed in a number of publications that "directorial personality" resides in the style evident in that director's films. Sarris elevated auteur theory as a means of evaluating and interpreting films, arguing for "the distinguishable personality of the director as a criterion of value."[7] For Sarris, a film is ultimately "the expression of a director's vision."[8]

But auteur theory's conviction that the director is the author of the film has never been widely accepted; indeed it has met with fierce criticism. The first objection has been that it is inappropriate to transfer the concept of author from the field of literature – where it has been most commonly applied – to the altogether different domain of film. Aaron Meskin notes this concern in his 2008 essay on film authorship, pointing out that the traditional notion of authorship, applicable to "the sphere of the high or fine arts," may be inappropriately applied to film, "which is often characterised as a popular or mass art."[9] The film theorist Karen Pearlman has suggested that "author," drawn from literary authorship, is an inappropriate analogy for the film director; she suggests that the conductor is a better analogy, as this cultural practitioner organizes movement, and the input of other practitioners, as does a film director.[10]

If film is a mass art, it is also an art with a mass of creators. Cinema is an industrial art, formed in the early twentieth century, employing the new industrial means of production of the moving image, then sound. Twenty-first century cinema could be termed a post-industrial art, deploying digital technology including Computer-Generated Imagery (CGI), and streamed over the internet to digital devices (as well as exhibiting in cinemas, in the twentieth century manner). Whereas a novel, poem, short story, or play is usually written by one person, the personnel contributing to the production of a contemporary feature film numbers in the hundreds. Indeed, the production credits at the end of feature films frequently take at least ten minutes to run through to the final credit. The critics of auteur theory argue that a novel may be written by one "agent" who can reasonably be described as its "author"; yet a film is made by hundreds of craftspeople, which makes it highly unreasonable to ascribe its authorship to one individual agent.

Rosebud

Another objection has been that auteur theory privileges the director as author of a film, discounting the contribution of the actual authors (in a literary sense): the writers of the film script. The script contains the narrative and structure of the film, as well as the dialogue: the core of any film. Most film scripts have more than one author; indeed a contemporary Hollywood film may list in its credits multiple authors, including the writers of the story treatment, teams of scriptwriters, as well as specialist writers brought in to polish the script in its final stages. Scriptwriting is a collaborative process in most cases, and it can be argued that the director further collaborates with the writers in realizing the film script in visual terms.

Debate over the relative contributions of scriptwriter and director in the authorship of the film has occurred in the context of many film works, most notably the 1941 film *Citizen Kane*. This film was not rapturously received by critics on its release, winning only one Academy Award. However, in subsequent decades it regularly topped international film critics' polls as the greatest film ever made. *Citizen Kane*'s enduring greatness as a work is often attributed to the daring visual style achieved by Orson Welles, in his first feature film as director. Yet many film critics and theorists have pointed to the central importance of the screenplay, credited to the writer Herman J. Mankiewicz and Welles as co-authors. In fact, the only Academy Award received by *Citizen Kane* in 1942 was for Best Screenplay, shared by Mankiewicz and Welles.

The narrative of *Citizen Kane* (as originally written by Mankiewicz) concerns the quest by an investigative journalist to solve the mystery of the tycoon Charles Foster Kane's dying word: "Rosebud." Who or what is Rosebud? This mystery underpins the narrative of the film concerning the rise and downfall of Kane; in the end, the investigator fails to solve the mystery – although it is revealed to the audience in the film's final shot. Critical and theoretical analysis of *Citizen Kane* has pursued its own mystery, its own version of Rosebud: who was the true author of this celebrated film?

Debate on this issue has raged since 1971, when the American film critic Pauline Kael argued in her article "Raising Kane" that Mankiewicz, officially only co-author of the screenplay, was in fact primarily responsible for the script of *Citizen Kane*. It is known that Mankiewicz created the first draft of the script; it is also known that he was a frequent guest of William Randolph Hearst at his San Simenon mansion in the 1930s: Hearst became Charles Foster Kane, and San Simenon became Xanadu, in Mankiewicz's screenplay.

But a counter-view of the authorship of the *Kane* script was proposed by Robert Caringer in his 1985 book *The Making of Citizen Kane*. Caringer asserted that Welles fundamentally reshaped the script over many drafts after receiving it from Mankiewicz. The debate has never been resolved. The 2020 film *Mank*, directed by David Fincher and written by his father Jack Fincher, adopted the Kael critical perspective. This film emphasized Mankiewicz's role as the primary author of the *Kane* screenplay.[11]

It should occasion no surprise that the film critics and theorists have failed to solve their mystery; Rosebud remains unresolved. Proponents of auteur theory firmly believe that Welles, with his extraordinary – and radical – visual flair, is the true auteur of *Citizen Kane*, as well as the shaper of its script in the final stage. Supporters of Mankiewicz uphold the primacy of the script, which is the backbone of the film; Mankiewicz should therefore be considered the author of the film. Film theory has divided along the lines of this discord. The playwright and screenwriter Howard Koch was adamant that the scriptwriter is "the primary creative source" of a film. But Bordwell and Thompson, in their film studies text *Film Art: An Introduction,* state that within the film industry, the director "is considered the single person most responsible for the look and sound of the finished film."[12]

Genius of the System

When the law has been asked to decide in an issue of disputed ownership of a film, it has found, at least in one case, not in favour of the director, or screenwriter, but the producer. Daniela Simone notes that because copyright law emphasizes individual authorship of a work, courts have at times sought to determine the "dominant author," who is accorded ownership of a film. In one case, the court found against a director's claim to co-authorship of a film, determining instead that it was the producer who had: initiated the project, acquired rights to the script, selected all cast and crew – including the director, controlled film production, publicity, and release. This sustained control over the creation of the film was deemed sufficient for the court to define the producer as the "dominant" – and sole – author of the film.[13]

However, Simone makes the further point that in European and UK copyright law, authorship of a film is generally vested in both the producer and director of the work (the UK copyright act of 1988 initially designated the producer as author of a film, but later added the director as joint-author, in line with EU copyright law). In the American film production system, production companies maintain ownership of rights through contracts with all contributors to the film; this system ensures that producers are "unimpeded in their exploitation of the final product – so they are best-placed to recoup their investment."[14] Indeed, the legal concepts of sole ownership/authorship of a film (the producer) or dual authorship (producer and director) are largely founded on consideration of the huge financial scale – and risk – of film production. In this legal/economic model, the claim of producer or film company to authorship is based on their financial investment and overall control of the production process, while the director's authorship claim relates to their control of the creative film-making process.[15]

But many critics, theorists and film industry practitioners have contested the attribution of authorship to a single film-maker, or dual film-makers, positing instead a collaborative or distributed authorship of films. Simone summarizes this viewpoint: "Recent trends in this industry and in film scholarship are for a more inclusive notion of authorship in line with the reality of the film-making process."[16] James Naremore has described this reality of film creation as a mix of industrialized, technical, theatrical and artisanal practices.[17] The authorship of a film in this view is shared by all the practitioners working on a film project, including scriptwriter, cinematographer, production designer, composer, costumes designer, editor, sound designer, and numerous other specialist technicians.

The cinematographer, also known as director of photography, is in many instances responsible for the "look" or visual style of the film. Indeed, film historians have suggested that Greg Toland, cinematographer on *Citizen Kane*, was directly responsible for the visual style and techniques – including deep focus and camera placement – of that great work (especially as Orson Welles at that stage was an inexperienced director). A case has even been made for considering actors as co-authors of the films in which they appear. Berys Gaut, in his essay "Film Authorship and Collaboration," has proposed that actors should be considered "co-creators" of films, because their performances are integral to the film, and because actors partially determine the characters they play in performance.[18] It could be added that major actors – or "stars" – have been used as selling-points for films since Hollywood adopted a "star system" around 1910.

An alternative to auteur theory was proposed in the pages of *Cahiers du Cinéma* by André Bazin, who did not share the wholehearted auteur commitment of his *Cahiers* colleagues. Bazin sought to situate film theory within a social context, which meant that his focus was not so much on the individual director, but on the system of film production. Bazin wrote that the success of Hollywood was: "only incidentally technical; it lies much more in what one might call the American cinematic genius, something which should be analysed, then defined, by a sociological approach to its production."[19] This industry-wide analysis of film creation became known as the "genius of the system" approach, particularly as applied to the "Golden Age" of the Hollywood studios in the 1930s and 1940s.[20]

In this period, the five major Hollywood studios controlled all aspects of a film's production and distribution, operating a strict division of labour in which all contributors – including screenwriters, actors, technicians, and directors – were contracted to the studio. Films could be identified as issuing from a particular studio, based on the studio's favoured genre, style and stable of stars: MGM: opulent, extravagant films; Paramount: sophisticated comedies; Warner Brothers: dark, gritty dramas; Fox: westerns; RKO: film noir and challenging dramas including *Citizen Kane*.[21] The "genius of the system" approach suggests that the studio – not the director – was responsible for the distinctive style of the films it produced. Unlike auteur theory, this alternative viewpoint locates authorship of films within the broad system of the studio itself. It replaces the individualist bias of auteur theory with a model of collective authorship, founded on the "industrial complex" of film production (as film theorist Jim Kitses has described the Hollywood production system).[22]

In this regard, the model of film authorship is not the lone auteur but rather the factory. The industrial factory was the driving force of industrial capitalism in the early twentieth century. The modern factory, employing technologies such as the conveyor belt, and enforcing strict division of labour, was deployed with spectacular success early in the twentieth century by Henry Ford: Ford's automobile factory manufactured Model T Ford cars at an unprecedented rate and scale of production. The Ford-style factory was a highly rationalized version of the labour process, as theorized by Frederick Taylor in his 1911 book *Principles of Scientific Management*. In a Taylorized factory, the work process was organized around an assembly line, while each worker had one basic and repetitive task to perform. Workers were reduced to the function of cogs in a gigantic mechanism, as satirically portrayed in Charlie Chaplin's 1936 film *Modern Times*.

The Hollywood studio system, which was extremely productive in releasing high volumes of popular and celebrated films, ran film production as a form of cultural factory. Simone has described the process of creating a film, in which "a large number of individuals" with "very specialised skills" are involved, requiring "a division of labour that is organised hierarchically."[23] This is a description of the industrial factory process. The Hollywood studio oversaw all aspects of film production according to a strict and tight schedule, in which creative practitioners including script writers and even directors had limited creative freedom. It could be argued by auteur theory proponents that the director was still able to impose a singular vision on this industrial process, in the manner of a factory foreperson, overseeing the entire labour system. However, it could equally be asserted that the heads of the studios – whose number included high-profile moguls such as Louis B. Mayer and Daryl F. Zanuck – were ultimately responsible for the style of films released by their studios.

The studio-as-cultural-factory system was so successful – and so productive – in the Hollywood golden age that it was adopted in other areas of cultural production in the twentieth century. The Motown record company was enormously successful in popular music throughout the 1960s, achieving many hit records on both the rhythm & blues and pop charts. Motown's production mogul, Berry Gordy, modelled his record company on the local car manufacturing plants in Detroit: Motown stood for 'Motor Town"; it was also known as the "hit factory." Gordy produced pop records as if on an assembly line, with a strict division of labour between songwriters, singers, musicians, and producers – all contracted to the Motown label.

Gordy's prodigious music factory system only began breaking down when specialists on the assembly line – songwriters, then performers – demanded greater control of the production process. Motown's leading songwriting team, Holland-Dozier-Holland, entered into a bitter dispute with Motown over royalties and profit-sharing; the team left Motown in 1968 to form its own production company. In the early 1970s, leading performers Marvin Gaye and Stevie Wonder demanded far greater control in the creation of their own records; by this stage the genius of the Motown system had dimmed, replaced by individualized creative control by recording artists.

The genius of the system has been evident in the animation industry, since the spectacular success of the Disney studio animations in the early twentieth century. Walt Disney Animation Studio was founded in 1923 by the Disney brothers Walt and Roy; in the studio's early years, Walt Disney worked as animator, but soon withdrew from drawing to concentrate on organizing the studio, as it produced feature length animations – beginning with *Snow White and the Seven Dwarves* in 1937. A case could be made for Walt Disney as auteur-producer in his lengthy career as overseer-mogul of Disney studios; Paul Wells, in his book *Animation: Genre and Authorship*, proposes that "Disney's auteurial status resides on his own personal sense of ownership and control of his studio's work."[24]

However, animation is such a difficult creative process, requiring the collaboration of hundreds of highly skilled specialist technicians, that the "genius of the system" is a better description of the production process of animation, including the distinctive styles and approaches that can be attributed to different studios or companies. Authorship is difficult to ascribe even in print comic-books, in which characters and plots are generally created in collaboration between artist and writer. Many of the Marvel comic super-hero narratives – involving Spider-Man, Hulk, Thor, X-Men, and other characters – were created in a collaboration between writer Stan Lee and artist Jack Kirby; but the co-creators later disputed authorship of the Marvel characters and story-lines. Lee progressed from editor-in-chief to president and publisher of Marvel Comics; his role at Marvel has been described not as author but as "orchestra conductor, coaxing talent from others."[25] Marvel came to be associated with a distinctive style of comics and animation, involving flawed super-heroes; the genius of the system is a more appropriate description of Marvel's distinctive approach than attribution to a single author such as Lee. The studios specializing in animation likewise developed characteristic styles of animation: Warner Bros cartoons, for example, featured perennial contests between pairs of cartoon animals – Wile E. Coyote vs. Road Runner – in surreal settings. Japanese anime achieved world-wide success with distinctive styles; Studio Ghibli's feature-length animations, for instance, draw on the other-worldly spirit-zone of Japanese mythology.

In the twenty-first century, the video game industry dwarfs both the film and music industries in sales; in the US alone, there are more than 2,500 companies producing or publishing video games. But who authors a video game? The issue of authorship is even more complex for video games than in the domain of cinema. The team of video game developers includes specialist technicians such as programmers and graphic designers, as well as audio-visual technicians and script writers as in film production and animation. This team of developers and technicians is overseen by a number of producers working for the video game company, which then publishes, distributes, and markets the game. Scripts for video games have been adapted from films and novels, but have also been original narratives (which in many cases have then been novelized or adapted into films). Because the design of video games incorporates both a narrative and a game-playing element, the construction of the work is a complex interplay between programming and narrative; in this industry, it is unreasonable to pinpoint a single auteur of video games, and plausible to posit the "genius of the system" at work.

If large-scale industries – including video games, animation, and cinema – create cultural works through collaborative authorship, why did auteur theory seek to elevate the film director as individual author of the work? John Caughie, in *Theories of Authorship,* describes auteur theory as "the installation in the cinema of the figure who had dominated the other arts for over a century: the romantic artist, individual and self-expressive."[26] This figure of the Romantic artist – inspired, possessed of a unique vision – was an attractive version of the author-function to apply to a massive industry, whose production process resembled that of a factory.

This point has been made by Andrew Bennett in his book *The Author*: Bennett suggests that the privileging of the director as author involved "a conscious resistance to the industrial film production of 1940s and 1950s Hollywood."[27] That is, while film was a collaborative, commercial, and industrial medium, it needed "its own version of the myth of the solitary genius" to be taken seriously as an art form alongside literature and visual arts. The concept of the auteur implies an "organic, controlling personality," an "ordering agent" projecting a "coherent and unified" vision. Bennett concludes that the project of imposing an "individual subjectivity" onto a collaborative work such as a film indicates "the seemingly ineluctable desire for the author."[28] Dana Polan has made a similar point in film theory, suggesting that auteur theory betrayed a "desire" for the director to be credited as author, so that films could be seen as "having an originary instance in the person who signs them."[29]

But in the case of film, the notion of an individual author is an illusion, as numerous film theorists have argued. Auteur theory dismisses the contributions to authorship of the many practitioners working on a film production. Robert Self has claimed that "the apparatus of film, with its mix of many crafts … quite literally models the idea of the multiauthored text."[30] Georges Sadoul has also made the case for collective authorship of films: "each collaborator, from the least technician to the most famous star, in small part or large, is one of the authors"[31] In their 2021 essay "Reframing the Director: Distributed Creativity in Filmmaking Practice," Karen Pearlman and John Sutton propose that film authorship is a case of "distributed creativity" among all practitioners contributing to the production, so that "a Scorsese film" should instead be credited as "a film by Scorsese et al."[32]

Feminist film theory has argued that auteur theory's privileging of the director – at a time when directors were almost entirely male – obscured the contributions made by women working in the film industry in the roles available to them from the early twentieth century. Julia Wright has proposed that a corrective to the theoretical frameworks – including auteur theory – that efface women in the film industry would be: "a paradigm shift away from authorship and textual analysis and a move toward analysing industry practices and cultures of film and media production."[33] This would make visible the achievements by women in the history of film production, in many cases in roles other than that of director. The 2010 book *Reclaiming the Archive : Feminism and Film History,* edited by Vicki Callahan, published research into the archive of film history, uncovering the many contributions of female film practitioners; along the way, Callahan advocated a "re-writing" of authorship, deemphasizing the centrality of directing and screenwriting as authorship of films.[34] In her 2015 essay "Feminist Media Historiography and the Work Ahead," Shelley Stamp made a similar proposal:

> We must also fundamentally reconceive authorship. The true scope of women's engagement with, participation in, and production of early movie culture comes into view only when we move beyond a focus on female directors and screenwriters.[35]

Karen Pearlman, a filmmaker as well as film theorist, concentrates on the role of editor as major contributor to films in her 2021 essay "Editing and Authorship." The editor is a major contributor to any film, establishing the rhythm of the work and creating meaning through

Figure 3.1 Karen Pearlman, *I Want to Make a Film about Women* (2019), still. Actor: Victoria Haralabidou as Esfir Shub.

the sequencing of shots. Pearlman made a trilogy of films – *Woman with an Editing Bench* (2016); *After the Facts* (2018); and *I Want to Make a Film About Women* (2019) – about Russian women editors working in the Soviet Montage era of the 1920s, when editing was elevated to a prominent position in Soviet film theory and practice. These female editors, including Elizaveta Svilova and Esfir Shub, remain little known, despite the fact that Shub was an esteemed and influential colleague and teacher of the directors Sergei Eisenstein and Dziga Vertov. Pearlman shows that these editors – in common with all film editors – should be considered co-authors of the films they edited.[36]

One of the factors preventing a more wide-spread acceptance of film authorship as a collaborative or distributed process is the individualist bias of copyright law, as Martha Woodmansee and other theorists have argued. One of the aims of Daniela Simone's 2019 book *Copyright and Collective Authorship* is to press for reform of copyright law pertaining to the creation and ownership of films. Simone asserts that copyright law "should seek closer alignment with the creative reality of film authorship."[37] This closer alignment would entail the extension of rights to the actual creators of films, rather than a concentration of rights in the owners – studios and film companies. Simone argues that copyright law "should embrace an *inclusive, contextual* approach to determining the authorship of a film as a dramatic work." Such an inclusive approach would involve recognition that: "a film is actually created by a range of collaborators inputting a variety of skills (each with some autonomy in shaping the form of their contribution), and recognizing these contributors as joint authors of that film."[38]

Reform of copyright law along these lines would ensure legal recognition that a film has not one but many authors.

Collective Intelligence

One of the earliest celebrations of the internet as a site of collaborative cultural expression was made in 1994 by the French media theorist Pierre Levy. Speaking at the International Symposium on Electronic Arts in Helsinki, Levy rhapsodized on the potential of the internet to generate a new "superlanguage" of dynamic hyper-text writing and "multimodal simulations."[39] He spoke optimistically of the "collective intelligence" activated on sites across the World Wide Web, which was for him "the best use the cyberspace can be put into." By "collective intelligence," Levy meant "intelligences distributed everywhere, active everywhere" across the web;[40] he developed these thoughts on internet-based collaboration in his 1996 book *Collective Intelligence: Mankind's Emerging World in Cyberspace*.

"Collective intelligence" was an early instance of the "wisdom of the crowd"/gift economy rhetoric employed by internet optimists after 2004, when "Web 2.0" emphasized user-generated content, and social media was inaugurated with the launch of Facebook. A flurry of theoretical works applauded the enhanced democracy and freedom of expression created by the open system of communication called the internet. The participatory nature of the internet meant that "the people formerly known as the audience" (Jay Rosen) were now known as "prosumers" – that is, both producers and consumers of information.[41]

The huge volume of new online communication was frequently collaborative in nature, whether expressed in messaging groups, online chat rooms, email threads, collaborative blogs, or websites. The collective authorship implicit in much online writing – along with utopian hopes for the promise of the internet – were expressed in the titles of theoretical works published in the half-decade after 2004. These books included: James Surowiecki's *The Wisdom of Crowds* (2004); Glenn Reynolds' *An Army of Davids: How Markets and Technology Empower Ordinary People to Beat Big Media, Big Government, and Other Goliaths* (2006); *Infotopia: How Many Minds Produce Knowledge* by Cass Sunstein (2006); Clay Shirky's 2008 book *Here Comes Everybody: The Power of Organizing Without Organizations* (the title *Here Comes Everybody* derives from James

Joyce's *Finnegans Wake*); *Wikinomics: How Mass Collaboration Changes Everything* by Dan Tapscott and Anthony D. Williams (2008); Jeff Howe's *Crowdsourcing: Why the Power of the Crowd Is Driving the Future of Business* (2008); and Shirky's 2010 book *Cognitive Surplus: Creativity and Generosity in a Connected Age*.[42] These and other theoretical works assumed that internet connectivity was a good in itself, empowering users as citizen journalists, amateur creators, bloggers and small online businesses. Most importantly, the internet fostered mass collaboration, creating "an army of Davids" to short-circuit the old networks of mass media and government.

However, this internet optimism did not survive to the end of the next decade. By 2019, journalism and media theory conveyed disillusionment with the monetized, commercialized nature of the World Wide Web, while Facebook, Apple, Google, and Amazon were now known as "Big Tech." These organizations had become some of the largest and most powerful corporations in the history of capitalism – and were subject to increasing criticism from journalists, theorists, and politicians. Revelations in 2016 that voters in the US Presidential election were targeted by a "data analytics" firm, using data harvested from users' social media, prompted alarm that the internet could pose a danger – rather than a benefit – to democracy. The realization that data mining or harvesting was continually deployed against users – either as direct advertising or attempts at political influence – led to severe critiques of the "Big Tech" corporations and their social impact.

Other criticisms of the internet-based Big Tech organizations included: widespread intrusions into users' privacy; the prevalence of unchecked misinformation and "fake news" on social media; the parasitical online use of copyrighted material drawn from traditional media, including news, music, film, and literature; and the monopoly status of Big Tech corporations, achieved by means of absorbing competitors. In 2017, Jonathan Taplin made the case against the major internet-based organizations in his book *Move Fast and Break Things: How Facebook, Google and Amazon Have Cornered Culture and What It Means for Us*. Timothy Wu's 2017 book *The Attention Merchants: The Epic Scramble to Get Inside Our Heads* levelled a critique at the "attention economy," in which internet users are targeted with campaigns based on their own social media use. In 2019, Shoshana Zuboff coined the term "surveillance capitalism" to describe the techniques of data mining – used by corporations and government – in *The Age of Surveillance Capitalism: The Fight for a Human Future at the New Frontier of Power*. Even Tim Berners-Lee, architect of the world wide web, publicly criticized the Big Tech "silos" in 2021: too much power and too much personal data, he declared, had

Who Is the Author / Who Are the Authors? 57

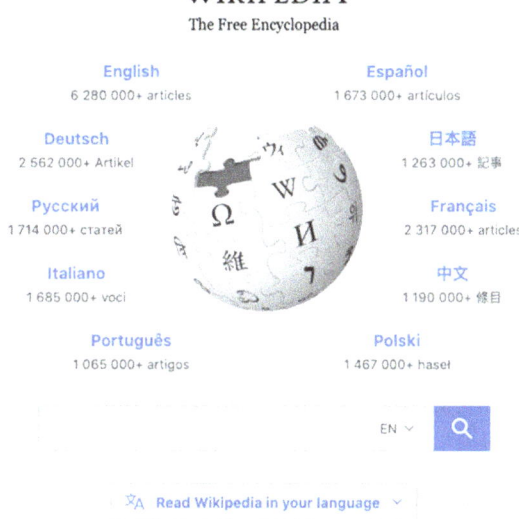

Figure 3.2 Wikipedia homepage. Creative Commons CC BY-SA 3.0.

become concentrated within a few gigantic corporations, which had become "surveillance platforms and gate-keepers of innovation."[43]

By 2021, then, the commodification and exploitation of the internet had formed not an army of Davids but a new Goliath. Certainly the utopian hope for the internet as a site of democratic empowerment and mass collaboration had faded appreciably compared to its height in 2008. But there was one exception to this pervasive disappointment with what the internet had become: Wikipedia.

Wikipedia was launched in 2001; a collection of scholarly articles – *Wikipedia@20: Stories of an Incomplete Revolution* – was published in 2020 to mark twenty years of the online encyclopaedia. While some writers in this collection make criticisms of Wikipedia's biases along the lines of gender and race, the consensus view is that it is "the major success story of the Internet era."[44] Wikipedia is not monetized; it carries no advertizing; its many volunteer contributors are not paid; and every online entry is freely available to be used without copyright restrictions. The vast enterprise of Wikipedia has two names attached as founding editors – Jimmy Wales and Larry Sanger – and is hosted by the Wikipedia Foundation; but it has no single author – indeed it has many tens of thousands of different contributors or editors. It is the most impressive realization of the collaborative authorship envisioned for the internet in the 1990s; it is a highly visible demonstration of "collective intelligence," "the wisdom of the crowd," and "the army of Davids" of internet users.

The editors of the book *Wikipedia@20* – Joseph Reagle and Jackie Koerner – note approvingly that Wikipedia is an instance of "commons-based peer production,"[45] the principle that almost anyone can write or edit an entry. They quote Jimmy Wales's 2004 articulation of Wikipedia's founding vision: to "imagine a world in which every single person on the planet is given free access to the sum of all human knowledge."[46] This lofty, idealistic aim is an internet-enabled updating of the eighteenth-century Enlightenment project: the creation of a better, fairer world through the application of reason and the widespread distribution of knowledge. And it is to the great Enlightenment-age encyclopaedias – vast compendiums of all knowledge – that Wikipedia is most often compared. The *Encyclopédie* edited by Denis Diderot and launched in 1751 – representative of the French Enlightenment – and *Encyclopedia Britannica*, first published in 1768 and representing the Scottish Enlightenment, aimed to make "the sum of all human knowledge" available to all readers, and employed the technique of cross-referencing of articles: a pre-internet version of linking.

But the limitations of print publishing mean that even the compendious *Encyclopedia Britannica* was dwarfed in its knowledge base by Wikipedia, which has no publication end-date and is continuously expanding. *Encyclopedia Britannica* had 65,000 articles in its last printed edition; in 2020 Wikipedia claimed to host more than 55 million articles in 313 languages.[47] The fundamental difference is in the contributor base: the editors of the Enlightenment encyclopaedias commissioned academics, scholars, and professional experts to write articles summarizing knowledge in their respective fields; contributors to Wikipedia do not require such qualifications. In this regard, a more appropriate precedent for Wikipedia is not *Encyclopedia Britannica*, but the *Oxford English Dictionary (OED)*, which was compiled over a seventy-year period with many thousands of contributions from volunteer members of the public.

The *OED* project commenced in 1858 under the editorship of Herbert Coleridge (the poet's grandson); its seemingly impossible – and unprecedented – ambition was to document the totality of the English language. The goal was to provide a definition and etymology for every English word, with quotations from English language texts to demonstrate meaning and change of meaning over time. The founders of the project realized that this aim could not be achieved without "the combined action of many" – that is, a vast team of unpaid amateur volunteers who would send in quotations from books making use of words listed in the new dictionary.⁴⁸ A circular was widely distributed, calling for volunteer readers in Britain; in 1879, the newly appointed editor James Murray sent out another appeal for volunteers throughout America and the British colonies, thereby further expanding the volunteer base.

This entirely new approach proved a spectacular success: more than six million slips of paper containing quotations were submitted by volunteers (one of the most prolific volunteers, as described in Simon Winchester's book *The Surgeon of Crowthorne*, was a convicted murderer imprisoned in an asylum for the criminally insane). The *OED* project was so gigantic that it wasn't completed until 1928, when 12 volumes of the dictionary – comprising over 414,000 word definitions, and over 1,800,000 definitions – were published. Even then, the English language kept growing and changing; a number of *OED* supplements were issued, and a twenty-volume second edition was published in 1989.

The *OED*, then, was constructed using a "rather noble idea" with a "rough, rather democratic appeal," as Winchester has characterized it – volunteer contributions.⁴⁹ But Wikipedia goes further. The volunteer contributions to the *OED* were sifted and selected by James Murray and subsequent editors, in a filtering process; and the professional editors were responsible for the actual definitions of words. Wikipedia entries, by contrast, are entirely written and edited by volunteer contributors, with only minimal editing intervention to eliminate unlawful content: discriminatory, defamatory, or offensive material. Wikipedia is a profound test of the wisdom of the crowd, of collective intelligence; and there have been many sceptics doubting that the crowd of volunteers could be capable of producing a reliable "sum of all human knowledge."

From the beginning of Wikipedia, critics doubted the ability of amateur volunteer contributors to create encyclopaedia entries without bias or subjective emphases. But all Wikipedia contributors are bound by three core policies of the online encyclopaedia: no original research, verifiability, and neutral point of view. These practices, including the use of existing information from – for example – other encyclopaedias, have produced entries with remarkably few errors or obvious biases, a feat which has won over many academics – initially suspicious of Wikipedia – to the project. (In 2005, a study in *Nature* journal found that science articles in Wikipedia averaged four errors per article, while *Encyclopedia Britannica* averaged three).⁵⁰

Every page of Wikipedia is a work in progress shaped by many contributors over time. As Daniela Simone observes, Wikipedia operates on the assumption that: "many different users will refine or 'refactor' each individual page until the page stabilises and comes to represent the voice of the community." Contributors feel strongly that they are part of a massive altruistic project of disseminating knowledge, and therefore strive to maintain standards of accuracy and reliability. As Simone comments, Wikipedia "has organised itself over time through the consensus-driven activities of its community of regular contributors."[51]

But what of authorship in Wikipedia? Can an individual contributor – or team of contributors – consider themselves authors or joint-authors of specific Wikipedia pages? Simone considers "the dynamics of authorship on Wikipedia" as a case study in collective authorship and copyright. She finds that copyright, and therefore individual authorship, is "ill-adapted" to Wikipedia, for two principal reasons. First, each page is a product of collaboration, by individuals from around the world who may never have met; and secondly, each page is never finished, but is "a perpetual work in progress,"[52] composed of ongoing and expanding collaboration. Simone notes that almost every page on Wikipedia invites the reader – or "prosumer" – to interact with it, thereby editing, altering, or adding to the entry. Because each page is never fixed, it is difficult to conceive of copyright subsisting in any entry, unless it were to apply to succeeding "draft versions" of the one page.[53]

All Wikipedia pages are in fact copyleft – that is, licensed to alternative schemes such as Creative Commons, which allow any user to copy or modify material (copyleft and Creative Commons are discussed in more detail – as alternatives to copyright – in chapter 6). Wikipedia content is co-licensed to the GNU Free Documentation Licence (GFDL) and the Creative Commons Attribution-Sharealike 3.0 Unported licence (CC-BY-SA); this means that any user may copy or make use of Wikipedia entries, so long as they acknowledge the original Wikipedia page, and re-licence any modifications under the CC-BY-SA licence.[54]

This is the gift economy of mass collaboration at work, as it has also functioned in open source software. On Wikipedia, individual authorship is discarded in favour of an ethic of sharing. This is the realization of the hopes held for internet use by theorist Sean Cubitt, in his 1998 book *Digital Aesthetics*. Cubitt posited that networked activity, "formed outside the managed webs of globalization," partakes of "the very purpose of making: to share."[55] The notion of ownership of copyrighted works, central to the concept of the modern author, has no purchase in the Wikipedia sharing economy. As Simone remarks, contributors to Wikipedia write and edit pages for free, and expect their work to be modified by others; Wikipedia "is thought of as owned by no one, to be shared by all." The earliest statement on ownership posted by Wikipedia, in 2003, explicitly addressed the refusal of individual authorship: "No one person 'owns' the articles in the Wikipedia. They are the common property of all humankind."[56]

Figure 3.3 *The Noon Quilt*, edited by Teri Hoskin and Sue Thomas. The trAce Online Writing Community, 1998.

Befitting the gift economy and digital commons in operation in Wikipedia, authorship of Wikipedia entries needs to be considered in different terms. Simone characterizes Wikipedia authorship as the "donation of creative efforts to an altruistic community project."[57] The author-function in the domain of Wikipedia should be considered as author-as-donor, donating to the internet commons for the benefit of the community.

Multimodal Authors

Wikipedia is the largest, and most visible, example of collaborative writing on the internet – but there are many other websites devoted to collective expression. The "superlanguage" of online writing envisioned by Pierre Levy in 1994 developed rapidly in succeeding years; this superlanguage utilized the properties of digital media, in which text could be combined easily with still image, moving image, sound, music and graphic design. Theorists attempted to describe the properties and potential of "hypermedia" communication. Gregory Ulmer wrote in his 2003 book *Internet Intervention: From Literacy to Electracy*, that literacy in the context of hypermedia had become "electracy." Gunther Kress outlined the new zone of online communication in his 2010 book *Multimodality*; Kress proposed that diverse incoming channels – comprising image, text, and audio – produced multimodal "ensembles," generating "a rich orchestration of meaning."[58] Mark Amerika wrote in 2000 of multimodal online works that "defy categorization," incorporating "the suppleness of nervous words, sonorous syntax, vocal microparticulars, animated imagetexts, and unsung e-motions."[59]

The trAce Online Writing Centre in the UK operated, from 1995 to 2005, as a site for experimentation by international writers and artists in multimodal internet writing (many of the resulting digital works are housed in an online archive). The works produced were collaborative in spirit, comprising multiple authorship in a range of media forms. The work *The Noon Quilt*, for example, published online in 1998, is an interactive digital mosaic: users click on individual squares of the electronic quilt, opening works-within-the-work. The editors of *The Noon Quilt*, Teri Hoskin and Sue Thomas, asked writers from around the world to describe the view outside their window at noon; these short prose pieces form "an assemblage of patches," in the words of the editors, within the work. Each square of the quilt encloses three smaller squares of visual art; by clicking on one of these images, the user summons a small prose piece. The authors of these texts have donated their writing to form part of a work of electronic literature. As in the many other electronic literature works published online, *The Noon Quilt* is multimodal as well as multi-authored.

Chapter Four

A Brief History of the Author

Who was the first named author? If authors are "heroes with names," as I have suggested, who is the earliest named author whose work has survived? Archaeologists and literary historians generally agree that this honour belongs to Enheduana, an Akkadian high priestess and "the world's first poet known by name," who lived from c. 2285 to 2250 BCE.[1] The Akkadian civilisation flourished in the third millennium BCE in Mesopotamia; Enheduana was the daughter of the Akkadian king Sargon and high priestess of the moon god Nanna. She wrote 43 hymns for the Akkadian and Sumerian temples, in honour of Inanna, the goddess of love and war. In addition, she wrote poetry, creating templates for poems, psalms and hymns used by later poets. Many of her works, inscribed on clay tablets, were signed with her name; and there is even a surviving picture of her – testament to her eminent status in Akkadian society. The fact that the earliest named poet was female also attests to the status of women in ancient Akkadia, at least within the ruling royal house and aristocracy.

But it would be a mistake to begin a history of the author with Enheduana. She may be the first poet whose works survive in written form – but there were many earlier poets and storytellers who created major works – including epic poems *Gilgamesh* and *The Iliad* – in the oral tradition. Oral poets deserve to be recognized as authors, as do literate poets such as Enheduana; the respective author-functions, however, are significantly different. The literate poet writes as an individual, even signing her own name as an individual poet; the oral poet contributes to a grand unfolding storytelling tradition, which expresses something of the identity and memory of the social group. The names of the individual oral poets have not survived, in part because their names were not important; they were, however, highly valued as transmitters, preservers, and co-creators of great narrative traditions.

Shamans, Poets, and Painters

A literate bias attends much intellectual and cultural history – including the history of authorship. This bias is reflected in the nomination of Enheduana as the first named author, when she is more accurately described as the earliest literate poet whose writing has survived. Writing developed in the civilizations based in settled communities founded on agriculture; in Mesopotamia by the middle of the third millennium BCE – the time of Enheduana – the technique of writing had acquired sufficient sophistication to convey creative literature. But there were countless poets, painters, musicians, dancers and storytellers who created cultural works – often of central importance to their communities – well before 3,000 BCE. These were the authors of prehistory.

This period, incorporating vast expanses of human experience – tens of thousands of years – is named "prehistory" simply because it predates the invention of writing, so that there are no historical records of the time. In his book *Ideas That Changed the World*, the historian Felipe Fernández-Armesto seeks to overturn intellectual historians' prejudice against pre-literate cultures. Fernández-Armesto locates many of humanity's most powerful and influential ideas – including the symbol, magic, afterlife, and heredity – in prehistory, in "the mind of the hunter"; he insists that "some of the best ideas were the earliest."[2]

Creative practitioners – including shamans, poets, and painters – were regarded in hunter-gatherer societies as important conduits to the spirit-world, home of spirit-ancestors and spirit-animals. The poets and storytellers were oral practitioners who subsumed their oral poetry within mythical narratives; the artists, including the painters of the famous Neolithic caves, did not sign their names. But they were all creative artists exemplifying a prehistoric author-function; and their achievements helped shape much of the later literature and visual art of literate societies.

In *A Short History of Myth*, Karen Armstrong identifies the shaman's central role in hunter-gatherer societies; his visions "encapsulated the ethos of the hunt, and gave it a spiritual meaning."[3] Roy Willis has observed that the shaman's social role was a composite of priest and artist: the shaman was concerned with "the domain of spirit" like a priest; and possessed a degree of creative freedom, like an artist, in describing visions and spirit-quests, including communion with spirit-animals.[4] Armstrong finds the underground caverns at Altamira and Lascaux (36,000 years and 15,000 years old respectively), richly painted with images of animals, hunters and shamans, to be the equivalent of "the very first temples and cathedrals." The paintings depict bison, deer, and ponies; hunters with spears; and men wearing bird masks, suggesting spiritual flight: these were most probably shamans. These painted caves opened up a ritualistic place, a meeting space between humans and the "godlike, archetypal animals" adorning the cavern interiors.[5] In the twentieth century, Pablo Picasso was so overwhelmed by these anonymous paintings that he famously declared: all art since Altamira is "decadent."[6]

Poets and storytellers, like shamans, were believed to connect with the spirit-world in narrating events of the mythic past, including the feats of spirit-ancestors. The ancestral events, continuously recounted through oral narration, were understood as foundational events existing simultaneously in past, present and future; they contained the memory and identity of the social group. Mircea Eliade, in *The Myth of the Eternal Return*, finds many hunter-gatherer rituals in which creation myths were narrated by the shaman in ceremonies for cure or rebirth. The participants in the ritual "are transplanted into the mythical epoch in which its revelation took place,"[7] so that the culture is regenerated by accessing its origin myth.

The conviction that shamans, poets, and artists were relaying or recounting emanations from the spirit-world or the divine realm was an integral part of the prehistoric author-function. These practitioners were not valued for their original creations, in the manner of the modern author. Rather, they performed a crucial cultural function in transmitting spiritual truths. In his 2019 article "What is an Author? Old Answers to a New Question," Sophus Helle finds that prehistoric and ancient authors were commonly described as "relaying words revealed to them in dreams by a god or as binding the tangled threads of received material into new compositions." Both these elaborations of the prehistoric author-function construe the storytellers as "textual transmitters rather than original creators." Helle suggests that attributing creativity solely to inspiration "relocates intention, agency, and self-knowledge away" from the author, "leaving inspired authors with only partial access to their words."[8] This limited agency in creative expression was part of Plato's critique of the Greek oral poets, meaning that for Plato the poets had no real authorship or control of their works.

Helle argues that a more appropriate model for describing premodern authors is as mediator of received materials. Metaphors of authorship as textile labour – current in the ancient world – offer a "better framework for writing the history of authorship." Helle notes that Enheduana was referred to as a "weaver of tablets," and that the word for a written "text" derived from the Latin for "woven." But textile metaphors also applied to the oral tradition: the great epic poems, recited by innumerable oral poets, were each known as a "rhapsody," from the Greek meaning "a song sewn together."[9]

The conception of a huge epic poem as a rhapsody – or stitching together of many pieces – points to the other key element of the prehistoric author-function: the idea that each poet, singer, or narrator was a contributor to an enormous enterprise. The epic poems of ancient Greece – *The Iliad* and *The Odyssey* – were created by collective and collaborative authorship. The realization that *The Iliad* was an oral composition, constructed by many oral poets over a long time-span – and not the work of a single poet called Homer – came relatively late, in the twentieth century writings of classics scholar Milman Parry and other literary historians.

The belief, even in the ancient world (Plato refers to "Homer") that these verse epics were written by one poet, indicates the ideological force of the "seemingly ineluctable desire for the author," as Andrew Bennett terms it. The desire for a single author is felt in literate cultures, where texts are signed by individual authors – heroes with names – and is applied to premodern times, where it does not belong. The Homeric epics were composed by multiple oral authors, as Parry persuasively showed.

In *The Making of Homeric Verse*, initially published in 1928, Parry demonstrated that "virtually every distinctive feature of Homeric poetry is due to the economy forced on it by oral methods of composition."[10] Standardized verbal formulas were used by the oral poets in reciting the verses, which were committed to memory by other poets; the formulas make memorizing of the whole easier – and account for the repetitive expressions in the epic poems. The metrical formulas also facilitated composition by the oral poets while reciting, as the set expressions occurred in expected places within the line of verse. In this way, lengthy sections of the epic could be "preserved and/or reworked" in recital by the poets.[11]

Walter J. Ong, in *Orality and Literacy*, has summarized the "psychodynamics" or characteristics of oral compositions, which were created, memorized, and transmitted orally. These psychodynamics include: formulaic thought-processes and descriptions, repetitive locutions, agonistic narratives, external rather than internal crises, aggregative rather than analytical descriptions, situational rather than abstract thinking, a subjective rather than objective orientation.[12]

In considering the methods of individual "rhapsodes" – or song-stitchers – Ong also focuses on individual poets in their act of reciting epic verses. Studies of recitals by twentieth century oral poets revealed a level of originality in the telling – or transmitting – of poems handed down by tradition. Ong observes that in different recitals, the same formulas and themes recurred, but were: "'rhapsodised' differently in each rendition even by the same poet, depending on audience reaction, the mood of the poet or of the occasion, and other social or psychological factors."[13] That is, although the poet is working with "pre-fabricated materials," committed to memory, each recital will be slightly different, in diverse contexts, which accounts for the gradual change to oral compositions over time.

Originality for the oral poet is not the creation of new works, as it is for the modern author; rather originality consists in "fitting the traditional materials effectively into each individual, unique situation and/ or audience."[14] Ong finds this principle of oral composition – as transmission and slight modification of tradition – to be true for all forms of oral expression, from the bards of Europe to the griots of West Africa. Helle, likewise, finds the principle of premodern authorship – as "mediation," "transmitting" or "weaving" of existing materials – to be distributed across cultures, including Arabic and Indian civilisations, as well as ancient China: Confucius wrote that "I transmit and do not create; I trust and love the ancient."[15]

In the culture of prehistory, individual authors – including poets – are subsumed within the greater transmission of tradition. This principle applies not just to oral poets or bards, but to other cultural practitioners, including dancers and painters. In the oral culture of ancient India, the great literary and philosophical works were anonymous, while in the traditional Balinese culture, all art was communal-oriented, made as "the expression of collective thought."[16]

Indigenous cultural practices are not restricted to prehistory; Indigenous artists and authors create cultural works in the age of the internet. In many instances, those cultural works are created with the same communal or collective practices pursued tens of thousands of years ago. In *Collective Authorship and Copyright,* Daniela Simone considers the authorship of contemporary paintings in Aboriginal Australia, contrasting the communal ownership practised in Indigenous cultures with the modern conception of copyright. For traditional Indigenous communities, a painting is an act with religious significance, as it expresses the community's relation to the land and to spirit-ancestors.

An individual artist within the social group earns the right – through initiation by elders – to depict in visual form some of the ritual knowledge belonging to the group. But paintings maintain the cultural heritage and beliefs of the community, so that painters are not expected to deviate far from pre-existing designs, forms, and styles. And the artist is understood as merely a "delegate of the tribe," permitted to create an artwork that is "seen as owned by the community as a whole." Simone summaries the traditional conception of creation and ownership (or authorship): "Although a painting results from an individual's hand, from an Indigenous point of view the whole community is involved in its creation."[17] These communal values of collective authorship contrast with the contemporary model of authorship protected by copyright, which emphasizes the individual author as originator of works. As Simone details, this clash between values of authorship has resulted in legal disputes over the ownership of Aboriginal art works, as the collectivist approach to culture – stretching back to prehistory – comes into conflict with the modern, individualized, legal conception of the author.

A similar clash – between the communal authorship practised by Indigenous communities and the individualized concept of authorship enshrined in copyright law – attends the authorship, and ownership, of Indigenous dance. The Bangarra Dance Theatre, an Aboriginal and Torres Strait Islander modern dance company in Australia, takes many of the stories and dance movements for its works from the Munyarrum Clan. However, Australian copyright law is more likely to recognize the choreographer of a dance work as its individual author; communal or collective authorship of the work, developed through movements and narratives within communities over thousands of years, is not recognized under copyright.

Jo Dyer, the former general manager of Bangarra Dance Theatre, has stated that despite the lack of legal acknowledgment of this communal ownership, "there was no one individual who owned or choreographed the dances: they belong to the Clan and they have done for thousands of years."[18] To overcome the shortcomings of copyright law, the Bangarra Dance Theatre entered into a private agreement with the Clan, developed through negotiation with community elders, recognizing that copyright properly belongs to the Clan as a collective. Bangarra pays a fee to the community to use "themes of traditional song and movement" in its performances.[19] This is an instance of creative practitioners acknowledging – and recompensing – communal and traditional authorship of works; this acknowledgment operates outside the limitations of copyright law.

What We Owe to Mesopotamia

In the ancient world, Mesopotamia was the region circumscribed by the Euphrates and Tigris rivers, in the area now known as Iraq. Mesopotamia was the base of several great early civilizations: Sumer and Akkad in the third millennium BCE, and Babylonia in the second millennium

A Brief History of the Author 69

Figure 4.1 Cuneiform script, clay tablet, from Northern Mesopotamia Media-Assyria Kingdom, second half of the second millennium BCE. From Wikimedia Commons, Creative Commons CC0 1.0 Universal Public Domain Dedication.

BCE. Mesopotamia bequeathed a number of extremely significant legacies to later civilizations, the most important of which was writing, developed by the Sumerians in the fourth millennium BCE. Another legacy from ancient Mesopotamia is the very idea of the author itself – or at least, of the named, individual writer.

Writing appears to have been invented independently in at least three global locations: Mesopotamia, China, and Central America (with Egypt a possible fourth independent location).[20] The Sumerians in Mesopotamia invented the first systemic writing method from around 3700 BCE, developing it gradually so that cuneiform script, as it has been named, was "capable of conveying 'any and all thought' by around 2500 BC."[21] The word "cuneiform" derives from the Latin cuneus or "wedge"; cuneiform script, adopted throughout Mesopotamia, inscribed wedge-shaped signs representing sounds, with auxiliary phonetic and grammatical signs, allowing for sophisticated literary nuance. Much of the writing from the civilizations of Mesopotamia was preserved because it was inscribed using reeds on clay tablets, which when dried proved remarkably durable.

The first use of writing was for record-keeping – inventories of land or livestock. Writing appears to have been invented to meet the needs of a large-scale settled community based on agriculture, primarily the need to register and record ownership of land and property. But by the middle of the third millennium, writing moved beyond "mere record keeping" to encompass "creative literature" as well as medical, legal, astrological, and magical inscriptions.[22] In Mesopotamia, only specially trained individuals could become scribes, creating a new literate elite; from the copious inscriptions on tablets, made by these scribes, later civilizations absorbed many key ideas. This is some of what we owe to Mesopotamia: the positional number system; the division of time into 12 units in the hours of clocks and the months of calendars, and sixty units in the minutes and hours of clocks; the representation of space in maps; astronomy and astrology, both of which continue to flourish in the twenty-first century; the first transcribed epic poem in *Gilgamesh*; and – in relation to authorship – the first named author in world literature.

In his book, *The Babylonians*, H.W.F. Saggs notes that the epic poem *Gilgamesh* was probably complete in oral form by around 2200 BCE. The epic was a "stitching-together" or rhapsody of at least four separate Sumerian stories, including a narrative of a great flood (another version of which would later be included in the Hebrew Bible or Old Testament). The whole epic was transcribed onto tablets in Akkadian around 2000 BCE, bequeathing humanity a great verse epic in which the central figure Gilgamesh (one-third human and two-thirds divine) is eventually reconciled to his mortality.[23] The creative literature of Mesopotamia, preserved on clay tablets, also included many shorter works created by literate poets including Enheduana. These works included books of wisdom in the form of proverbs and advice; love poems; humorous stories; psalms and hymns; and religious texts dealing with theodicy, or the problem of evil and suffering.

Saggs observes that some tablets remained anonymous, ascribed directly to a god – with the implication that the scribe is merely the vessel transmitting the words form the gods. But many other tablets are "attributed to specific authors," who are named as the creators of the texts.[24] In *A History of Reading*, Alberto Manguel focuses on the "colophons" at the end of tablets, which included the name of the scribe, the date, and the town where the writing took place. For Manguel, the very idea of the author is born here. When the poet signed his or her name at the end of the tablet, this identification "enabled the reader to read a text in a given voice – in the case of the hymns to Inanna, the voice of Enheduana – identifying the 'I' in the text with a specific person and thereby creating a pseudo-fictional character, 'the author,' for the reader to engage with."[25] Manguel concludes that this device, "invented at the beginning of literature, is still with us more than four thousand years later."[26]

Plato vs. the Poets

Literacy spread throughout the civilizations of the ancient world. The ancient Greeks developed a fully phonetic alphabet by the eighth century BCE, derived from the earlier Phoenician alphabet. *The Iliad* and *The Odyssey* were written down and attributed to an individual poet named Homer. The ancient civilizations of Greece and Rome celebrated individual authors known by name, including, in the classical period of Athens in the fifth century BCE: the tragedians Aeschylus, Sophocles and Euripides, the comedic playwright Aristophanes, the historians Herodotus and Thucydides, and – in the fourth century BCE, the philosophers Plato and Aristotle. Their works survived, recorded on papyrus scrolls, and preserved in libraries owned by wealthy citizens, and then in public libraries. In first-century CE Rome, the codex book form emerged as an alternative to the scroll, most commonly using parchment pages. Paper was invented in China in the second century, there replacing silk as the medium for written texts; paper later reached the Muslim world by the ninth century, and Europe in the twelfth century, adopted in place of the more expensive vellum as the material used in books.

If playwrights, poets, historians, and philosophers could be said to be authors in fifth century BCE Greece, their author-function differed radically from that of the modern author. There were no publishers, no mass production of their works, no market to buy and sell copies. The lyric poet Simonides was reportedly the first author to accept poetic commissions for a fee, in the fifth century BCE, making him something like a professional writer.[27] Patronage by wealthy aristocratic supporters was the primary source of income and financial support for writers – and would remain so in Europe until the eighteenth century, when finally replaced by the legal-economic system of copyright and royalties. Playwrights had their works performed at festivals in honour of the god Dionysus; wealthy citizens paid the production costs of staging the plays. The dramatists competed for prizes awarded to the best play performed at the festival; plays were known to the public through performance rather than as texts.

Because there was no legal means in the ancient world of establishing ownership of a work – no copyright – there was no legal avenue to protect a work from theft or copying. The first century CE Roman poet Martial coined the idea of "plagiarism" to denounce rival poets who stole his poems and passed them off as their own (*plagiarus* is Latin for "kidnapper" or thief). A plagiarist – or kidnapper – of another's work could be the subject of moral censure, but there was no legal recourse for the victim of the theft.

The status of the author was in a fundamental way conditioned by the advent of literacy in the ancient world. This shift in the concept of the author – from oral poet to writer – is evident in Plato's exclusion of poets from his ideal state in *The Republic*. As already mentioned, Plato's rather dismissive account of oral poets was based on his conviction that their inspiration was a form of possession, so that they were mere transmitters of divine words rather than authors. In *The Republic*, Plato goes further in his critique of the oral poets. He rejects the popular belief that Homer is "the educator of Greece"; indeed, he bans the poets from his ideal city-state altogether: "the only poetry that should be allowed in a state is hymns to the gods and paeans in praise of good men."[28]

Part of Plato's antipathy towards the poets stems from his suspicion of their inspiration, an irrational force that results in highly emotional works of poetry. The poet, according to Plato, "gratifies and indulges the instinctive desires of a part of us," "infecting" and "corrupting" our reason with emotional responses.[29] Plato's ideal state is a domain of rationality and enlightened thought, presided over by "philosopher-rulers" who know best how to guide their fellow-citizens. This paradise of reason would be ruined if oral poets were allowed entry as citizens: "once you ... admit the sweet lyric or epic muse, pleasure and pain become your rulers instead of law and the rational principles commonly accepted as best."[30] Plato has another criticism of the poets: that their basic procedure is to lie or deceive. Plato's philosophy was founded on his concept of The Ideas or Forms – perfect, ideal types of all things which have representations – objects – in the material world. For a poet to sing of those objects is to create a mere representation of another mere representation, "at third remove from reality." The true reality is the thing-itself, the Form, which the philosopher may discern through rational inquiry, making this reality apparent to others. But the poet, like other artists, does the opposite, further blinding listeners to reality: "So the tragic poet, if his art is representation, is by nature at third remove from the throne of truth; and the same is true of all other representative artists."[31] This is Plato's main intellectual reason for proscribing the poets: that their verses obscure the truth – relating to the Ideal Forms – thereby undoing the noble work of philosophers to enlighten the people. This conviction prompts a more scathing indictment of all poets, including Homer: "all the poets from Homer downwards have no grasp of truth but merely produce a superficial likeness of any subject they treat."

Poetry may have a bewitching quality, in its "metre and rhythm and music" that allows the poet to "persuade people as ignorant as he is"; but, Plato cuttingly remarks: "Strip it of its poetic colouring, reduce it to plain prose, and I think you know how little it amounts to."[32] Poets convey superficial, "ill-informed" – and worse, misleading – ideas; accordingly, they are to be banned from the ideal republic.

But there is a more profound process underpinning Plato's exile of the poets: the transformation of consciousness – and authorship – effected by literacy. This idea has been advanced by Walter J. Ong, Eric Havelock, and others. For Ong, "more than any other invention, writing has transformed human consciousness." He postulates that the radical impact of writing derives from "the reduction of dynamic sound to quiescent space, the separation of the word from the living present."[33] A written text is a new form of space: a space for knowledge. It is a container of knowledge, an artificial memory, whereas previously the knowledge and history of a people had been conveyed in the narratives of storytellers and poets.

New attributes of thought and expression are made possible when information is contained – not in poets' memories – but in a text that can be re-read and analysed. These attributes include: critical analysis, objectivity, precision, linearity, and abstraction. Ong's interpretation of Plato's proscription of the poets is that it represents a conflict between oral and literate sensibilities. Plato's philosophy, involving "patiently analytic, lengthily sequential thought processes," had been shaped by "the ways in which literacy enabled the mind to process data." Plato ejected the poets from his ideal state because "they stood for the old oral, mnemonic form of communication." This oral communication was "traditionalist, warmly human, participatory"; these values were antithetical to Plato's "analytic, sparse, exact, abstract, visualist, immobile world of the 'ideas.'"[34]

In this respect, Ong follows Eric Havelock, who argued in his 1963 book *Preface to Plato* that literacy itself was the preface to Plato's philosophy. Havelock posited that Plato's abstract philosophical thought – even the idea of the Forms themselves – was conditioned by the properties of writing. The Forms or Ideas are visually based, like words on a page; they are "voiceless," unlike oral poetry with its base in sound.[35] Despite his professed hostility to writing in *The Phaedrus*, Plato is in fact fully shaped by the characteristics of literacy.

Plato excludes the poets not just because they are poets but because they are *oral* poets. His banishment of the poets is his rejection of the oral tradition, his attempt to replace Homer with philosophy as the true educator of Greece. Literacy enables the objectification of knowledge, even the objectification of the self as an object of study; it enables thought to conceive of abstractions and concepts, such as the Forms, which exist outside concrete reality. In preferring logic to narrative, the abstract to the concrete, the literate Plato usurps the oral poets as the educator of Greece. Authors resident in the ideal republic will be writers, not speakers.

Scriptor/Auctor

The periodization of the "middle ages" is a Eurocentric construction: the term is meant to denote the long middle period between the glories of ancient Greece and Rome and the "rebirth" of those glories in the European Renaissance – from the fall of Rome in the fifth century CE to the flowering of Renaissance culture in the fifteenth century. Because of this Eurocentric bias, world historians avoid "medieval" as a periodization, preferring "post-classical" or "premodern" as classifying terms. The concept of the "middle ages" – the first few centuries of which were previously known as the "dark ages" – has connoted a long period of cultural decline in Europe, before a reawakening in the Renaissance. But this characterization of the centuries following the final collapse of Rome in 476 does not apply – in any way – to the other great civilizations of this time, including China, India, and the Islamic world.

In this period, Indian scholarship made many advances in mathematics which eventually found their way to Europe. In China, the span between the seventh and tenth centuries was not a dark age, but rather "the golden age of classical poetry," as well as a time of new developments in the writing of history.[36] Chinese civilization also produced extraordinary technological innovations, including, in the ninth century, books made with woodblock printing (six centuries in advance of the Gutenberg printing press in Europe). The Islamic Golden Age occurred over a similar time-frame, when Islamic scholarship flourished in science, medicine, algebra, astronomy, architecture, and other fields. Islamic scholars also preserved classical texts from Greece and Rome in translation, at a time when most of those works disappeared from view in Europe. Medieval Europe was, by comparison with the achievements of these other civilizations, an intellectual and cultural backwater.

Knowledge was preserved in Europe in the monasteries, where specially trained monks copied manuscripts in scriptoriums, and – from the twelfth century – in universities. In the monasteries, the skilful decoration of Christian texts resulted in glorious illuminated manuscripts such as the *Book of Kells* and the *Lindisfarne Gospels*. The texts painstakingly copied by monks included works of exegesis – that is, interpretation and commentary – of the scriptures. Occasionally, scribes did more than copy manuscripts in the scriptoriums: they wrote new words.

All histories of authorship refer to one particular document from the thirteenth century. This document is a commentary by the Franciscan monk St Bonaventure on the four different ways of "making" a book. Bonaventure helpfully lists and describes these four modes of writing: the first is the *scriptor* or scribe, who simply copies texts and "add[s] nothing and change[s] nothing." The second is the *compilator* or compiler, who "put[s] together passages" from texts which are "not his own." The third is the commentator, or exegete, who adds his own commentary to the words of others. Finally there is the *auctor*, who writes "both his own words and others," with his own words in primary place and the words of others added "for purposes of confirmation."[37]

There has been voluminous scholarship on this particular thirteenth century commentary, as it articulates key aspects of the medieval author-function. Andrew Bennett observes that Bonaventure does not privilege the *auctor* category, which of the four modes of writing is closest to the modern conception of the author. J.A. Burrow notes that even the *auctor* is understood as a scribe who writes others' words as well as his own, so that the *scriptor* and *auctor* are not regarded as entirely separate functions: "Bonaventure's scheme combines into a single continuum two functions which seem fundamentally different to us: composition and the making of copies."[38] Bennett further remarks that the medieval *auctor* is remote from the modern sense of the author as "a personalized individual expressing intentions and a particular subjectivity."[39] The *auctor* does not express a subjectivity or sense of individualized personhood, nor does the *auctor*'s writing "entail verbal inventiveness"[40] – and the basic reason for this relates to the authority – or *auctoritas* – of the *auctor*. As Seán Burke remarks, the *auctor* "designated less an empirical self than a seal of religious authority."[41] The *auctor* was a scribe writing in Latin, understood as a writer whose authority derived from God. *Auctores* possessed the authority to establish "the founding rules and principles" of disciplines and to augment "the knowledge and wisdom of humanity" within those disciplines.[42] The sense of religious authority also brought with it the conviction that knowledge was received from tradition, that "the great *auctores* of the past, Christian and pagan, have already said almost everything there is to say."[43] The role of the *auctor*, writing in the "dead" languages of ancient Greek and Latin, was to preserve – and at most augment – this received ancient knowledge.

Bennett makes the additional point that the *auctor* was almost always anonymous, as the manuscript itself was the important cultural and religious form; the identity of the various scribes who may have contributed to this manuscript was in most cases irrelevant. In this regard, the medieval scribes performed a function similar to that of medieval artists: they were considered tradespeople, practitioners of crafts devoted to the glory – and authority – of God, without the need of individual fame – or naming. In 1550, when Giorgio Vasari celebrated the heroic feats of the Renaissance artists in his book *Lives of the Artists*, he looked back in wonder – and dismay – at the large-scale anonymity of medieval art. Having examined the buildings and sculptures of the middle ages, Vasari could find no trace of authorship, so that he could only "marvel at the simplicity and indifference to fame exhibited by the men of that age."[44]

As George Henderson and other scholars of medieval culture have asserted, Vasari probably did not look very hard, as he was predisposed to dismiss the middle ages as a dark period of European culture. Certain highly skilled artisans, such as Matthew Paris in the thirteenth century, *were* singled out at the time and named for their accomplishments, and the greatest achievements of the age – the magnificent Gothic cathedrals – in some cases bore inscriptions naming the various master architects overseeing construction. But it is also true, as Henderson remarks, that the names of these masters is all we know of them, whereas a great deal more is known of Brunelleschi as Renaissance architect – individual and heroic – of the dome of the Florence cathedral, completed in 1436.[45] In addition, the Gothic cathedrals could take several centuries to complete, so that individual master architects were understood as contributors to a vast, long-running collaborative enterprise.

In *Gothic Art and Civilisation*, Henderson finds that artists in the period of the Gothic cathedrals – from the twelfth century – were for the most part anonymous, and historical records of artists are "at best scant and fragmentary." Patronage was central to the life of the artist, in a near-feudal relation between artist and patron: "the artist expends his best skill in return for favour and support"; and the art work created "is the patron's due." As a result of this relationship, art works such as paintings and tapestries could be inscribed as belonging to the patron, with no signature by the artist: "the owner's ownership is not obtruded upon by the maker's name."[46] If the artist's name could be subordinated to that of the patron, artists and scribes working for the glory of the church similarly subsumed their individual identity within the greater authority of God. Medieval artists were not cultural heroes, the subject of admiring biographers, as artists and writers would become in the Renaissance and later. Henderson makes the telling point that in the middle ages, "the art of the biography" was applied not to writers or artists but "solely to a special kind of hero, the saint."[47]

In his revisionist approach to the history of authorship, Sophus Helle cautions against positing a "radical break" or rupture between the medieval *auctor* and the modern author, formed by the eighteenth century. Instead, he proposes that the modern author emerged after a long, gradual process of "evolution" from its medieval precursor.[48] Several literary scholars have in fact charted aspects of this gradual transition. A.J. Minnis describes a shift in the thirteenth century towards a focus on individual *auctores,* effected in part by the rediscovery of Aristotle's texts (provided by Muslim scholars). Aristotle had described four major causes of change and activity; within this framework, late medieval scholars construed the *auctor* as "efficient cause" or motivating agent of the text. As a result of this emphasis, in the thirteenth century "focus had shifted from the divine *auctor* to the human *auctor* of Scripture." The intention of the *auctor* in interpreting scripture becomes of greater interest; the *auctor* gradually develops into an individual whose "human qualities" are valued.[49]

Another gradual change in authorship has been identified by Bianca Del Villano, centred on the idea of "invention." Del Villano shows that "invention," from the Latin for "to find," originally meant – in the context of the *auctor* – the recovery and re-arrangement of older material. But over time this word came to mean the opposite: artistic creation or originality by authors.[50]

In the later medieval period, texts reflected a tension between self-effacement and self-assertion of the authorial personality, particularly in works by vernacular writers. Danielle Bohler claims that medieval French authors alternated between a "profile" pose – subservient to the received manuscript and tradition – and a "frontal" pose, in which the author assumes a more dominant position. Helle notes a similar oscillation between effacement and assertion of the writing self in Dante's *The Divine Comedy*, written in vernacular Italian in the fourteenth century. In the *Inferno*, Dante addresses Virgil, the great poet of ancient Rome, as his "teacher" and "author": "you alone are the one from whom I took the beautiful style for which I am renowned." As Helle observes, Dante here defines himself as mediator of a tradition originating with Virgil; but at the same time, he foregrounds his own renown as a contemporary poet.[51]

A similar manoeuvre was made by the English poet Geoffrey Chaucer, writing in the late fourteenth century, as Andrew Bennett has observed. In the Prologue to *The Canterbury Tales*, Chaucer describes himself as merely the person who has "compiled" the text from multiple sources. He thereby aligns himself with the *compilator* author-function, as defined in St Bonaventure's classification. But, as Bennett and numerous literary historians have shown, this is in fact a knowing disguise adopted by Chaucer for his own authorial presence. It is "knowing" because it depends on the readers' awareness of the "compiler" authorial function as a literary convention; readers also know that Chaucer is the author of the tales. Bennett describes the "authorial game" played by Chaucer: "it is the very modesty by which he explains his humble position as "compilatio" that is itself an *assertion* of authorship ... it is this knowing fiction of authorial modesty that allows us to recognize the elaborate authorial game that is set in motion in *The Canterbury Tales*."[52] Numerous scholars have located Chaucer, writing in the late fourteenth century (the *Canterbury Tales* stories were written between 1387 and 1400) at the very beginning of the modern conception of the author. Stephanie Trigg has observed that a distinctive feature of Chaucer's works is the "sympathetic readerly identifications" with a narrator-figure, who functions as a stand-in for the author.[53] A.J. Minnis likewise remarks that by the late fourteenth century, the author "is becoming the reader's trusted friend."[54] J.A. Burrow also notes that Chaucer, and other late fourteenth century poets including Langland and Gower, are "poets with names and identities who speak in distinctive voices." Burt Kimmelman finds a "poetics of authorship" in the later middle ages, along with the "emergence of the modern literary persona." Writers such as Chaucer could create, through "the very craft of authorship," opportunities for their own "self-advancement" and for their "recognition as individuals." They were becoming, in other words, heroes with names.[55]

The Author Pre-copyright

The printing press changed everything. Gutenberg's mechanical printing press was active in Germany from the middle of the fifteenth century; by 1500, printing presses across Europe were producing multiple copies of Bibles, other religious texts, and – increasingly – diverse types of books, pamphlets, and other printed texts. The cultural and intellectual ramifications of mechanical printing were profound. Elizabeth's Eisenstein's 1979 two-volume work, *The Printing Press as an Agent of Change*, details the cultural changes effected by the printing press in the domains of literature, science, religion, economics, politics, and exploration. Eisenstein argues for "the advent of printing as inaugurating a new cultural era" in world history.[56]

The mechanical reproduction and distribution of texts removed the control of knowledge from specialist scribes in monasteries and universities; the exactitude of printed copies facilitated the development of modern science, and encouraged global exploration through the accuracy of printed maps; mass printing made universal literacy a goal of nations; the circulation of religious tracts and pamphlets underpinned the Protestation Reformation; political pamphlets and texts helped develop nationalist political sentiment; the printing press created new media forms in the newspaper and the magazine; and made possible the widespread popularity of the novel, a printed form that developed in the eighteenth century and reached huge circulation in the nineteenth, as mass literacy grew in industrialized nations. Walter J. Ong lists further consequences of the printing press: the drive to fix and document languages through printed dictionaries; and the fostering of a growing sense of privacy and individualism, encouraged by the practice of individual, silent reading of printed books.[57]

In the sixteenth century, printers and publishers were selling works of poetry, fiction, and drama in increasing quantities; Ong observes that typography "had made the word into a commodity."[58] However, the benefits from the sale of these commodities flowed not to authors but to "stationers" – the term for printers, printer-publishers, and booksellers. A printer could secure a royal privilege, or monopoly, to print and publish a specific book; this privilege protected against the unlawful piracy of the book by other printers. The Stationers' Company was formed in London in 1557 to oversee the rights of printers and booksellers; at this stage, author's rights – copyright – did not exist.

What then, was the status of the author in the sixteenth and seventeenth centuries, pre-copyright? And how did an author make a living, in lieu of royalties?

The one-word answer to the second question is: patronage. To be successful – to be published – an author needed an aristocratic patron, as did a composer or an artist. In some cultures, the fine arts remained the preserve of the aristocracy even into modern times; the "gentleman writer" or artist of the aristocratic class lived not "by the pen," as Roger Chartier has observed, but by landholdings and investments. The aristocracy was also the main source of patronage for authors and artists who were not themselves born into that class. In *The Order of Books*, a study of readers and authors in Europe between the fourteenth and eighteenth centuries, Chartier finds that in this period, "the author-function had no trouble harmonizing with the dependency instituted by patronage."[59] He cites as an example the title page of one of the greatest, and most famous, works of literature, Cervantes' *Don Quixote*, published in 1605. Under the author's name is the dedication to Cervantes' patron, the Duke of Bejar, whose other aristocratic titles as Marquis and Viscount are listed in full. Chartier's commentary is that: "The upper third of the title page is thus given over to the fundamental relationship that dominated literary activity until the mid eighteenth century: the connecting of an author ... to a protector from whom he expected support and gratifications."[60] The bottom of the title page lists the printer and the royal privilege that made publication possible, along with the address at which the book could be bought.

Other means by which a professional writer could make a living were related to the theatre. A playwright could augment his income if, for example, he were an actor in the theatre company performing his plays, and, even more, if he were a member of a successful theatre company. This was true of William Shakespeare, a playwright and poet active in London at the end of the sixteenth and beginning of the seventeenth century; Shakespeare serves as a case study in both how an author earned a living in this period, and in the status of the author itself.

Shakespeare is no ordinary author, of course, and no ordinary case study. Shakespeare is almost universally acclaimed as the greatest writer in the English language, and the greatest playwright in any language. His tragedies *Hamlet* and *King Lear* are regularly included in critics' most exclusive lists, of the grandest achievements of world literature. Shakespeare takes his place in this exalted field, alongside oral epics *Gilgamesh* and *The Iliad*, and literary works including Dante's *The Divine Comedy*, Cervantes' *Don Quixote*, and Milton's *Paradise Lost*. But in his own time, Shakespeare was not considered a giant of world literature; indeed, his plays were not even considered literature, and there was no complete publication, in his lifetime, of the plays that would make Shakespeare "the central figure of the Western Canon," in the words of the twentieth century critic Harold Bloom. Bloom's reverence for Shakespeare's plays is so compete that he elevates the playwright to the status of universal genius of literature: "Shakespeare sets the standards and limits of literature." Bloom goes so far as to claim that Shakespeare "invented," in his plays, the very idea of the modern human being.[61]

In his own time, however, Shakespeare was not considered a genius, as that term was only applied to cultural practitioners later, from the eighteenth century. He was not celebrated as a great exponent of world literature, as that concept, like the "genius," had not yet been born. He was known as a popular and successful playwright, a skilled craftsman who took stories from the public domain (as did all playwrights) and shaped them into plays that captivated audiences at the Globe and other theatres. But beyond that, there was no great critical or public interest in Shakespeare the author. There was no contemporary biography, and information on his life is so scant – in comparison with the volume of biographical information on later authors – that within this void of biography, several later speculative theories on the "real" authorship of his plays have flourished.

As for those tragedies, histories, comedies, and romances – the plays that later became the cornerstone of Western literature – their actual treatment as texts in Shakespeare's time is – from a modern perspective – astonishing, even shocking. Shakespeare ensured that much of his poetry was published, but when he retired as a playwright in 1613, there was no definitive, or even respectful, publication of his plays. Roughly half of them had been "published" in quarto format: these were cheap, small, unbound, disposable, pamphlet-like publications, described by Gerald Bentley, in *The Profession of Dramatist in Shakespeare's Time,* as "looking like almanacs, joke books, coney-catching pamphlets, and other ephemera."[62] Bentley quotes Sir Thomas Bodley's denigration in 1611 of the quarto play publications as "riff-raffs" and "baggage books," not suitable for inclusion in the new Bodleian Library.[63] Worse, the versions of Shakespeare's plays published in these quarto versions could be extremely abbreviated and inaccurate. Some of the quartos could have been edited by Shakespeare himself, or by other members of his theatre company; some may have been transcribed from performances by members of the audience. "To be or not to be, that is the question" is perhaps the best-known line from any play – but the text of the quarto *Hamlet* read: "To be or not to be, aye, there's the point."[64]

Many of Shakespeare's plays may have been lost, and others survived only in truncated, squalid quarto versions, if two of Shakespeare's fellow actors in the King's Men theatre company – John Hemynges and Henry Condell – had not managed to assemble accurate texts of 36 Shakespeare plays in *The First Folio*, published in 1623, seven years after Shakespeare's death. Hemynges and Condell drew on Shakespeare's original manuscripts, held by the King's Men; in their preface they sound almost relieved to replace the "diverse stolen, and surreptitious copies, maimed and deformed by the frauds and stealths of injurious impostors" with versions of the plays "cured, and perfect in their limbs, and all the rest absolute in their numbers as he conceived them."[65]

The *First Folio* ensured the preservation of Shakespeare's plays for posterity; but the fact that it was published after Shakespeare's death is one indication of the lowly status of playwrights as literary practitioners in Shakespeare's time. The collection of Shakespeare's plays, in the dignified folio format, followed the publication in 1616 of fellow playwright Ben Jonson's collected plays in folio; but Bentley places these publications in a cultural context, in which playwrights were ranked well below poets, philosophers and other authors: "the increased dignity which the appearance of the Jonson and Shakespeare folios

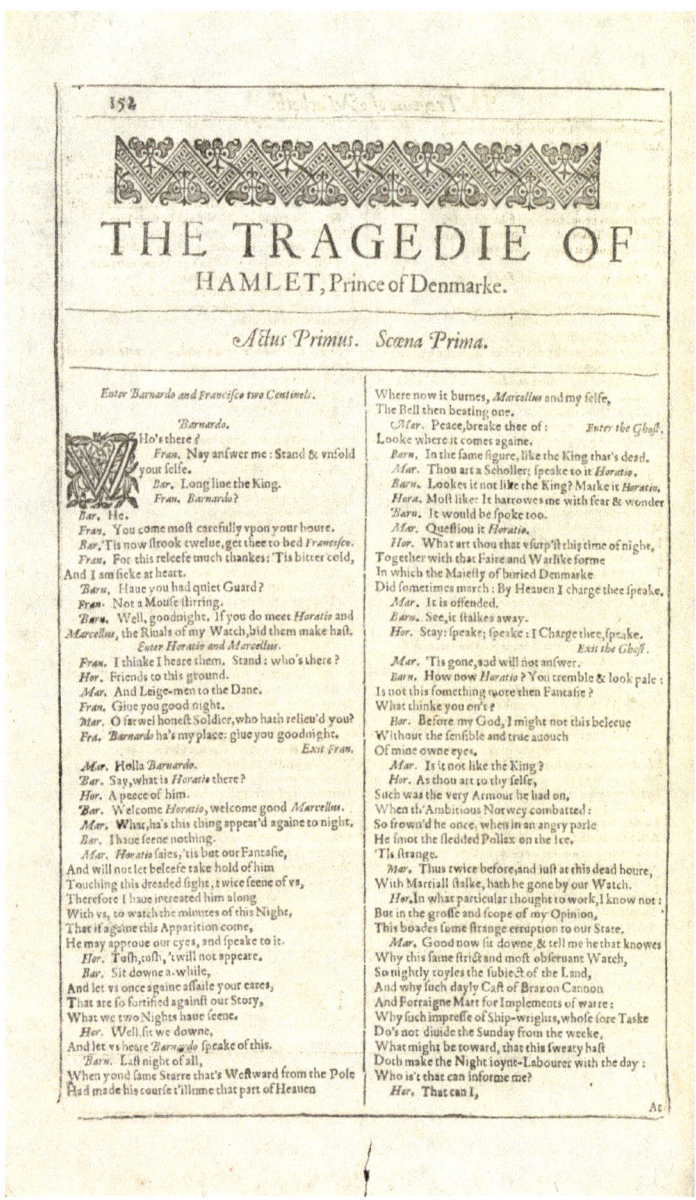

Figure 4.2 William Shakespeare, *Hamlet* in *First Folio*, 1623. From the Bodleian First Folio: digital facsimile of the First Folio of Shakespeare's plays, Bodleian Arch. G c.7, http://firstfolio.bodleian.ox.ac.uk/, Creative Commons licence CC BY 3.0.

brought to plays and playwrights must be seen only as a rise from an exceedingly low status to a moderately low one."[66] Shakespeare made nothing from the publication of his plays, as he did not own them; how, then, did he make a living? Shakespeare benefited throughout his career from patronage. He was a member of the Lord Chamberlain's Men, a theatre company formed in 1594 in an act of patronage by Lord Hundson, the Lord Chamberlain. In 1603, this company was renamed the King's Men, enjoying royal patronage; there are records of Shakespeare acting in performances of his plays at the royal court. Early in his career, Shakespeare was supported as a writer by the third Earl of Southampton; Shakespeare's published poems *Venus and Adonis* and *The Rape of Lucrece* were dedicated to this patron.

It has been suggested that the financial support Shakespeare received from his patron may have included the 50 pounds Shakespeare paid, in 1594, to become a "sharer" in the Lord Chamberlain's Men. However he raised the money, this decision set Shakespeare on a professional path within the theatre: he would write plays for the Lord Chamberlain's Men, act in their performances, and share in the company's profits. In effect he abandoned a career as a poet for a career as a playwright, even though plays were regarded as a much lower form of creative expression than poetry: plays were not considered literature at all. In his Shakespeare biography, Peter Ackroyd speculates that perhaps Shakespeare: "considered that his life with the Lord Chamberlain's Men offered him financial security, away from the perilous world of private patronage; in this, his judgement proved to be correct."[67] Shakespeare earned income as an actor within the theatre company, while his shares in the company – as well as shares in the Globe and other theatres and property investments – proved lucrative over time, allowing him to retire in comfort to his birthplace Stratford-upon-Avon, where he bought the second-most expensive property in the town. Throughout his career as a playwright, he sold his plays to the theatre company, earning himself additional income – but this practice effectively meant that he lost control of his own works, which became the property of the company. Bentley remarks that some theatre companies altered plays without any negotiation with their author, a custom which "offends the modern concept of literary property": "The dramatist sold his manuscript to the acting company for which it had been prepared; after that it was no more than the cloak that he might have sold to the actors at the same time."[68] Shakespeare's plays, even the greatest works such as *Hamlet*, were shortened and altered in performance by the theatre company; indeed, it is thought that performances never exceeded a two-hour limit on stage – necessitating the editing of many of Shakespeare's dramatic works. There is no record of Shakespeare, or any other playwright, protesting this treatment of the plays. In the cultural economy of the time, such a protest would have been futile: the plays were owned by the company, which bought each work from its author.

It is likely that some of the "significantly shorter" quarto versions of the plays may have been actual performance scripts of the plays. Ackroyd observes that these stage versions illustrate "the somewhat brutal way in which Shakespeare's texts could be treated." Soliloquies could be removed, lines re-arranged, and whole scenes transposed. But Ackroyd also remarks that in all likelihood, Shakespeare himself must have concurred with these changes, indicating that he was "an eminently practical and pragmatic man of the theatre."[69] His livelihood, after all, depended on the successful performance of these plays.

Author's Rights

One cultural ramification of the printing press, noted by Elizabeth Eisenstein, was the forging of the modern author, as a writer – and owner – of books whose copies are sold in the market. Before the printing press, medieval culture was founded on the principle of a public domain or literary commons, in which traditional songs and narratives resided, to be borrowed and adapted by storytellers and bards – but these cultural forms remained anonymous, constituent parts of tradition. Medieval scriptor/auctors copied and/or added to existing manuscript texts, with little concern for authorial attribution: writing was a collective enterprise for the glory of God, not an expression of individual authors. All this began to change when an author's name appeared on the cover of printed books, which fixed the text in permanent form – to be distributed to masses of readers. An emphasis on novelty and originality developed along with the market for printed books. Eisenstein poses the question: until books were classified by their authors' names, with the understanding that the text inside the book was newly composed and not copied, "how could the modern game of books and authors be played?"[70]

The eighteenth-century legislation establishing the law of copyright effectively transferred the ownership of a literary work from its printer and publisher to the individual who had created the work: its author. For Mark Rose, the inauguration of copyright is fundamental to the very concept of the modern author: by endowing authorship with "legal reality," copyright "helps to produce and affirm the very identity of the author as author." Copyright is based on "the concept of the unique individual who creates something original and is entitled to reap a profit from those labors" – that is, the author.[71]

The history of the invention of copyright has been thoroughly recounted; in chapter 1, I sketched the convergence of economic, legal, and technological factors that culminated in the first copyright legislation, the Statute of Anne in England in 1710. But this legislation was only one step on the difficult path to establishing authors' rights in their own works. As numerous historians have shown, the idea of the "modern proprietary author" was born, in England, France and elsewhere, out of a protracted legal tussle involving publishers and booksellers.[72]

The motivating factor in England was the expiry in 1695 of the Licensing Act, which had controlled publishing since 1662, by ensuring a near-monopoly of printing by the Stationers' Company. The philosopher John Locke was one highly public critic of the Licensing Act, which for him concentrated too much publishing power in "ignorant and lazy stationers." With the demise of the Act, those stationers lost their exclusive right to print and sell books; fearful of piracy, they agitated over the next fifteen years for a new legal regime of printing regulation. In a number of pamphlets from 1704, the writer Daniel Defoe developed the idea of authorial property rights, for the "Encouragement of Letters and all useful Studies"; several commentators have suggested that the stationers adopted the cause of authors' rights as a strategy in pursuing their own interests.[73]

Certainly authors' rights were a key component in the copyright legislation advocated by the stationers, eventually forming the Statute of Anne in 1710, which legislated copyright protection of new books for a term of fourteen years. Proponents of authorial rights were extending to authors the ideas of liberty and possessive individualism – including the right to private property – propounded by Locke and others as cornerstones of a liberal society. It may have been that newly defined author's rights were used as a legal ploy not only by the stationers but also against them. It has been suggested that legislators in Parliament worded aspects of the new Act – including the limited fourteen-year term and the emphasis on author's rights – as weapons in the fight to break the stationers' monopoly.[74]

However, the idea – and legal reality – of proprietary authorship was not so easily established. A number of court cases were needed to confirm the legal principle that authors were now the proprietors of their works. One of those cases, in 1741, found that the poet Alexander Pope owned copyright in his letters, which had been published. This decision established the idea of literary property as an abstraction,[75] so that copyright was understood to inhere in the work at the moment of its creation by the author.

By the 1750s, a "new, print-based, author-centred literary system," based on a market for literary works and the law of copyright, had emerged – at least for the leading authors of the time. In his study of the prolific author and editor Samuel Johnson, Alvin Kernan emphasizes the link between a market for works and the affirmation of the author. The year 1754 marks a symbolic turning-point – from the old world of patronage to the new world of author-entrepreneurs, whose success in the market freed authors from ties to patrons. In 1754, Samuel Johnson wrote a letter to Lord Chesterfield, declining an offer of patronage to help finance Johnson's great *Dictionary*; Kernan calls this letter "the Magna Carta of the modern author."[76] From this point onwards, the market gradually replaced patronage as the pathway to publication and literary success.

The other significant development in eighteenth century thought was a new privileging of originality; this concept became central to discussions of literary property, copyright, and the author itself. In law, a literary work was construed as the property of its author; in the sense that John Locke had asserted an individual's "person" as that individual's property, so an author's personality was thought to be imprinted on a text, forming a "work of original authorship" to be protected by copyright.[77] From around 1750, originality was increasingly upheld as the distinguishing characteristic of the best literary works. In 1753, the author and printer Samuel Richardson railed against the attempted piracy of his new novel by declaiming: "Never was Work more the Property of any Man, than *this* is his." Richardson then suggested to Edward Young that he write a treatise on originality – *Conjectures on Original Composition* – which Richardson printed in 1759.[78]

Young's text defined – through a series of extravagant metaphors – the modern author as "original," in contrast to the earlier medieval writer, defined as "imitator." Originals are upheld as "great benefactors" who "extend the republic of letters, and add a new province to its dominion." Imitators are denounced as writers who "only give us a sort of duplicates of what we had, possibly much better, before; increasing the mere drug of books."[79] Young celebrates the modern author as a figure whose originality liberates the writer from the burden of literary tradition. Only such a writer, who rejects borrowings from the past and publishes instead original thoughts, can be considered a true author: "His works will stand distinguished; his the sole Property of them; which Property alone can confer the noble title of an *Author*."

As Mark Rose remarks, Young's metaphors here draw on the notion of the literary work as an estate, connected to the aristocracy as the "noble" landed, propertied class.[80] For Young, the modern author, creator of original works, has become an elevated social figure, a new type of cultural aristocrat. Ironically, Young's paean to the "noble" modern author came at the very time when authors, artists and composers were detaching themselves from the aristocracy as source of patronage.

The rhetoric surrounding the modern author in the second half of the eighteenth century increasingly drew on the idea of "genius" and organic metaphors: Young wrote of the "vegetable nature" of originality, which "rises spontaneously from the vital root of genius."[81] The mystification entailed in the concept of genius, and the use of organic imagery (intensified in the Romantic period), can be regarded as responses to the economic reality of the author mid-eighteenth century: authors were now dependent on the commodification, and sale, of works to make a living. Terry Eagleton has remarked that the notion of the transcendent genius emerged "just when the artist is becoming debased to a petty commodity producer," so that this mystification is partly a "spiritual compensation for this degradation."[82] The greatest authors – geniuses – were considered the most original authors. Rose declares that by the 1770s, the doctrine of originality had become "orthodox," citing as an instance of this orthodoxy Samuel Johnson's statement in his "Life of Milton," of 1779, that the "highest praise of genius is original invention."[83]

Authors' rights were legislated in France in 1793, while in the US the Copyright Act of 1790 granted copyright in works for a period of fourteen years. In 1842, Charles Dickens witnessed, on a reading tour of the US, numerous pirated versions of his books; the prevalence of international piracy indicated the need for binding copyright agreements between countries, or – even better – an international copyright treaty. The Berne International Copyright Convention was launched in 1886; member nations agreed to respect the copyright, within their own jurisdictions, of international authors (the US did not become a signatory to Berne until 1989). Other international copyright agreements have included the Universal Copyright Convention (1952) and the World Intellectual Property Organization (WIPO) Copyright Treaty (2002).

Copyright has been formulated in different legal frameworks around the world since its inception. Moral rights protecting the integrity of copyrighted works, for example, exist in many national legislations, but not in others. National copyright legislation was amended repeatedly throughout the twentieth century – often to extend the term of copyright protection, at other times to adjust to the properties of new media technologies. Computer-based information – essentially a string of zeroes and ones – needed to be legally defined as a form of writing so that electronic texts could be granted copyright protection. Copying technologies marketed in the second half of the twentieth century – audio and video tapes and cassettes, photocopiers – posed problems for the policing of copyright law: these technologies made infringement of copyright much easier for individual consumers. Various strategies were adopted to meet the threats of these technologies, including levies on recordable tapes, cassettes and tape machines: these were first introduced in Germany in 1965, when manufacturers of tape recorders were required by law to pay 5 per cent of revenue to copyright collecting societies.[84] In some countries, including the UK, Canada and Australia, copyright collection societies were formed with the authority to collect fees – on behalf of authors – from institutions such as libraries, schools and universities which copy and distribute texts – either by photocopying or electronic copying. These fees, distributed to author members, are intended to compensate for the loss of sales – and royalties – of the copied works.

Lawrence Lessig wrote in 1999 that "copyright has always been at war with technology."[85] By 1999, it was evident that the internet was a much greater foe than the photocopier. Copyright was effectively overrun in the late 1990s, as online peer-to-peer file-swapping networks allowed users to share music files; each "sharing" represented an infringement of copyright. The loss of royalties resulting from the illegal distribution of copyrighted works on the internet is the primary factor in the "near-death of the author" in the twenty-first century. I discuss this issue in detail in chapter 6, along with the argument that copyright – invented in the wake of the printing press – is obsolete in the wake of the internet.

What We Owe to the Romantics

The modern author – founded on the legal institution of copyright – was firmly established by the end of the eighteenth century. The Romantic period – from the end of the eighteenth century to the early nineteenth century – made other contributions to the idea of the author. These were not so much legal or economic contributions as they were ideological: the Romantics elevated the author or artist figure to the status of cultural hero.

Romanticism was in part a reaction against the veneration of reason in the eighteenth- century European Enlightenment; in response, the Romantics lauded imagination and emotion. Whereas the great British scientist Isaac Newton was a hero to Voltaire and the other *philosophes* of the French Enlightenment, that same scientist was a villain of cosmic proportions for the Romantic poet and artist William Blake: Blake's 1795 portrait of Newton depicted a secular demigod, sectoring – and disenchanting – the world with his instruments and calculations. Mary Shelley's novel *Frankenstein*, published in 1818, is the classic science fiction work, a moral warning against the ambitions of the "Modern Prometheus": reason and science.

A Brief History of the Author 89

Figure 4.3 Illustration from the frontispiece of the 1831 edition of *Frankenstein* by Mary Shelley. Published by Colburn and Bentley, London 1831, licensed from Project Gutenberg.

The philosophical underpinning of this period was the German idealistic philosophy of Kant and Schiller, with its positing of innate faculties of mind, including the creative faculty; and Rousseau's commitment to writing as self-expression, most evident in his posthumous *Confessions*. The Romantics emphasized imagination, spiritual vitality, and the natural "sublime"; affinity with nature was sought in art, poetry and music, as remedy for the alienation of humanity from its natural environment, wrought by the industrialization of the nineteenth century.

The Romantic poets also sought an intensity of subjective, emotional experience: in 1800, William Wordsworth described poetry as "the spontaneous overflow of powerful feelings," and the writing of poetry as "emotion recollected in tranquillity." Inspiration was a mysterious spiritual force lifting the poet into a heightened creative state: William Blake stated that he wrote his poetic work *Milton* "from immediate Dictation ... without Premeditation & even against my Will." Samuel Taylor Coleridge defined the poet as an elevated representative of the human race, an artist who "brings the whole soul of man into activity."[86]

The exaltation of the poet – meaning the creative writer or artist – reached its height in the poet Percy Bysshe Shelley's "A Defence of Poetry," published in 1821. Shelley positions poetry at "the centre and circumference of all knowledge," above science and reasoning, since science itself must be "referred" to the creative inspiration of poetry. Employing the organic imagery beloved of Romantics, Shelley avers that poetry is "the root and blossom of all other systems of thought," due to the mysterious powers of inspiration that motivate a poet; this power "arises from within," unpredictable "like an inconstant wind," the source of "the original conception of the poet." In situating poets as the "unacknowledged legislators of the World," above scientists and philosophers, Shelley reverses the hierarchy established by Plato in *The Republic*; and the unpredictable, uncontrollable inspiration of poetry – one of the reasons for Plato's banishment of the poets – is the foundation for Shelley of poetry's central cultural role, as the "influence which is moved not, but moves."[87]

"Poetry is indeed something divine," Shelley states in "A Defence of Poetry," connecting to another cultural development in the eighteenth and nineteenth centuries. This was the gradual process of secularization, resulting in the assumption by art of some of the social role previously reserved for religion. The philosophers of the Enlightenment were in many cases critical of religion; some espoused agnostic or atheistic viewpoints. As the influence of organized religion declined, art for the Romantics functioned in part as a substitute. As has been remarked of Romantic music, art was "a kind of religion" for the Romantics.[88]

The music of Beethoven soared with an emotional power that was also felt as a spiritual force; Wordsworth's "crisis lyrics" were long, deeply subjective poems that probed spiritual depths previously deemed the province of religious thought. This quasi-religious aspect of the Romantic artist's mission was another reason for the lofty social role assigned to poetry by Shelley: poets, artists and composers acted as spiritual guides for modern society. Shelley declared that poets "are the hierophants of an unapprehended inspiration," meaning that they are the expositors or explainers – to the rest of society – of spiritual mysteries.[89]

The Romantics embraced the idea of genius to describe the singular vision of the greatest artists. Originality was a key component of genius for the Romantics, as Wordsworth wrote in 1815: "Genius is the introduction of a new element into the intellectual universe." A genius in the arts has the rare ability to do "what was never done before," thereby "widening the sphere of human sensibility, for the delight, honour, and benefit of human nature."[90]

In his book *Divine Fury*, Darrin McMahon provides a history of the idea of genius, noting that the word originated with the ancient Romans, for whom "genius" meant "guardian spirit." McMahon shows that the modern sense of genius, as "an individual of exceptional creativity and insight," was forged in the eighteenth-century Enlightenment, and further "stylized and mystified" by the Romantics. William Blake wrote of the "universal Poetic Genius," a "principle of individual creation" active throughout history.[91] Romantic painters including Delacroix and Casper David Friedrich depicted heroic individuals, transcendent in their solitude before nature, or as the suffering genius, alone and misunderstood. Martha Woodmansee has noted that the idea of genius and the law of copyright both emerged in the eighteenth century, both resolutely focused on the individual author.[92]

All of these factors combined to render the genius Romantic author an extraordinary figure: a cultural hero benefiting society through original works of art, but also a figure so unique as to isolate the author from society. Andrew Bennett describes the Romantic author as an "outstanding" figure, a kind of superhuman individual, "above or beyond the human."[93] The genius, like the hero espoused by Thomas Carlyle, was a gendered construct in the nineteenth century: the writers, composers and artists described as geniuses or cultural heroes were almost exclusively male. The genius was considered so visionary as to be ahead of the time; this could result in the author being misunderstood or rejected by the mainstream of society. The Romantic idea of the misunderstood genius was later applied to various figures, including

Vincent Van Gogh and Friedrich Nietzsche: largely unappreciated in their own time, championed as geniuses after their deaths.

The Romantic genius was thought to so inspired as to be possibly unstable; possibly a little mad; possibly touched by the divine: a wildly exciting type of cultural hero. Because the genius author was construed as the individual creator – the sole genesis – of original works, literary critics came to recognize the author's intention as central to an understanding of the work. (This critical focus on the author's intention developed despite the evident complication that Romantic authors, including Shelley, insisted on the "instinct and intuition of the poetical faculty," so that the author's mind is "incapable of accounting to itself for the origin" of a work: inspiration was too mysterious a force to be understood).[94]

The ideal of the Romantic author is well summarized by Bennett: "original, autonomous, and fundamentally expressive of a unique individuality"; also "a personalized individual expressing intentions and a particular subjectivity."[95] This ideal became so dominant in Western culture that its legacy has been profound. Rock music, for example, follows a purely Romantic ideal of authorship, of the songwriter and singer conveying an authentic, emotional, personalized vision. The Modernist art movements of the twentieth century adopted the Romantic idea of the genius author, particularly in an era when Modernist art seemed avant-garde or ahead of its time. Picasso was celebrated as the great genius of Modernist art in the early twentieth century; then Jackson Pollock was lionized as the genius of abstract expressionism in the 1950s: projecting his complex, inspired, even tortured subjectivity into paint.

The modern-artist-as-genius trope was countered, however, in the early 1960s, in the persona of pop artist Andy Warhol. Here was a decidedly unheroic, unRomantic version of the artist: cool, dispassionate, ironic, not conventionally masculine in the manner of the heroic Picasso and Pollock. Warhol painted the surface rather than the depths, drawing on found images from commercial media rather than probing spiritual mysteries. Warhol prefigured the post-modern artist as processor of information: a post-Romantic rendering of the author. The twentieth century in fact generated several versions of the post-Romantic author, in literary theory and the avant-garde (examined in the next chapter). But the concept of the Romantic author remained culturally dominant throughout that century. When Roland Barthes published "The Death of the Author" in 1968, the author he had in mind for assassination was indeed the Romantic author.

Chapter Five

The Alleged Death of the Author: Post-structuralism and Postmodernism

Roland Barthes wrote his essay "The Death of the Author" in 1967, but it wasn't published in France until 1968. "The Death of the Author" thereby gained a readership in that tumultuous year, the height of the "Age of Disruption" in the late 1960s: student uprisings and political protests in France, race riots and political assassinations in the US. Barthes's essay proved to be a major disruptive force in literary theory, cultural studies, and the conception of the author. As Seán Burke has wryly observes in his book *The Death and Return of the Author*, many literary and cultural theorists in the 1970s and 1980s, including practitioners of "euphoric American deconstruction," accepted the death of the author as proven in Barthes's text, as well as in the post-structuralist writing of Foucault and Derrida.[1] The author, it seemed, had been theoretically terminated as a viable concept by French post-structuralism, and would cease to function as a term of analysis in theory and criticism – and perhaps even in culture generally.

But what did Barthes mean when he announced the death of the author? And what effect did post-structuralist theorizing have on the concept and practice of the contemporary author?

What We Owe to the Russian Formalists

Barthes's essay was the culmination of decades of theoretical developments in the twentieth century – in formalism, literary theory, structuralism, and post-structuralism – that devalued the importance of the author in the interpretation of texts. The cumulative effect of these theoretical developments was a decentring – or exclusion – of the author in consideration of the generation of cultural works themselves.

The first, highly influential, steps taken in this direction were made by the Russian Formalists, a group of loosely affiliated literary theorists practising in Russia from around 1915, until the suppression of their activities by Soviet authorities in 1930 (Soviet aesthetic orthodoxy by 1930 viewed any emphasis on formalism with official disapproval). As a result of this suppression, much of the Russian Formalist writing remained unknown outside the Soviet Union, although their approach was continued in the later Prague Structuralist school, influencing structuralist and semiotic analyses of cultural texts in the 1950s and 1960s. A broader awareness of the Russian Formalists' methods did not emerge until 1965, when a selection of their writings, translated into French, was published by Tzvetan Todorov – in time to inspire and influence French post-structuralist approaches to literature and language.[2]

The Russian Formalists' goal was to establish a science of literature; their approach was morphological – that is, pursuing the study of forms and structures. The poetics of a literary work entailed the detailed analysis of the work's structural components and their function – without recourse to the author of the work or the author's intentions in creating it. Osip Brik wrote in 1916 that "the social role of the poet" cannot be determined by study of the poet's "individual qualities and habits"; rather, it was now essential for literary theory "to study on a mass scale the devices of poetic craft."[3]

The poetics pursued by the Russian Formalists yielded some profound insights, adopted by generations of later cultural theorists and artists. Viktor Shklovsky proposed that the most important function of creative art is *ostranenie*, or "making strange." By this he meant the capacity of literature or art to defamiliarize the world, by rendering everyday routinized reality in a startlingly new way. The idea of "making strange," as the radical potential of art to shape perception and cognition, has been embraced by many theorists and practitioners, including Bertolt Brecht, whose "alienation effect" was an application of "making strange" in his dramatic works.[4]

Mikhail Bakhtin developed a theory of the novel as a polyphonic text, which incorporates all available modes of discourse as voices in the novel. Bakhtin also used the terms "heteroglossia," the "carnivalesque" and "dialogistic" to describe the great diversity of discourses circulating in the text: "every novel," he wrote, "is a dialogized system made up of the images of 'languages.'"[5] Bakhtin's ideas, when discovered in France in the 1960s, heavily influenced the post-structuralist concept of intertextuality, while the post-structuralist theorist Julia Kristeva developed Bakhtin's idea of the carnivalesque in relation to cultural texts. Bakhtin's dialogic conception of the text, in which multiple voices are engaged in a complex dialogue, entailed a new formulation of the author: not the Romantic intentional author but a dialogic author, who may find the voices of characters or discourses in the text broadening – even contesting – the authorial perspective. For Bakhtin, the author remains active, but "this action takes on a specific dialogic character."[6]

The most well-known work of Russian Formalist poetics is Vladimir Propp's *Morphology of the Folktale*, originally published in 1928. Propp believed that a scientific analysis of a folk tale's structural elements would be the equivalent of a botanical analysis of a plant's biological forms; his aim was "an examination of the forms of the [folk] tale which will be as exact as the morphology of organic formations."[7] He broke down the structure of Russian fairy tales into a number of recurring components: seven character functions – including hero, villain, helper, princess (or sought character); six plot stages – including preparation, struggle and return; and 31 plot functions based on those plot stages. Propp concluded that all folktales are based on the sequencing of these set character functions and a selection from the possible set of plot points.

From the perspective of the author, the most striking feature of Propp's analysis is that there is none. Propp chose oral Russian folktales for his study; these narratives were passed orally through generations by storytellers: they were anonymous tales. With no individual author attached to these stories, and no authorial intention to consider, Propp was free to build a poetics through a study of the structural components of the narratives. The author is missing in analysis because there was no individual author in the first place. Instead, the folktales are shown as arrangements of character and plot functions; they have been composed by drawing on the reserves of story elements present in the culture. Propp's narrative analysis exerted a powerful influence on later literary and cultural theory. Joseph Campbell devised his own set of narrative components for the analysis of myths and other narratives in *The Hero with a Thousand Faces* in 1949. In the 1960s, semioticians including Umberto Eco conducted narrative analyses of popular films such as James Bond movies, drawing heavily on the stock of character and plot types first identified by Propp.

Structuralists and Post-structuralists

The narrative analysis conducted by the structuralist anthropologist Claude Lévi-Strauss took as its object mythological narratives, generated in oral cultures over generations. These myths, like the Russian folktales, had no individual authors: they were anonymous. But the structuralist analysis of narrative functioned at a different level to that of the Russian Formalists. Whereas Propp achieved a morphology of narrative, revealing the structural components of story, Lévi-Strauss aimed to demonstrate how meaning is generated in myth narratives – primarily through the structural play of opposite terms. Lévi-Strauss argued that myths work by reconciling opposite concepts – human/animal, nature/culture, mortal/immortal, the raw/the cooked – to produce narratives meaningful to their community. From an exhaustive examination of myths, Lévi-Strauss isolated a number of recurring functions in myth narratives, but his focus was on the underlying symbolic function of the narrative, creating meaning through the contrast of opposites.

The most profound legacy of structuralism for post-structuralist thought was the radical decentring of the individual subject in analysis. The subject – including the author – was replaced by a study of the cultural form itself as "autonomous object, independent of any subject," as Lévi-Strauss wrote in *The Raw and Cooked*, published in 1964. Lévi-Strauss claimed that his structuralist anthropology showed "not how men think in myths, but how myths operate in men's minds without their being aware of the fact." He took the further step of suggesting that analysis should disregard "the thinking subject completely," proceeding instead "as if the thinking process were taking place in the myths, in their reflection upon themselves."[8] Culture itself speaks through the myths, and analysis may glean the meaning of those narratives through attention to deep structures within the language of the culture – without the need of considering individual agents, such as authors. The structuralism of Lévi-Strauss therefore incorporated a post-humanism, evident in his declaration in *The Savage Mind* (1962) that "the goal of the human sciences is not to constitute man, but to dissolve him."[9]

Semiology – or semiotics – was foreseen by the linguist Ferdinand de Saussure as a "science of the life of signs within society" as early as 1915, in his *Course in General Linguistics*.[10] Semiology flourished decades later, in the 1950s and 1960s, as a form of structuralist analysis applied to all forms of communication in modern societies. Semiology developed a complex classification of signifiers, signifieds, referents, syntagm and paradigm, denotation, and connotation, as well as cultural codes embedded in a text; the work of a skilful semiotician was to reveal how the play of signifiers and codes produced meaning, subliminally, in the text. Roland Barthes was certainly a skilful semiotician; his 1964 book *Elements of Semiology* was his detailed elaboration of the semiotic method, with perhaps a slightly apologetic acknowledgment that "the binary classification of concepts seems frequent in structuralist thought."[11]

The transition from structuralism to post-structuralism took place in the years following publication of this book; this transition is reflected in the change in Barthes's works – from the scientific rigour of *Elements of Semiology* to "The Death of the Author" (1968), *Sade/Fourier/Loyola* (1971) and *The Pleasure of the Text* (1973). These and other later works were premised on the elusiveness of meaning, and on the conception of language itself as the generator of texts and new works. Post-structuralist writing was influenced by the psychoanalytical theory of Jacques Lacan, who fused structuralist linguistics with Freud's theory of the unconscious. Lacan's dictum that "the unconscious is structured like a language" was a theoretical support for the idea that language itself – speaking through individual subjects, even the unconscious – was the creator of culture in a ceaseless flux of discourse, whose meanings could not be discerned or fixed by structuralist analysis.[12]

In *Sade/Fourier/Loyola*, Barthes expressed the post-structuralist conviction that Text (or language) "is the destroyer of all subject," including the authorial subject. He also distanced himself from his earlier structuralist self when he declared that "nothing is more depressing than to imagine the Text as an intellectual object (for reflection, analysis …)"; instead, the text, for a post-structuralist theorist, is "an object of pleasure." The flow of language in texts produces a subject for analysis that is "dispersed, somewhat like the ashes we strew into the wind after death."[13]

Modernists, Feminists, and Marxists

Other currents in twentieth-century thought – in literary theory, avant-garde Modernism, Marxism, and feminism – also contributed to the rejection – or modification – of the author as a theoretical concept. Anglo-American literary theory increasingly focused analysis on the text itself, marginalizing the biographical emphasis on authorial intention. This approach was most clearly articulated in the 1954 essay "The Intentional Fallacy" by W.K. Wimsatt Jr and Monroe C. Beardsley. Wimsatt and Beardsley asserted that "the design or intention of the author is neither available nor desirable as a standard for judging the success of a work of literary art."[14] They did not deny authorial intention in the creation of a work, but rather dismissed it as a criterion in the reception – including the critical evaluation – of that work. This theoretical move decentred the author in the domain of interpretation and evaluation of texts: the author's intention was granted no more authority than a reader's judgment of the text.

In the avant-garde of Modernism in the early twentieth century, a post-Romantic conception of the artist/author could be found. The 1919 Manifesto of the newly opened Bauhaus design school in Germany asserted a new unity – of art and craft. This manifesto, written by Walter Gropius, the first director of the Bauhaus, demystified the artist and defined art's social role in the terms of craft or industry. For Gropius, the artist was not a divinely inspired seer, as the Romantics had professed: "There is no essential difference between the artist and the craftsman. The artist is an exalted craftsman." As the Bauhaus increasingly emphasized applied design in the 1920s, Gropius shifted its slogan to "art and technology, a new unity."[15]

Marxist theory stipulated that the author should be conceived as a servant of the collective – the proletariat – rather than as the individual hero of bourgeois capitalist culture. Accordingly, in the 1920s the Soviet Constructivist artists considered themselves engineers, working for the benefit of the Bolshevik revolution, constructing the new communist state. The poet Mayakovsky and the artist Rodchenko collaborated on posters to promote Lenin's Economic Plan; these propaganda/artwork/Communist advertisements were attributed, in the Constructivist manner, to "Advertisement Constructors, Mayakovsky-Rodchenko."[16] Outside the Soviet Union, the artists George Grosz and John Heartfield espoused Communist values, declaring that "the title 'artist' is an insult."[17] Walter Benjamin's 1934 essay "The Author as Producer" defined the author as a cultural producer engaged in the class struggle, not as an individualized creative genius. In the 1960s, Marxist theory incorporated aspects of structuralist linguistics, particularly in the theory of ideology developed by Louis Althusser. Ideology for Althusser spoke through institutions and individuals, constituting the latter as subjects. The Marxist theorist Pierre Macherey wrote in *A Theory of Literary Production* (1966): "the proposition that the writer or artist is a creator belongs to a humanist ideology."[18] Post-humanist structuralist Marxist theory stripped agency from the individual subject – including the author. Texts and cultural works were generated by ideology through the operation of language; the author was merely part of the mechanism of cultural production.

Feminist literary theory from the 1960s onwards critiqued the author as an inherently gendered concept, as mentioned in chapter 1. Sandra Gilbert and Susan Gubar, in their 1979 book *The Madwoman in the Attic* noted that one of the early meanings of "author" was "begetter": the author was thought to "father" his texts.[19] The patriarchal character of authorship was also reflected in the establishment of literary canons, constructed by male critics, and comprising almost exclusively male authors. Much of the work in feminist literary theory was to reclaim female authors, identifying women writers whose work had previously been suppressed or ignored, building a canon of female authors.

At the same time, it was observed by many feminist theorists and critics that just as feminism made an intervention into the patriarchal construct of the author, the author was declared dead as a concept by Roland Barthes. There have been many divergent strands of feminist thought; some feminists argued that Barthes's destruction of the author should be celebrated, because the Romantic, God-like Author in Barthes's sights was also an intrinsically patriarchal author. Other feminists, including Nancy K. Miller in "Changing the Subject: Authorship, Writing and the Reader" (1988), advocated for a reconstituted author, one capable of incorporating a "female writing identity" and, more broadly female agency and subjectivity.[20]

Volumes of theoretical writing in the twentieth century – formalist, feminist, structuralist, post-structuralist, Marxist and other – targeted the traditional concept of the author. But it was only Roland Barthes who, in 1968, hit this target so unerringly that he was emboldened to announce "the death of the author."

a/A

Barthes's essay is a short text of only seven pages. This brief work, however, is probably the most widely read text on the topic of authorship; it is also, probably, the most misunderstood. Barthes begins with a mini-history of the author, which he describes as a "modern figure": post-medieval, the product of Renaissance rationalism and the Reformation's "personal faith," resulting in the "prestige of the individual" applied to authorship. Barthes acknowledges that this figure of the modern author "still reigns" in literary history, biographies, and criticism, where explanation of a work "is always sought in the man or woman who produced it" – that is, the author's intention. Barthes then compiles a somewhat longer mini-history of writers – Mallarmé, Valéry, Proust – who dislodged or "loosened" the centrality of the author in literature, by emphasizing the generative flow of language in producing texts.[21]

These writers serve as support for Barthes's central argument – that for Mallarmé, and "for us too," it is "language which speaks, not the author." Further support is taken from linguistics, which has shown that "enunciation is an empty process," functioning perfectly well without the need for an individual author: "language knows a 'subject,' not a 'person.'" For Barthes, the removal of the Author is a profoundly significant process, which "utterly transforms the modern text." Barthes nominates a new term to replace the author: the "modern scriptor." This revival of the medieval term for one of the possible author-functions – a scribe who simply copies the words of others – is a deliberate ploy by Barthes to strip away the Romantic glorification of the author. The Author, Barthes states, is "thought to *nourish* the book" by existing before the work, creating it in a process of inspiration, toil, and suffering, thereby offering explanations for the meaning of the text. But the modern scriptor, by contrast, is merely the enunciator of what is written, a vessel for the process of language which has created the work. The modern scriptor generates texts in "a pure gesture of inscription," with "no other origin than language itself."[22]

Barthes then attacks the quasi-religious aspect of the Romantic author, as a figure divinely inspired, endowed with the authority of an "Author-God." He asserts that interpretation of a text should not look for a single "theological" meaning emanating from the Author-God. Instead, a text should be understood as: "a multi-dimensional space in which a variety of writings, none of them original, blend and clash. The text is a tissue of quotations drawn from the innumerable centres of culture."[23] This is the classic post-structuralist characterization of the text as inter-textuality. Barthes deploys the medieval concept of scriptor as copyist within a post-structuralist setting: contemporary authors are scriptors because they copy words – "none of them original" – and displace them into new texts, which are "tissues of quotations." The writer-as-scriptor can only "imitate a gesture" that is "never original"; the modern scriptor's "only power is to mix writings." The Author is thus succeeded by the scriptor, who bears within not inspiration and originality but an "immense dictionary from which he draws a writing that can know no halt."[24]

Barthes takes a passing shot at the "Critic" who has been in league with the Author, in the way that a priest is in league with a divinity. When belief in the Romantic author was unqualified, the critic's role was to discover the author within the text, thereby providing explanation of the work. In the post-Author world of literature, Barthes insists, the "multiplicity of writing" is not to be "deciphered" but rather "disentangled." There can be no "final signified" of meaning drawn triumphantly from the text; instead, "the space of writing is to be ranged over, not pierced" by critics and readers. This is because no definitive meaning can be fixed in texts perpetually based on other texts, as "writing ceaselessly posits meaning ceaselessly to evaporate it, carrying out a systematic exemption of meaning."[25]

Barthes concludes his essay by focusing on the reader, who will occupy a new cultural role after the demise of the author. Indeed, Barthes declares that the reader is now the point that unifies the text, replacing the previous unifying-point, the author. Barthes reiterates the post-structuralist conception of the text as "made of multiple writings, drawn from many cultures," but adds that "there is one place where this multiplicity is focused and that place is the reader." Barthes replaces the previously omnipotent author with a new, active form of the reader, so that now "a text's unity lies not in its origin but in its destination." This theoretical move is underlined with the resounding sentence that closes the essay: "we know that to give writing its future, it is necessary to overthrow the myth: the birth of the reader must be at the cost of the death of the Author."[26] Barthes provided a brilliant, sustained exercise in the reading – and unifying – of a text in his 1970 book *S/Z*, a detailed analysis of the novella *Sarrasine* by Balzac. The first sentences of "The Death of the Author" in fact refer to *Sarrasine*; Barthes was working on his virtuoso dissection of the novella while writing the famous essay. In *S/Z*, Barthes offers a line-by-line (sometimes word-by-word) analysis of the Balzac text according to five cultural codes which speak through the prose; he also pays particular attention to the interplay of the letters s and z. Z is "the letter of mutilation," Barthes notes; it performs a significant role in the relationship between the castrato Zambinella and the novella's male protagonist Sarrasine, who mistakes Zambinella for a woman. Barthes stages a confrontation of s and z within the text as "a panic function" in the work; the s/z opposition is the core of his reading of the 1830 novella as a crisis text, inscribing repressed values of identity and sexuality within the novella.[27]

Barthes conducts his own interplay of letters within the seven pages of "The Death of the Author" – but this game of a and A was largely undetected by early readers of the essay. Seán Burke, in his book *The Death and Return of the Author*, certainly noticed the "curious play of capitalisation and decapitalisation which Barthes studs into his text"; he also remarked that "scrupulous attention" to this play may have prevented the "literal reception" of the essay in Anglo-American theoretical schools.[28]

Barthes uses "author" six times and "Author" sixteen times in his essay. The six appearances of "author" occur in the first two pages, including the brief historical background on the formation of the author as writer of books. "Author" makes its first appearance on the second page, and is used exclusively from the third page to the end, as Barthes's argument becomes polemical. The capital A is in effect in the essay's final pronouncement: "the birth of the reader must be at the cost of the death of the Author." The "Author" is the object of Barthes's fiercest critique, particularly regarding the "theological" meanings drawn from the words of the "Author-God." The Author, then, stands for the Romantic author: genius, divinely inspired, unique, personalized, "original, autonomous, and fundamentally expressive of a unique individuality" (Andrew Bennett's summary). This is the author-function that Barthes condemns; he consigns the Author to retirement, to be replaced in literary service by the more humble modern scriptor – a transmitter of language and its flow of meanings that will allow greater scope for the reader's engagement with texts.

Barthes has not destroyed the very concept of the author, as many post-structuralist enthusiasts assumed in the 1970s, based on a literal reading of the essay. Instead, he has dismantled the Romantic Author as individual creator of original works. In its place is a focus on the inter-textuality of all texts, their origin not in the mind of a lone creative genius but in the ceaseless flux of language itself.

That Barthes had not intended – or effected – the demise of the author as a concept and social reality is evident in several post-structuralist texts published in the years following "The Death of the Author." Jacques Derrida, whose philosophy of deconstruction observed the post-structuralist emphasis on the generative nature of language, in which meaning is infinitely deferred, did not nevertheless dismiss the concept of the author. In 1977, Derrida maintained a (qualified) role for authorial intention, declaring that intention will not disappear, although "it will no longer be able to govern the entire scene and system of utterance." In 1984 he even remarked of the alleged death of the author that "too much of a case" had been made for that "death or omission."[29]

Barthes himself wrote of the author – alive and not quite deceased – in the years after his controversial essay. In *Sade/Fourier/Loyola* (1971), Barthes wrote that the pleasure of the text now includes "the amicable return of the author." He describes this author not as the "biographical hero" of traditional literary discourse; rather, this returning author is a reconstituted figure, a post-structuralist version of the author: "The author who leaves his text and comes into our life has no unity; he is a mere plural of "charms," the site of a few tenuous details ... a discontinuous chant of amiabilities."[30] And in *The Pleasure of the Text* (1973), Barthes first reiterates his act of literary homicide: "As institution, the author is dead: his civil status, his biographical person have disappeared; dispossessed, they no longer exercise over his work the formidable paternity." But he then acknowledges a wistful longing for the idea of the author, testifying to the persistence of some form of the old author-function: "but in the text, in a way, I *desire* the author: I need his figure (which is neither his representation nor his projection), as he needs mine."³¹ The author survives, then, even in the longings of its alleged assassin – but this author is now thought to be a radically altered version of its former self.

Author as Processor

The notion that Barthes could have literally dispatched the legal-economic entity of the author is absurd. In the decades following "The Death of the Author," the author attained new heights of cultural and economic importance in Western culture. Hollywood cinema in the 1970s vested increased prestige in the director-as-author, celebrating a new generation of film auteurs: Coppola, Scorsese, de Palma, Lucas, Malick. In the 1980s, the publishing industry and media conspired to elevate book authors to celebrity status, approaching the celebrity of pop stars and actors. The adaptation of novels into films and television series further lifted the profile of many authors, both writers of popular fiction such as J.K. Rowling and Stephen King, and authors of literary fiction. In 2007, Lorraine York published a study of three successful authors in her book *Literary Celebrity in Canada*. Through an examination of the careers of authors Margaret Atwood, Michael Ondaatje and Carol Shield, York analysed the contradictions and difficulties involved in literary fame, including the need to preserve privacy behind the public persona of the celebrity.

Indeed, publishing success and literary celebrity often proved onerous for high-profile authors of literary fiction. In 2001, the novel *The Corrections*, by Jonathan Franzen, was selected by television celebrity Oprah Winfrey for her book club, ensuring a huge new readership for the book and enhanced fame for its author. When Franzen expressed unease at the book's selection, however, his invitation to appear on Oprah's television show was rescinded. Franzen was roundly criticized for his elitist attitude in rejecting television exposure; nevertheless, the book became a best-seller, perhaps boosted by the Oprah controversy.

But problems such as these for literary authors were barely problems: they were the function of great success in the book industry. They did not herald the death of the author; rather, they attested to the extreme good health of authors, at least best-selling writers. On the other hand, there was one cultural development that did seem to reflect the influence of Barthes's essay: this was the emergence of the postmodern author.

Postmodern culture gained prominence in the 1970s, particularly in architecture and design, and a postmodern aesthetic was apparent throughout the 1980s and 1990s in visual art, music, literature, and other forms of expression. Postmodernism in general reacted against the singularity, austerity, and avant-garde sensibility of Modernism; in their place were a pluralism of styles, more accessible works, and a recycling or quotation of previous forms, drawing on a data bank of images, sounds, techniques and texts. Postmodern artists took their cue from Andy Warhol in the 1960s: they appropriated existing cultural forms with a cool irony, quoting, fragmenting, and displacing pre-existing texts, which functioned as found objects of culture. This aesthetic of eclecticism was further enabled in the 1980s by the widespread availability of new digital devices, the sampler (used in music) and the scanner (visual art). These digital recording devices were quotation instruments: they made the copying and adaptation of cultural texts easy to achieve by electronic means.

As a result, a new text or artwork was reconfigured not as an original work but as a mosaic of quotations from other texts. Barthes's definition of the modern scriptor's text – "a tissue of quotations drawn from the innumerable centres of culture" – was entirely apt as a description of postmodern works. The quotations were most evident in electronic popular music of the 1980s, which deployed the sampler as an appropriation device. The 1987 song "Pump Up the Volume" by the British group MARRS stitched together 30 samples from other songs into a musical tissue of quotations; this appropriation-text was a number one hit in many countries in 1987. The 1996 album *Entroducing …* contained the boast by its creator DJ Shadow that "This album consists entirely of samples."[32] In other words, sample-based pop music contained little or no original material; rather, it was premised on the skilful arrangement of found material: other texts. The postmodern artist was not so much a genius creator of original works (the Romantic author) as a processor of information, forging hybrid works.

Cultural theory of the time noticed the correlation between post-structuralist inter-textuality and postmodern practice. Andrew Goodwin wrote in "Sample and Hold," his 1990 essay on sampling in hip hop and electronic pop music, that: "postmodernists and devotees of Walter Benjamin's cultural analysis could be forgiven for patting themselves on their theoretical backs and ruminating on the strange prescience of these two bodies of theory."[33] The reference to Walter Benjamin is to the 1934 essay "The Work of Art in the Age of Mechanical Production," in which Benjamin celebrated the loss of "aura" of original artworks in the wake of mass copying. Postmodern aesthetics also realized Barthes's post-structuralist appreciation of a work as a "multi-dimensional space in which a variety of writings, none of them original, blend and clash."

The idea of the author was transformed in the postmodern period, in line with Barthes's conception of the modern scriptor. New criteria of creativity for the artist or author emerged: musicians and DJs were evaluated not on their originality, but on their judgment and skill in assembling found texts into a "new" work or assemblage. However, the free-wheeling postmodern aesthetic, founded on the creative use of appropriation, met a stumbling-block in the 1980s in the form of copyright law. Many musicians and DJs were sued for infringement of copyright due to their unlicensed sampling of musical works (including MARRS for its hit "Pump Up the Volume"). At one point, there were so many suits for copyright infringement in sample-based pop that it was wryly observed: "Where there's a hit, there's a writ." The skill of the artist as processor/sampler of musical information came to include the disguising of samples, using the sampler's capacity to alter the sampled musical items.

The postmodern artist's function as modern scriptor was also evident in appropriation visual art of the 1980s and 1990s. Much postmodern art comprised the copying of older works; these copies could then be displaced as fragments within a collage of quoted fragments. In some instances, the new artwork was simply a copy of an old work. Sherrie Levine created controversy with her works such as *After Walker Evans* (1980), which were her photographs of famous Walker Evans photographs, originally exhibited in the 1930s; after photographing the Evans images from catalogues, Levine exhibited them as her own work.

The principle underlying rephotography, as practised by Levine and other artists including Richard Prince (who rephotographed advertising imagery in his work *Untitled (Cowboy)* of 1990), was recontextualization. The original image is recontextualized in the act of copying and displacement: the identical image can take on new meanings in a new context. This principle of appropriation as recontextualization had been demonstrated in 1939 in the short story "Pierre Menard, Author of Don Quixote" by Jorge Luis Borges (a writer beloved of post-structuralists and postmodernists). In this story, Pierre Menard is a modern scriptor, who copies pages word-for-word from Cervantes' novel *Don Quixote*, with the paradoxical result that the copied work "is almost infinitely richer." This is because the novel has been recontextualized in time, from the seventeenth century to the twentieth. A statement in the original text on "truth, whose mother is history" is mere rhetoric in the seventeenth century, but when copied in the twentieth century it conveys an "astounding" idea, within a different intellectual context.[34] The recontextualization of images in the work of artists in the 1980s often had a feminist motivation: famous images made by male artists in the predominantly male Western canon were imbued with new meaning when rephotographed by female artists. Indeed, there were many more prominent female artists – including Cindy Sherman, Sherrie Levine, Barbara Kruger, and Jenny Holzer – in the postmodern period than had been the case within modernism.

Appropriation art and rephotography devalued both the original work and the idea of originality itself; in this they were partly inspired by the writing of Benjamin and Barthes. In "The Death of the Author," Barthes wrote that the modern scriptor – successor to the Romantic Author – is little more than a copyist, empowered only to "imitate a gesture" that is "never original." This serves as a description of the postmodern appropriation artist, who copied the works of others and presented the copies as new – but non-original – works. However, the rephotography artists, like the sampler-equipped electronic pop musicians, were frequently confronted by the law of copyright. The estate of Walker Evans considered Sherrie Levine's *After Walker Evans* an infringement of copyright; the estate acquired all the works in this series to prevent sale. Richard Prince was sued for copyright infringement in 2008, although the court's initial finding of infringement was appealed, and the case eventually settled.

Mere Irony Is Loosed upon the World

A central feature of postmodern aesthetics was the use of irony. Previous works were appropriated and recontextualized in a spirit both affectionate and ironic. In a general climate of intertextuality, influences were foregrounded rather than disguised in postmodern works. An ironic perspective pervades the intertextual cinema of Quentin Tarantino, Baz Luhrmann, and the Coen Brothers, while the long-running animated TV show *The Simpsons* (beginning in 1989) was laden with sophisticated – and ironic – quotations and parodies of popular culture. In literary fiction, an ironic self-reflexivity within texts was given the name "metafiction." Novels by John Barth, Richard Brautigan, Thomas Pynchon, Paul Auster, and others played with narrative conventions and intertextuality in a playful metafiction mode. Italo Calvino's 1981 novel *If on a Winter's Night a Traveller* took self-reflexivity and intertextuality to their furthest extremes: in this work, the narrative is constantly interrupted by the beginning of different narratives inserted into the text; the reader is even addressed in the novel as the possible means of unifying the fragmented, multiplicitous text.

Irony, however, was also held to be the weakness of postmodern works by the critics of postmodernism. The relativism of values and a protective screen of irony yielded works lacking in critical edge, according to Terry Eagleton, while Frederic Jameson critiqued the ironic referencing of texts as "blank parody" or "pastiche."[35] As the 1990s progressed, it was increasingly concluded that mere irony had been loosed upon the world by postmodernism, and that postmodern irony had become a trap to be avoided. In 1993, the novelist David Foster Wallace, weary of postmodern metafiction, proposed as its replacement a "new sincerity"; writers including Zadie Smith, Dave Eggers and Jonathan Franzen later aligned themselves with the new sincerity movement in literature. The 9/11 terrorist attack on New York in 2001 was claimed as a terminal point for postmodernism, as irony and self-reflexivity were now deemed inappropriate cultural strategies.

The postmodern era had ended earlier, however, around the middle of the 1990s: this date coincided with the rise of network culture. The world wide web was opened to commercial traffic in 1994; from that year internet use increased exponentially, and culture was increasingly conducted online. All cultural forms became data, to be transmitted, bought, and sold, consumed, and analysed on the internet. There is no post-postmodern period other than the era of network culture from around 1995; and it is from the late 1990s that the illegal downloading of copyright material on the internet had a major impact on authorship, resulting in the "near-death of the author." In the early twenty-first century, postmodernism was widely thought to have expired; but one of its aesthetic strategies – appropriation – was retained and repurposed as adaptive reuse, or creative reuse, of found – often copyrighted – works.

Chapter Six

The Author and Technology: Downloading vs. Copyright

In 2011, the Spanish novelist Lucia Etxebarria, author of several award-winning books, retired from writing, complaining that illegal downloads of her books outnumbered sales.¹ In 2012, the film production company Village Roadshow sold 50 per cent of its stake in Golden Village (Hong Kong) due to film piracy. In his 2020 book *The Death of the Artist*, William Deresiewicz interviewed 140 authors, artists, filmmakers, and writers, all of whom reported extreme difficulty in maintaining an artistic career in the context of greatly diminished income from royalties.

Some of Deresiewicz's interview subjects had already abandoned their career in the arts. One example is song-writer and musician Martin Bradstreet, founder of rock band Alexei Martov, who spent years trying to sustain a career through performing and touring – to compensate for the lack of royalties. But by 2019, Bradstreet had "moved on to other pursuits." He told Deresiewicz, wistfully, that: "It does seem like playing music for a living would be a nice thing to have done."² Another rock musician – Kim Deal of the Pixies – was more rueful than wistful in describing her plight as a musician depending on royalties that are no longer paid: "I'm just another person in the history of the world where their industry has become archaic, and it's gone."³

Roland Barthes did not kill the author, nor did post-structuralist theory. But in the early twenty-first century, many authors and artists discontinued their artistic careers, discouraged by the deleterious effects of illegal downloading and streaming on their royalties – that is, their income as authors. The examples noted above represent only a tiny selection of instances whereby authors and artists have terminated their careers because of the persistent infringement of copyright in their works. These are actual cases of the death of individual authors – or, less dramatically, of the cessation of authors' careers.

Figure 6.1 Download progress bar. Image courtesy of Steve Collins.

The Millennium the Music Died

There are numerous reported instances of financial hardship confronting song-writers, at times causing the termination of careers in music. This is because the music industry was the sector of the cultural industries that was first – and hardest – hit by internet-enabled infringement of copyright, around the turn of the millennium. In the late 1990s, it was widely publicized that online peer-to-peer file-swapping networks such as Napster were encouraging the free sharing of MP3 music files. This practice was reported to be rampant among young music fans; it was also being conducted in brazen disregard of copyright.

In 2000, the major record companies responded forcefully, prosecuting Napster for breach of copyright. But this recourse to the law did nothing to prevent the practice of peer-to-peer file-swapping: Napster may have been sued out of business, but there were many other file-swapping networks to take its place. Legal action failed to inhibit millions of illegal downloads – and, from around 2005, the illegal streaming of copyrighted audio-visual works including TV programs and films.

Music streaming services such as Spotify, founded in 2006, were supported by the record companies as a means of using online technology to pay royalties to musicians (Spotify pays royalties to record labels based on the number of an artist's streams, as a proportion of the total streamed songs; the labels distribute this revenue to the artists). But the tiny amount paid per stream on Spotify – estimated at less than half a cent – has been widely criticized by musicians, who regard the service as little more than a "digital tip jar." Canadian musician Tracy MacNeil told media in 2020 of her resentment at having to ask fans for donations at concerts, which wouldn't be necessary "if Spotify was paying artists properly in the first place."[4]

There are statistics that starkly demonstrate the rapid downturn in the music industry, corresponding to the jeopardizing of careers in music. In 1999, the year that Napster made its debut, global revenue for the music business peaked at $39 billion US. In 2014, that figure fell to $15 billion. From 2001 to 2018, the number of people employed as musicians in the US fell by 24 per cent. From 2000 to 2015, the number of full-time songwriters in Nashville dropped by 80 per cent. For musicians to survive in the industry, many played more concerts, asked for donations from fans at performances, and sold merchandize to counter the loss of revenue from royalties. For those who struggled even to perform concerts, their business model – as David Remnick of *The New Yorker* has remarked – "is giving music lessons."[5]

Because many musicians have come to depend heavily on live performance to generate income, the inability to perform at concerts or festivals can have a catastrophic impact on musicians' careers. This plight afflicted all musicians and songwriters during the COVID-19 pandemic beginning in 2020. Social restrictions and lockdowns meant that music venues closed, festivals were cancelled, and musicians were prevented from performing at live events. A report published by the UK Music organization in 2020 found that musicians and songwriters would lose 65 per cent of their income in 2020 due to COVID-19 social lockdowns. That figure rose to 80 per cent for those most dependent on live performance and studio recording work.[6]

Even previously successful musicians have endured ruinous loss of income from royalties as a result of illegal downloading and streaming. In 2017, Jonathan Taplin published an excerpt from his new book, *Move Fast and Break Things: How Facebook, Google and Amazon Have Cornered Culture and What It Means for Us,* in *Rolling Stone* magazine. Taplin tailored this excerpt to the concerns of a rock music magazine and its readership. To demonstrate "the human cost of the Internet revolution," Taplin focused on the plight of Levon Helm, member of the successful rock group The Band.

In the article, Taplin quantified the impact of illegal downloading on the income of a musician such as Helm. Members of The Band received a "decent royalty income" of around $100,000 per year throughout the 1970s (there are various types of royalties – including performing on the recording as well as song-writing – paid for every copy of a recording sold). This annual revenue from royalties increased in the 1980s, as The Band's albums were bought in the new CD format. The steady royalty stream continued "right up until the introduction of Napster in 2000," after which it declined to "almost nothing."

Taplin notes that new generations of music fans listened to The Band in the early twenty-first century, but "because fans listened on pirate sites or on YouTube, Levon had no income stream from this amazing catalog." After Helm was diagnosed with cancer in 1999, he staged concerts in his barn to cover medical costs; but after he died in 2012, it was feared that his widow would lose their house in Woodstock. To prevent this loss of home, Helm's musician friends held a benefit concert, with proceeds going directly to Helm's widow.[7] In this emotional article, Taplin identifies the "human cost" of copyright infringement conducted on an enormous scale on the internet.

The End of Copyright, the End of Authors?

The persistent infringement of copyright, in the illegal transmission and reception of digitized works across the web, has been the most contentious aspect of network culture. In her 2019 book *Authors and Apparatus*, Monika Dommann records that copyright has been fundamentally disrupted by the World Wide Web since the mid-1990s. Dommann notes the various defenders – and detractors – of copyright since that time, summarizing their view as a declaration of "the end of copyright as we know it."[8] A diverse array of reformers, critics and denouncers of copyright have pronounced that copyright – an eighteenth century legal invention to meet the demands of the printing press and the book market – is outmoded in the age of the internet.

Certainly the sheer ease of transmitting and downloading data across the internet, and the sheer difficulty in preventing copyright infringement, are crucial factors. Lawrence Lessig identified these factors in 1999, in his book *Code and Other Laws of Cyberspace*: "For the holder of the copyright, cyberspace appears to be the worst of both worlds – a place where the ability to copy could not be better, and where the protection of law could not be worse."[9] The realization that this was an entirely new situation confronting copyright holders prompted the initial panicky response by record companies in 2000. They and other rights holders in the culture industries, fearful of a cataclysmic loss of revenue, deployed the law in a desperate – and failed – attempt to stem the illegal transmission and reception of works.

But if copyright can be considered a cornerstone of the modern author as legal-economic entity – as argued in chapter 1 – what does the consistent violation of copyright law in the internet age mean for the contemporary author? Mark Rose asserted that the fundamental characteristic of the modern author is "proprietorship"[10] and that the law of copyright endows the author with the exclusive right to exploit their original works. Copyright as inaugurated and developed in the eighteenth century was designed to support the author in two ways. The first was to provide protection against the unlawful copying of the author's works, so that authors need not compete in the market against copies of their own works. The second was to provide a source of income – in the form of royalties for works sold on the market – to authors, artists, and other creators.

But both those aspects of copyright law have been greatly diminished in the internet age, to the extent that many authors – especially song-writers – have abandoned careers as authors altogether. This decision is made in the knowledge that copyright no longer functions as an economic-legal support: it is flagrantly violated in illegal streaming and downloading; and income in the form of royalties is drastically reduced or obliterated altogether. The contemporary author has in this way lost much of the proprietorship which Mark Rose considers the essential characteristic of the modern author. Authors are deprived of the exclusive right to exploit their works; this exploitation of works frequently happens elsewhere, on the internet, to the financial detriment of authors.

As William Deresiewicz points out, piracy websites – on which films, songs, texts, and other media forms can be streamed or downloaded for free – are not actually concerned with "free culture." Pirated content is posted wholesale on these websites, so that the online traffic – or volume of clicks – on the sites is monetized through advertising. Because these ads are brokered by Google, Deresiewicz can list the organizations which earn revenue from pirated works: Google; the pirate sites; credit card payment processors. The individuals missing out on revenue from online pirating are the creators of the works themselves: the "people who created the films and songs, of course, do not make any money whatsoever."[11]

In 2015, Scott Timberg published *Culture Crash: The Killing of the Creative Class*, in which he documented the disastrous effect of the online economy on authors, journalists, bookstores, record shops, other institutions and other creative individuals.[12] The cataclysmic tenor of this book – the "killing" of the creative class – is echoed in Deresiewicz's "death of the artist" and Taplin's "cornering of culture" and "undermining" of democracy. These books pursue a similar theme – the demise of creative individuals' careers resulting from online copyright infringement. For Taplin and Deresiewicz, the culprits behind this cultural catastrophe are primarily Big Tech corporations such as Google, which have facilitated online piracy and the large-scale disregard for copyright.

In *Move Fast and Break Things*, Taplin juxtaposes the severe decline in earnings by authors and artists since 2000, with the gigantic growth in annual revenue of Google over the same period (0.4 billion dollars US in 2002; 74.54 billion dollars in 2015). Noting a similar upward trend in the revenues of Facebook, Amazon, and Apple, Taplin concludes:

> What we have been witnessing since 2005 is a massive relocation of revenue from creators of content to owners of platforms.[13]

YouTube (launched in 2005, bought by Google in 2006) operates a "permissionless philosophy" in hosting copyrighted material without permission, typifying the attitude of the "tech elite" – characterized by Taplin as a "blatant disregard for the artist's intellectual property."[14] Taplin asserts that the founders of YouTube knowingly designed their platform to incorporate the consistent infringement of copyright, by publicly declaring that users posting videos – rather than the platform itself – are responsible for copyright permissions.

In this strategy, YouTube, Google, and other platforms were aided by the passing of the Digital Millennium Copyright Act (DMCA) in the US in 2005. This statute protected online service providers from prosecution for copyright infringement, provided that the provider does not have "the requisite level of knowledge of the infringing activity" and does not "receive a financial benefit directly attributable to the infringing activity."[15] As Taplin and other critics have pointedly observed, this allows a company to pretend ignorance of the incessant breach of copyright on its platform. Further, the "no financial benefit" clause is violated by the very business model of online platforms – to attract traffic through content, then monetize those clicks through advertising.

Taplin cites email correspondence between the co-founders of YouTube in 2005; these emails were made public during one of the early copyright infringement lawsuits brought against the company. In one email, one of the founders offers that "a way to avoid the copyright bastards" would be "to let the users moderate the videos themselves." Another email exchange between co-founders, as reported by Taplin, concerns the posting of full-length films on YouTube:

- "Steal it!"
- "Hmm, steal the movies?"
- "We have to keep in mind that we need to attract traffic."[16]

Deresiewicz endorses Taplin's harsh critique of the Big Tech companies' "cornering of culture" through copyright infringement on a colossal scale. Deresiewicz asserts that the tech giants – especially Google, Facebook, and Amazon – "have engineered a vast and ongoing transfer of wealth from creators to distributors, from artists to themselves." He notes that Facebook, like Google, benefits from piracy: a study in 2015 found that 725 of Facebook's 1,000 most popular videos infringed copyright.[17]

In the years 2019–2020, several governments around the world held inquiries into the unprecedented power, and monopoly status, of the "Big Tech" corporations. In 2021, legislation was passed in Australia compelling Facebook to pay news organizations for the content appearing in Facebook news feeds. At the same time, rights holders exerted public pressure on the online platforms to prevent piracy, particularly of films and TV programs. In 2018, the co-chief executive of Village Roadshow – a film production and distribution company – publicly attacked Google in the Australian press, accusing the company of "facilitating crime" by allowing piracy.

Roadshow CEO Graham Burke noted that there was provision in Australian law (since 2015) for rights holders to block pirate websites, through obtaining a court order. But because Google did not actively block pirate sites itself, Burke declared that "they are complicit and they are facilitating crime." The CEO demanded that Google take a more proactive stance to help eliminate piracy; but he did not believe that Google would act – "because piracy sites are popular, attracting 'eyeballs' to its search engine."[18]

However, after two more years of sustained public pressure, Google agreed in 2020 to remove hundreds of pirate film and TV program websites. This action also included the removal of proxy or mirror sites previously used by pirates once their websites were blocked.[19] In the global context of a vast pirate website industry, this was only a tiny victory for rights holders – but it was a victory nevertheless for copyright and creative artists, after two decades of heavy defeats.

Digitized Books, Google, and Non-Google

There are statistics indicating the often-dire financial circumstances confronting contemporary book authors. In a series of research papers published between 2015 and 2018, economists at Macquarie University in Sydney assessed the impact of digital disruption on the Australian book industry. In a 2015 industry briefing, *Australian Authors*, the researchers disclosed the findings of a survey of over 1,000 Australian authors: the average income derived from practising as an author is only $12,900 AUD. More than 25 per cent of these authors have had their work pirated; this figure is higher – 44.7 per cent – in the case of genre fiction authors.[20]

Even more alarming statistics were revealed in the US Authors Guild 2018 Author Income Survey of over 5,000 authors, which disclosed a 42-per cent drop in the median income from writing since 2009: the 2018 figure was a tiny $6,080 US. Revenue from books dropped to only $3,100, while writers of literary fiction suffered a significant drop of 27 per cent since 2013. This survey indicated that authors increasingly sought income from speaking engagements or teaching; even then, the median income for all writing-related activities was only $20,300.[21] In the US, the sale of books in bookshops plummeted by 39 per cent in the ten years after 2007, while 40 per cent of independent bookstores in the US closed in the years 1995–2000.[22]

The factors cited by the Authors Guild for the disastrous decline in authors' income include the dominance of Amazon in the bookselling market; the re-selling of books on Amazon for which authors receive no payment; the low royalties paid on e-books and discounted books; and the royalty-free electronic packaging of books by Google Books and other online outlets. Author Guild council members expressed their extreme concern at the plight of authors: "If even the most talented authors can no longer afford to write, who's going to provide the content?" declared vice president Richard Russo. Guild council member Nicholas Weinstock stated: "Reducing the monetary incentive for potential book authors even to enter the field means that there will be less for future generations to read: fewer voices, fewer stories."[23]

In the early twenty-first century, the digitization of books, and their availability on the web, created a major problem for authors and publishers, in which copyright – and its infringement – played a central role. Robert Darnton has described the conflict in which authors, publishers and Big Tech were involved, when huge numbers of books were digitized. Darnton characterizes this conflict as "democratization versus commercialization."[24]

The commercial aspect of the conflict can be charted, in the book industry, from 2004, when Google launched its Google Book Search project. Google proposed to digitize the collections of entire public libraries; the intention was to provide a search service, in which users could search for books stored in the enormous database. But authors and publishers around the world objected to this practice on the grounds that it infringed copyright. In the US, the Authors Guild and the Association of American Publishers sued Google in 2005 for massive copyright infringement. In France, the publisher Editions du Seuil successfully sued Google for copyright infringement in 2006; in 2009, Google's scanning of copyrighted books was stopped by a French court.

In the US, more than four years of difficult negotiations and legal actions resulted in a 2008 settlement between Google and publishers. In the terms of this settlement, Google would compensate authors and publishers for inclusion of scanned copies of works in Google Books; but the Google project had in the process transformed from a search service into "a gigantic commercial library." Darnton remarks that as a consequence, research libraries – which had originally supplied books free of charge to be digitized – would now be required to buy back access to those same digital books, "at a price that Google would determine."

This new arrangement engendered consternation in the book publishing industry, as well as in the library sector; but the arrangement was terminated in 2011, when a US federal court rejected the settlement because it would create a monopoly for Google, in violation of the Anti-trust Act. Darnton depicts this failed enterprise by Google as an "audacious" attempt to privatize "a vast stretch of the public domain," thereby collecting a toll "from anyone who tried to enter its fenced-off territory."[25]

As an alternative to the commercial monopolization of digitized books, Darnton points to the democratic, open-access model, in which "all of the material in all our research libraries" is available "to everyone free of charge." Several examples of this model already exist, including Kopinor in Norway and Copyswede in Sweden. The democratic version of the digital book database respects author's rights: Kopinor makes the total of Norwegian literature available in digital form to all Norwegians, while paying compensation to rights holders for the digital copying of their works.[26]

The US version of this model, as described by Darnton, is the Digital Public Library of America (DPLA), launched in 2013 and containing more than 17 million digitized books; the stated goal of the DPLA is "to make the cultural heritage of America available, free of charge, to all Americans and to everyone in the world." Lacking the collective licensing agreement with authors used by Copyswede and Kopinor, the DPLA relies on authors and publishers to license their books through Creative Commons, thereby making the texts available online on the DPLA. Darnton is optimistic that this online project will "satisfy authors and readers alike by bringing them together."[27]

The Internet Archive, founded in 1996 to archive the World Wide Web, expanded its collections from 1999 to become a free digital library of books, films, music, software, and websites; most of these materials were acquired by donation. In 2020, the Internet Archive launched its National Emergency Library in response to the social restrictions imposed during the COVID-19 pandemic. Borrowing restrictions on the 1.4 million digitized books held in the Archive's Open Library were lifted, allowing readers free access to the digital holdings. Responding to sensitivities concerning authors' copyright in digital libraries, the National Emergency Library extended an opt-out option to authors and rights-holders, removing their works from the Emergency Library if they wished.

How Copyright Broke, at Least Twice

Journalism and theoretical writing in media studies and digital technology studies began taking a critical stance against Big Tech in the years following 2015 – typified in Timberg's *Culture Crash: The Killing of the Creative Class* (2015); Taplin's *Move Fast and Break Things* (2017); Tim Wu's *The Attention Merchants: The Epic Scramble to Get Inside Our Heads* (2017); Shoshana Zuboff's *The Age of Surveillance Capitalism: The Fight for a Human Future at the New Frontier of Power* (2019); and Deresiewicz's *The Death of the Artist* (2020). Several of these books made a moral argument that the ongoing infringement of copyright on the web was an ethical – as well as legal – crime, that needed to be rectified for the benefit of society – and authors.

But earlier, in the first decade of the twenty-first century, the theme of critical theory had been markedly different. In the years following 2000, a welter of publications took the libertarian approach, vigorously arguing that free culture enabled by the internet was a social good. The stance taken in these books was that the ease of access to information on the web prompted the use, and creative reuse, of masses of newly available material – and that this reuse should be encouraged. It was postulated that remix and adaptive reuse of online works represented an expansion of creative practice, and was therefore a cultural and social benefit.

The moral position taken by the authors of these books, as well as by many commentators on online culture, was that the digital appropriation of found works – such as music samples, images, texts – was a cultural good, because it was part of online participation in culture made possible for millions of users. Jay Rosen was one of numerous commentators celebrating this new influx of online active and creative participation, when he wrote of "the people formerly known as the audience" in 2006.[28] In the years following Web 2.0 in 2004, more people than ever were active online, posting user-generated content, writing blogs, using social media, setting up their own websites – and reusing material found online.

The role of villain in the moral universe projected by this libertarian perspective was played by copyright – or at least, the restrictive enforcement by rights holders of copyright provision in online works. The existing intellectual property regime, in which copyright was predominantly administered by large corporations – publishers, record companies, film production companies – was frequently depicted as the enemy of free culture. These functionaries of "Big Media" prosecuted online users for infringement of copyright – but these legal actions were not applauded for their protection of author's rights. Their reception was quite the opposite: they were deplored as the heavy-handed punishment of creative online users, solely to increase the revenue – through court action – of already wealthy, bloated corporations. Copyright breach prosecution was equated with censorship of online free culture: it was vilified as a barrier, or block, to creative expression.

In the moral world view of internet libertarianism, the "overzealous" enforcement of copyright by rights-holding companies represented the enemy of creativity itself. This moral vision is evident in the titles of books published in the years following 2001; in these titles, "creativity" often stands for the hero of the story, while "intellectual property" or "copyright" play the role of villain. These book titles include: Siva Vaidhyanathan's *Copyrights and Copywrongs: The Rise of Intellectual Property and How It Threatens Creativity* (2001); Lawrence Lessig's *Free Culture: How Big Media Uses Technology and the Law to Lock Down Culture and Control Creativity* (2004); Kembrew McLeod's *Freedom of Expression: Overzealous Copyright Bozos and Other Enemies of Creativity* (2005); Joanna Demers' *Steal This Music: How Intellectual Property Law Affects Musical Creativity* (2006); and Matthew Rimmer's *Digital Copyright and the Consumer Revolution: Get Your Hands Off My Ipod* (2007).

Copyright has become "copywrong" in the early twenty-first century, according to the authors of these works. "How Copyright Broke" was the title of an essay by Cory Doctorow, originally published in 2006. Doctorow, a science-fiction author as well as commentator on online culture, argued that copyright broke when lawyers, operating for publishers, tech companies and other rights-holders, enforced restrictive license agreements on everyday users of the internet: "So this is where copyright breaks: When copyright lawyers try to treat readers and listeners and viewers as if they were (weak and unlucky) corporations who could be strong-armed into license agreements you wouldn't wish on a dog."[29] Doctorow argues that whereas corporations have their own lawyers to negotiate more favourable license agreements, ordinary consumers – of media works or proprietary software – have no means of negotiating less draconian copyright arrangements, and are liable for prosecution in the case of copyright infringement.

The core argument made by Doctorow and numerous other commentators and theorists is that copyright "broke" because of the way it was administered – and enforced. The key issue was the distinction between creators and rights owners; and the administering of copyright rather than the work itself. Copyright infringement was punished in repeated legal actions not by the authors or creators of works, but by the publishers or production companies to which rights in those works had been assigned. The approach taken by such rights-holders has been termed "propertarian,"[30] in that the protection of intellectual property is paramount, with no consideration for the benefits of free culture – if it involves creative reuse of proprietary copyright material.

This widely critiqued aspect of copyright regulation pre-dates online culture. In 1996 – pre-Napster, pre-illegal downloading and streaming – Ronald Bettig levelled trenchant criticism at the copyright regime in his book *Copyrighting Culture: The Political Economy of Intellectual Property*. Bettig states that if the copyright system works in the way it was intended when designed in the eighteenth century – to provide the incentive to create – then "it is functional in terms of the social good since it stimulates intellectual activity." But, he continues, evidence suggests that "the copyright system does not operate according to this ideal."[31]

Bettig offers two reasons for this shortcoming. First, contemporary cultural production differs greatly from that of the eighteenth century, when sole authors created works and negotiated with publishers. Creative productions such as films, TV programs, video games and animations involve many participants, complicating copyright agreements. Most important for Bettig's political economic critique is the discrepancy that arose in the twentieth century between creators and rights owners. "Ownership of copyrights," he observes, "increasingly rests with the capitalists who have the machinery and capital to manufacture and distribute works." Bettig identifies an "oligopolistic structure" of powerful media corporations – supported by teams of lawyers – that owns and controls rights in works. As a result, control of copyright "seeks to restrict the use of a work to those willing and able to pay for it." Bettig concludes that this exclusivity "can have the opposite result than that intended by the founders of the system." Looking ahead to the potential of the internet to "bring about an increase in the range and forms of intellectual and artistic creativity," he predicts that this potential will be "thwarted" by the aggressive assertion of exclusivity by rights holders.[32]

In his 1993 historical study of the advent of copyright, Mark Rose identified property – and property law – as the model for copyright. The discourse around intellectual property imported terminology from real estate, such as "public domain." (This adoption of real estate terms was repeated in internet culture, with its language of "domain names" and "sites.") Rose points out that copyright law casts author's rights as exclusive rights of control, treating violation or invasion of those rights as an actionable offence, equivalent to trespass onto an owner's land. This conception of copyright as a form of property, to which the author was naturally entitled, drew on the arguments of both John Locke and Adam Smith concerning property and individual's rights. The eminent eighteenth-century English jurist, Sir William Blackstone, upheld property – rather bombastically – as an individual's "sole and despotic dominion … over the external things in the world, in total exclusion of the right of any other individual in the universe."[33] Blackstone also advocated the recognition of copyright as a form of common-law property, which should be granted in perpetuity rather than for a limited term.

Rose makes the further point that in place of physical borders such as fences, intellectual property law imposed the notion of originality as a virtual border fencing off individual works. That is, for copyright law, originality is the fence. For legal purposes, "originality" simply means that a work differs from other works. This stipulation has been the trigger for thousands of copyright infringement law suits, in which a work – in part or in whole – is charged with not being sufficiently original: that is, it is the same – in part or in whole – as another work. Even if that part, deemed by the court to be the same as part of another work, is tiny in the context of the overall work, the court is likely to find that infringement of copyright is proven, that the fence has been breached.

Rose concludes that this emphasis on originality, as a prerequisite for a copyrighted work, has created difficulties in practice. This is because artistic production in reality is "typically a matter of appropriation and transformation rather than creation."[34] But the enforcement of copyright law, in the propertarian manner, has not concerned itself with aesthetic questions of transformation or appropriation. It has been solely committed to a question of property, its violation in infringement and – in many cases – a financial remedy ordered by the court.

In his 2008 book *Copyright's Paradox*, Neil Weinstock Netanel outlines the terms of the paradox: that copyright, with its inbuilt incentive to create, is not always aligned with freedom of expression – but its opposite. "In many ways, copyright now stands for private censorship, not public liberty," Netanel writes. This censorship occurs through prosecution for copyright infringement, which if successful can remove the offending work from the public sphere. Netanel blames the proprietary attitudes of rights holders – including "behemoth media conglomerates" which use prosecution for copyright infringement as a "tool to silence critics," thereby exerting control "over the images, sounds and texts that are the very language of our culture."[35] For Netanel, the main cause for copyright's "untoward chilling of speech" is its propertarian aspect, that it resembles "a full-fledged property right rather than a limited federal grant designed to further a particular public purpose."[36]

This property right is administered by publishers and "behemoth" media companies, making copyright in many ways a "publisher's right" rather than an author's right. The political power of the major media conglomerates can be detected in their successful lobbying of legislators in the twentieth century to extend the term of copyright protection. In the US, the copyright coverage of a work was set in 1831 at 28 years, with the option of a renewal of 14 years; this term was extended in 1909 to 28 years plus 28 renewal. In 1976, the US Copyright Act greatly increased the term of copyright to the life of the author plus 50 years. But media organizations successfully lobbied for a further extension of copyright in 1998, when the Sonny Bono Copyright Extension Act increased coverage to the life of the author plus 70 years.

This extension act is widely known as the Mickey Mouse Act, because it was considered the result of lobbying from the Disney Corporation, which feared that Disney creations such as Mickey Mouse were about to enter the public domain, where they would be free to be used and reused. The 1998 legislation allowed a further 20 years' exploitation of these creations in the market. (Copyright length is similarly life of author plus 70 years in Australia, the UK, and many European countries; it is life plus 50 years in Canada, China, New Zealand, and several other countries.) This lengthy term of copyright protection, administered by powerful media organizations, is one aspect of the "bloated copyright"[37] criticized by Netanel and other theorists.

The application of copyright as publisher's right throughout the twentieth century generated enormous wealth for many publishers and media conglomerates. This activity continues in the twenty-first century, at times pursued by companies whose only asset is a portfolio of copyrighted works. Steve Collins has recounted some of the legal actions launched by Bridgeport Music, a US company known for its prolific prosecution on the basis of copyright infringement. Steve Wu coined the term "trample troll" to describe Bridgeport's strategy of "trolling" the internet for unlicensed appropriation from its repertoire – then suing. Collins notes that in 2001 alone, Bridgeport launched almost 500 lawsuits claiming copyright infringement; its successes in the court included the awarding of $4.2 million US to Bridgeport for unlicensed sampling by Notorious B.I.G.[38] In cases such as these, copyright has become purely a publisher's right, and the exploitation of that right is solely of a pecuniary nature.

But the wealth generated by exploitation of copyright has not always been shared by authors, particularly in the music industry. Ruth Towse, an economist specializing in copyright, wrote in 2004 that copyright "generates more rhetoric than money for the majority of composers and performers in the music industry."[39] She noted that a tiny fraction of pop and rock stars became wealthy from astronomical royalties – but the great majority of songwriters and musicians received only a pittance.

This was partly due to the structure of recording contracts, in which the record company pays musicians an advance to record an album; but that advance, plus all production costs, must then be paid back by the musicians as recoupable expenses to the record company – from their royalties. This process left many songwriters and musicians not in a state of financial bliss, but in a state of debt. When the successful singer-songwriter Janis Ian complained of her financial situation in 2002, her grievance wasn't with illegal downloading, but with the music industry: "in 37 years as a recording artist, I've created 20+ albums for major labels, and I've never once received a royalty check that didn't say I owed them money. So I make the bulk of my living from live touring."[40] The widespread recognition that the administering of copyright by the record companies did not best serve artists, was one of the reasons copyright was disrespected by many commentators and cultural theorists in the 1990s and the first decade of the twenty-first century. It was one of the reasons that Joanna Demers advised music fans to "steal this music" in her 2006 book of that title. Another reason for the disfavour into which the copyright regime had fallen was the persistent prosecution of authors, artists, and internet users for copyright infringement – prosecutions launched by the rights holders: publishers, production companies, record companies, huge media conglomerates.

The Wind and the Kookaburra

Two widely publicized – and virulently debated – legal actions for copyright infringement concern, first, the 1936 novel *Gone with the Wind*, and secondly, a 1932 Australian song called "Kookaburra Sits in the Old Gum Tree." The first case is cited by Netanel in *Copyright's Paradox*; for him it encapsulates the "unacceptable burdens on speech" imposed by the current "bloated copyright" regime.[41]

Netanel's case study is *The Wind Done Gone*, a novel by African American writer Alice Randall published in 2001. *The Wind Done Gone* is a transformative work, in that it is based on – and transforms – a pre-existing work, Margaret Mitchell's 1936 Civil War novel *Gone with the Wind*. This novel won Mitchell a Pulitzer Prize in 1937, and was made into an extremely popular Academy Award-winning film in 1939.

Randall's novel reuses the setting and characters of *Gone with the Wind*, but shifts the perspective on the narrative. Whereas *Gone with the Wind* centres on Scarlett O'Hara, daughter of a prosperous slave-owner, *The Wind Done Gone* focuses on Cyanara, one of O'Hara's slaves. The adoption by Randall of this new point-of-view has a subversive impact on the material, in the manner of much other transformative fiction – primarily fan fiction – which often alters the point-of-view of published texts to that of a socially marginalized perspective.

In the context of the *Gone with the Wind* setting and narrative, an alternative perspective on race relations is opened up in Randall's novel. Whereas Mitchell's novel, and the film based on it, present a "romantic portrait of antebellum plantation life," *The Wind Done Gone* tells the story from the slaves' position, including their calculated manipulation of their masters. Randall acknowledged the subversive intention of her work, explaining that she wrote the novel to "explode" the racist stereotypes perpetuated in *Gone with the Wind*.[42]

The problem, however, was that Mitchell's estate did not approve of this transformation. The estate sued Randall and her publisher Houghton Mifflin for copyright infringement, seeking an immediate injunction of *The Wind Done Gone*. Randall had changed the names of characters and locations in *Gone with the Wind* in her own novel: Scarlett is known as "Other," and Rhett Butler as "R," in *The Wind Done Gone*. Nevertheless, a Georgia district court found that *The Wind Done Gone* was "unabated piracy" of *Gone with the Wind*. The court preliminarily enjoined the novel's publication. This legal action was a high-profile instance of the enforcement of copyright as a form of censorship, a practice castigated by Netanel and many other commentators.

Soon afterwards, the Eleventh Circuit Court of Appeals vacated the preliminary injunction. This court's finding reflected the copyright/freedom of speech paradox analysed by Netanel. The court held that by barring public access to Randall's "viewpoint in the form of expression that she chose," the trial court's order acted "as a prior restraint on speech." The initial ruling stood sharply "at odds with the shared principles of the First Amendment and copyright law."[43] The case was settled in 2002, when the publisher Houghton Mifflin agreed to make a donation to Morehouse College, a Black men's liberal arts college in Atlanta, Georgia, while Mitchell's estate agreed to drop litigation. *The Wind Done Gone* was further protected from prosecution for copyright infringement when it was defined as a work of parody: the cover of the book included a seal describing it as "The Unauthorized Parody." Parody in the legal sense refers to a work that comments or criticizes another work; parody is one of the uses included in the Fair Use provision of US copyright law, by which an original work may be reused or transformed without the prospect of prosecution for infringement of copyright.

The second case deals not with attempted censorship but with the punishment by financial means of authors for infringement of copyright. The original work is a song, "Kookaburra Sits in the Old Gum Tree," written in 1932 by Australian music teacher Marion Sinclair. This song has been a popular Australian nursery tune, from the 1930s to the present day. Marion Sinclair died in 1988; the copyright for "Kookaburra" was bought in 1990 by Larrikin Music Publishing (part of the multinational company Music Sales) for $6,100 AUD.

In 1978, the songwriters Colin Hay and Ron Strykert, later members of the internationally successful Australian rock group Men at Work, wrote a song called "Down Under." For the recorded version of "Down Under," Men at Work member Greg Ham added a brief – eight-second – flute instrumental to the song. This version was released in 1981 as a single, and was included on the Men at Work album *Business As Usual*. "Down Under" was a hugely successful single, reaching the Number One chart position in many countries, including the US, UK, Canada, Australia, Denmark, and other European nations.

For the next few years, no problem blighted the success of Men At Work and the popularity of "Down Under." The composer of "Kookaburra," Marion Sinclair, must have heard the Men at Work song, but found nothing objectionable in it. A problem arrived, however, in 2007, when a music quiz show on ABC TV, Australia, posed a question to contestants: "name the Australian nursery rhyme this riff has been based on." The riff in question was the flute instrumental section played by Greg Ham in the recorded version of "Down Under." One contestant answered, tentatively: "Kookaburra sitting in the old gum tree?" That one uncertain response by a contestant on a TV quiz show was the incident that launched a highly contentious legal action. Having been alerted to this similarity between the two songs, Larrikin Music instigated a law suit against EMI Songs, Colin Hay and Ron Strykert, asserting that the flute riff in "Down Under" appropriated the melody of "Kookaburra."[44]

Steve Collins has made a critical study of this case, concluding that it was an instance of legal "overkill." Collins cites the argument made by Patterson and Lindberg in their 1991 book *The Nature of Copyright*, that "there must be a distinction between the use of the copyright and the use of the copyrighted work."[45] In this case, Larrikin Music appeared to be exploiting the copyright, with little consideration of the copyrighted work – the song – and how little of it appeared in "Down Under." Collins reports that the eight-second flute riff – the only part of "Down Under" with any similarity to "Kookaburra" – appears only three times in the Men At Work song, comprising a total of 24 seconds in a song whose duration is 3'31." Furthermore, this brief flute instrumental is not structurally important to "Down Under"; indeed the song was written in 1978 – without the flute riff – before Ham had even joined Men At Work.[46] Collins makes the further point that the inclusion of the flute riff could be interpreted as a musical gesture towards Australian folk music, part of the "fusion of previously existing music" characteristic of all music composition.[47]

The court, however, disagreed. In 2010, the ruling in the Federal Court of Australia was that Hay and Strykert had copied a substantial part of "Kookaburra," so that they had infringed Larrikin's copyright in the song. The decision of the court regarding damages was that Larrikin would receive 5 per cent of royalties for "Down Under," back-dated to 2002. As was widely noted, Larrikin Music, which had bought the copyright for $6,100, will earn many hundreds of thousands of dollars through exploitation of this copyright.

This court ruling was controversial, and bitterly received by songwriter Colin Hay, who told BBC News in 2010: "When I co-wrote Down Under back in 1978, I appropriated nothing from anyone else's song. There was no Men At Work, there was no flute, yet the song existed." Hay was angered that the ruling, like many before it, had generated substantial income for the rights holder, based on a perceived copyright infringement: "what has won today is opportunistic greed, and what has suffered is creative musical endeavor ... It's all about money, make no mistake."[48] Greg Ham, who played the offending eight-second flute riff on the song, was reportedly deeply affected by the court ruling, distressed that his reputation had been tarnished by the imputation of plagiarism resulting from the court's decision. After Ham died in 2012, Colin Hay told media that his early death was linked to the stress of the court case.[49]

The "Kookaburra"/"Down Under" case attracted a great deal of attention, and controversy. As Collins notes, the court's judgment was based on "the law's narrow approach to creativity." It was a high-profile case of copyright as a publisher's right, with no author's right bearing on the case, since the songwriter was deceased. It was a case of "pure financial exploitation" of the copyright, to benefit the rights holder through receipt of a new, ongoing stream of revenue. Collins argues that such a case is unlikely to foster creativity, the social role envisaged for copyright. Instead, it is "more likely to have an adverse effect on the incentive to create and chill future creativity."[50] It is also the kind of case likely to bring the existing copyright regulation into further disrepute.

Copyleft, Not Right

The second time that copyright "broke" was in the late 1990s, when copyrighted works were distributed and downloaded – illegally and en masse – on the internet. The most spectacular manifestation of this process, as noted earlier in this chapter, was in the file-swapping networks trafficking in music files. There were so many transactions of this type that it was impossible to police – or prevent – them all as infringements of copyright. Many artists, theorists and commentators were convinced that digital and online technology had made copyright, and the conventional notion of authorship, obsolete.

Copyright had been conceived in the context of industrial technology – the printing press; in the 1990s, post-industrial technology – digital information and the internet – called for a new conception of intellectual property. The newly expanded online culture problematized the idea of information as commodity, as something to be owned; the libertarian rallying cry was "Information Wants To Be Free." This idea was articulated in a widely circulated essay by John Perry Barlow – "The Economy of Ideas (Everything You Know About Intellectual Property is Wrong)" – published in *Wired* magazine in 1994. Barlow argued that information is experienced, not possessed, and that the very fluidity of information flow makes copyright law outmoded.[51]

This online libertarianism in many ways inherited the counter-cultural values of the 1960s, especially the alternative, anti-establishment politics around San Francisco (near where Silicon Valley was later to emerge). The migration of counter-cultural, libertarian values to the online environment can be observed in the career of Stewart Brand, who began in 1968 as editor of the print publication *The Whole Earth Catalog*. This periodical publication advised on tools for communal living, intended for the alternative lifestyles of young "drop-outs" from mainstream society, many of whom lived in communes. Brand and other counter-cultural figures gravitated to the internet in the 1970s and 1980s, when the online network was still in a rudimentary, pre-World Wide Web, stage. Brand migrated the "Whole Earth Catalog" approach onto network culture when he founded the Whole Earth Software Review in 1984, specializing in computer-based media. In 1985 he co-founded the online community known as the WELL (Whole Earth 'Lectronic Link) and in 1988 co-founded the Global Business Network. In addition, in 1987 he published the book *The Media Lab*, describing developments in computer-based media – "inventing the future" – at MIT's Media Lab.

Meanwhile, libertarian approaches to software and intellectual property had taken public form by the mid-1980s. The Free Software Foundation, founded in 1985 by Richard Stallman, devised and supported alternatives to proprietary software. "Software should not have owners" was the declaration of Stallman's GNU software project; the GNU manifesto of 1985 announced that: "everyone will be permitted to modify and redistribute GNU ... all versions of GNU remain free." Importantly for free software and the later open source software schemes, "proprietary modifications will not be allowed."[52] Free software and open source operate in a manner directly counter to proprietary software, which Stallman condemned as "software hoarding." Shareware and open source software partake of a collectivist method, rather than a commitment to intellectual property as a commodity owned by one company or corporation.

Copyleft was a term increasingly used from the mid-1980s. The exact origin of this idea is disputed, but Stallman claimed that he first saw it used in a letter from Don Hopkins in 1984, in which Hopkins wrote: "Copyleft – all rights reversed."[53] Copyleft developed within the free software movement, at first associated with the GNU General Public License, written by Stallman. But it soon broadened to incorporate the free distribution and modification of other works of intellectual property.

Copyleft, free software and open source have been described as the basis of an electronic public domain – but this is an incorrect assumption. Copyleft does not consign works of intellectual property to the public domain; rather, it is a form of licensing that has some in-built restrictions (although these restrictions are far less restrictive than the conventional copyright license). A copyleft license grants the freedom to use, modify and distribute intellectual property, with the proviso that any derivative works will have the same rights. That is, any modification of the original work must itself be made available to be used, modified, and distributed in turn. Copyleft, then, makes possible not a new public domain, but rather a digital commons for the benefit of all online users, unrestricted by the regulation of copyright.

The Open Source Initiative, founded in 1998, clarified the collaborative, non-proprietary, process of software development. Under open source, the source code is released under a license to be used, changed, and distributed as software, so that any modified code is then to be made available to other users. The open source movement proposes that basic software and platforms should be freely available to all, developed freely within a network of benevolent programmers. The ever-expanding array of non-proprietary and endlessly mutable software was widely celebrated in the late 1990s. In 1999, the Prix Ars Electronica awarded its top prize in the *.net* category to the open source operating system Linux, for its fostering of collaboration which drew on thousands of volunteer programmers: "the community that has assembled around this anarchic effort demonstrates how strong an aesthetic can be in bringing a community, assets, ideas and attention together."[54] In further response to the practices of "overzealous copyright bozos" early in the twenty-first century, new means of licensing – and freely distributing – works were conceived. Creative Commons was founded in 2001 by Lawrence Lessig, Hal Abelson, and Eric Eldred as an alternative to the restrictive aspect and "possessive individualism" of copyright. Instead, Creative Commons aims to contribute to the building of a stronger online commons. The share-alike Creative Commons license is a form of Copyleft licensing suitable for the use of texts, images, and other media forms.

The six types of Creative Commons license range in gradation from most free or permissive at one end of the scale, to least permissive at the other end, close to the conventional copyright. The Creative Commons license often used by creators with the intention of encouraging creative reuse of their works is CC BY-SA, or Attribution Sharealike, which permits reusers to remix or adapt the work, including for commercial use, so long as credit is given to the creator. In addition, any modified material must be licensed under identical terms, in the manner of a Copyleft license. The most open Creative Commons license is CC-BY or Attribution, which requires only that credit be given to the creator of the original work. CC BY-NC, or Attribution Noncommercial, permits only non-commercial remix or adaptations of the work, while CC BY-ND does not permit adaptations or derivatives of the work.

In 2021, Creative Commons estimated that more than 1.4 billion works on the web were registered with Creative Commons licenses. In addition, Creative Commons has a CC Zero (CC0) option, which allows for the surrender of copyright altogether, enabling the work to enter a worldwide public domain – effectively as an authorless work, which can be adapted by others with no restrictions. Some theorists and commentators, inspired by the range of items available online with no copyright restriction, have speculated how culture would function with no copyright at all – and what that would mean for the author.

Imagine There's No Copyright

Imagine There Is No Copyright is the title of a 2009 book by Joost Smiers and Marieke Van Schijndel; the authors continue their play with John Lennon's hymn to wishful thinking by adding to their title: *and No Cultural Conglomerates Too*. Smiers and Van Schijndel take the position that copyright has become a publisher's right, mainly exercized by gigantic media conglomerates; their twin proposals to achieve a more "level cultural playing field" are to abolish copyright and to break up the huge cultural conglomerates through anti-trust laws.[55] Their optimistic view of a society structured in this way is that more culture will be made by more creative practitioners.

In one sense, it isn't difficult to imagine what a culture without copyright would look like: many areas of cultural practice already function without recourse to copyright law. This point is made by Aaron Perzanowski and Kate Darling in their 2017 book *Creativity without Law*. Perzanowski and Darling are unconvinced by the received wisdom that copyright is necessary to provide the "incentive to create." They challenge this "intellectual property orthodoxy" by pointing to the many artists, authors, and inventors who "are moved to create, not by the hope for monetary return , but by innate urges that are often quite resistant to financial considerations."[56] In particular, the contributors to this book offer case studies of specific types of cultural activity that currently flourish without the need of copyright law.

One example is graffiti art: as discussed in chapter 2, it is highly unlikely that a street graffiti artist will seek protection of their street art under copyright law, when the very practice of street graffiti is an illegal act. Nevertheless, as Marta Iljadica details in her book *Copyright Beyond the Law*, graffiti artists find their own ways to regulate their own prolific, illegal, activity. Other cultural examples showcased in *Creativity without Law* include: cooks and chefs; cocktail mixers; tattoo artists; fan fiction writers; and online pornography. All of these pursuits operate largely without copyright protection of works – yet they all organize their sectors of cultural practice according to codes and rules; and they are all culturally productive.

But what of authors who may hope to make a living from their work – or at least, make some income as authors? Smiers and Van Schijndel believe that authors could still earn revenue from their works with no copyright law in place – and therefore no protection from piracy. They argue that the author of an original work would have an advantage in the market over pirates of that same work: this is the "first mover effect," in which the original author is first into the market – an advantage over imitators.[57]

The New Patronage

However, income for authors – in place of royalties – would need to come from another source, and this source can be summarized in one word: patronage. A post-copyright world would return to the condition of the pre-copyright world, in which authors and artists were financially supported – and enabled to create works – by wealthy individuals or institutions. The new patronage in a minority of cases would emanate from wealthy philanthropists eager to support works of artistic creation; this philanthropy, not uncommon in the contemporary art world, would perform the patronage function previously performed by the aristocracy.

But the far more pervasive type of patronage in the internet age is of a more democratic temper: it is the crowd-funding technique made possible by online companies such as Kickstarter. Crowd-funding is patronage by the masses: thousands of fans and consumers can pledge small amounts of money to ensure that a project's minimum funding goal is met, and that the creative work will be made. Again, it is not necessary to imagine how this new online patronage would work, as authors, artists and producers have long used crowdfunding to generate the revenue no longer flowing from royalties.

In 1997, the British rock band Marillion, whose recording contract had expired, raised $60,000 via email by asking their fans to pay for their new album in advance. This early successful use of online crowdfunding set a precedent that was emulated many times, as artists used crowdfunding sites – such as Artistshare (launched 2001), Kickstarter (2009) and GoFundMe (2010) – to raise the funds necessary to record an album, make a film, publish a book, or create an art project.

The crowdfunding business model – Kickstarter takes 5 per cent of funds raised for a project, while Amazon takes 3 per cent – has proven successful as a means of raising revenue in lieu of royalties. William Deresiewicz acknowledges that crowdfunding has become a vital means of direct financial support, especially for young authors and artists. Funds raised by the publishing section alone of Kickstarter average $600 million US per year.

Another crowdfunding site, Patreon (launched 2013) emulates the old patronage model by requiring donors to pay a small monthly amount to an artist – in effect providing an alternative salary for that artist. Substack (launched 2017) provides a similar online platform for writers, especially journalists, as readers subscribe to the writer's online newsletters and writings – in effect becoming patrons of the writer. Substack later included novelists as well as journalists in its stable of writers. In 2021, Jeanette Winterson was a Substack writer in residence, sharing a series of ghost stories and a memoir essay, while Salman Rushdie serialized a novella and short stories for Substack subscribers in 2022.

However, Deresiewicz is sceptical about the long-term benefit of crowdfunding, especially if it is meant to replace the old-fashioned revenue stream provided by the exploitation of copyright. He notes that Kickstarter and other crowdfunding campaigns often fail: if the minimum funding target is not met, the pledged money is returned to donors. Deresiewicz cites statistics that in 2017 only 2 per cent of creators on Patreon brought in more than the US minimum wage of $1,160 per month. Many writers for Substack fail to build a subscriber base, effectively writing for free. In addition, crowdfunding has become increasingly crowded, as a high volume of authors and artists attempt to fund their creative works using this method. Deresiewicz notes reports, in 2020, of "Kickstarter fatigue," as fans and consumers weary of the constant calls on their generosity.[58] Copyright, in other words, has not been totally eclipsed by the new patronage as the means of funding art works, or an author's career.

The Blockchain Author: NFTs

One other instance of digital disruption – NFTs – emerged as a possible financial benefit for authors and artists in 2020, by offering a new means by which authors could monetize their work. An NFT – or non-fungible token – is a digital asset that is not fungible, that is, exchangeable; rather, it is held to be a unique object. An NFT is bought with cryptocurrency on a blockchain, where it is stored and verified as a unique digital object. The provenance of the NFT is guaranteed by the blockchain, ensuring that the purchaser is registered as the sole owner of the unique object. A blockchain is a shared database, a secure and decentralized digital ledger of transactions – such as the purchase of NFTs – across the blockchain network. Some proponents of blockchain technology have heralded the advent of Web3, a new version of the internet based not on the monopolizing power of Big Tech corporations, but on the decentralizing function of blockchains. The buying and selling of digitized works as NFTs on blockchain digital ledgers, has been hailed as a new – purely digital – domain for authors and artists.

The first NFT project appeared on the Ethereum blockchain in 2015, but NFT activity increased astronomically in the years 2020 and 2021. It has been speculated that the COVID-19 lockdown in those years was a motivation for this surge in buying and trading NFTs; Rebecca Tushnet observed in 2021 that during social lockdown, "people can't do many of the things they usually do for fun, so they trade intangibles instead."[59] Another contributing factor was a bull market for investors in 2020–2021. It was reported that sales of NFTs surpassed $2 billion USD in the first quarter of 2021 alone; these sales included spectacularly high prices paid for digital artworks as NFTs, notably $69.3 million USD paid for the work *Everydays: The First 5000 Days* by "Beeple" (Mike Winkelmann).[60]

In March 2021 the music trade publication *Music Business Worldwide* noted that music NFTs were rapidly increasing in blockchain sales: of the estimated $100 million USD generated by sale of digital collectables in the previous month, more than $25 million resulted from the sale of musical digital assets.[61] This activity included the sale at blockchain auction of music albums as well as individual music tracks; for some songwriters and musicians, this new source of revenue compensated for the income lost due to cancelled performances during the COVID lockdowns.

The celebration of the NFT as a unique digital asset, justifying the high prices paid for some NFT artworks, represents an inversion – or perhaps perversion – of Walter Benjamin's celebration of the copy over the original in his famous 1934 essay "The Work of Art in the Age of Mechanical Reproduction." Benjamin found something liberating in the mechanical reproduction of images, because the production of a multitude of copies would wither the "aura" of the original artwork. The aura of the unique and unattainable great work of art had sustained political and religious hierarchies for centuries; Benjamin applauded the democratic consequences of the wide distribution of photographic copies, which could be handled and owned by anyone: "the technique of reproduction detaches the reproduced object from the domain of tradition. By making many reproductions it substitutes a plurality of copies for a unique existence."[62] Proponents of NFTs – and, especially, investors in NFTs – are determined to move in the opposite direction to Benjamin: they aim to celebrate the originality – the uniqueness – of a digital object that can be easily copied, millions of times, and distributed. Despite the ease with which digital copies – or images – may be made of the original, the NFT establishes originality through the digital record of provenance as registered on the blockchain. In the age of digital reproduction, a new form of digital aura is manufactured around a digital asset that is claimed to be absolutely unique: such an aura is established in part by price tags such as $69 Million.

The NFT is a highly paradoxical entity, since it is held to be a unique digital object in an online environment where all digital objects are infinitely reproducible, and in which there is no difference between the original and the copy. The work of the blockchain is to establish a form of originality, through a unique identifying number for the NFT, recorded in the blockchain ledger. The NFT is a token, a proof of ownership, and a digital certificate of authenticity; it guarantees that this digital asset is a unique object – despite the fact that identical copies of that object could be circulating at any one time. Indeed, the creator of a musical work sold to an investor as an NFT could later release that musical work by conventional means; the owner of the NFT version is left with an "original" work no different to the copies owned by others. The NFT, however, is deemed to be more valuable because a high value has been conferred on the NFT by the artist, by social media influencers, or by the price paid for the NFT.

The significant factor for authorship regarding NFTs is that in most cases the author or artist retains control of the copyright, even once the NFT is sold on blockchain; this means that the creator of the work is free to sell more copies of the work by other means. Earlier forms of digital disruption – downloading and streaming – proved disastrous for the income of authors and artists, as detailed earlier in this chapter. But NFTs may offer the possibility of an alternative revenue stream for artists, musicians, and authors, who make sales of their works – tokenized as NFTs – direct to purchasers or investors. The disruptive aspect of NFTs affects not the author but the traditional gatekeepers and middlepeople in the creative arts industry: art dealers and galleries, music recording companies, studios, production companies and publishers. While these gatekeepers are circumvented and receive no financial gain from an NFT sale, the artist or author benefits directly from this sale. In 2021, Marc Hogan, writing in the online music magazine *Pitchfork*, expressed a cautious optimism regarding NFTs from the perspective of musicians, noting the possibility that NFTs "will give musicians the economic clout that they lack in the internet's most recent iteration." Observing that some platforms allow the artist to share in later secondary market sales of the work, Hogan held out the hope that Web 3.0 will be "better for recording artists than Web 2.0 has been."[63]

So long as the creator of the work retains copyright after the work is sold as an NFT, the author stands to benefit, possibly multiple times, from the existence of blockchains and NFTs. If the creator of the work is also the rights owner, in a position to exploit the copyright for direct financial gain, the author may be positioned more favourably than in the previous copyright regime, in which a separation between creator and rights owner (the publisher, the studio, the production company, the corporation) did not always benefit the author. It has been reported that "smart contracts" determining ownership of an NFT may allow the purchaser of the NFT to share future royalties with the creator of, for example, a musical work: this would constitute a new model of authorship, but one from which the author would continue to derive some financial benefit.[64]

NFTs remain a dubious proposition for many critics, and criticisms of the form have been widespread. The fundamentally irrational concept of the original digital object attaining extreme value has been thoroughly noted, as has the assigning of value to an artwork not by galleries, museums, and art critics but by influencers and wealthy investors. Art fraud and plagiarism have occurred in the NFT domain. The enormous levels of energy required for blockchain transactions has prompted a criticism on environmental grounds. Even those advocates of NFTs' potential to democratize the music industry through new sources of remuneration remain guarded on this potential, acknowledging that NFTs have mainly created only "a few more individual winners" profiting from the wealth of investors.[65]

But if NFTs – or other digital assets – continue to offer the possibility of financial benefit for authors in new incarnations of the internet – "Web3" or the "metaverse" – the crucial factor for authors is that they must maintain control of their copyright. Even if the creator comes to share copyright with the purchaser, some financial benefit will accrue to both parties. I return to considerations of copyright, and the author, in the final chapter, after discussion of the online culture of remix and reuse, in which copyright barely figures. I assess the arguments for and against copyright, along with calls for copyright reform, and proposals for a minimalist copyright regime. The future of copyright is assessed as a central component of the future of the author.

Chapter Seven

Big Data Writing: Author as Algorithm

Algorithms make the world go round. Or at least, algorithms perform the crucial function of sorting, organizing, and programming the data that swirls around the network-connected world.

Data is central to contemporary culture, contemporary business, contemporary banking, contemporary government, contemporary arts. In his 2002 book *The Language of New Media*, Lev Manovich identified the database as the core of contemporary media and arts, replacing narrative as the fundamental building block of culture.[1] Manovich later updated his analysis of digital culture, emphasizing the data stream – the constant stream of data presenting on Facebook, Twitter and other social media – as much as the database.[2] But data, whether assembled in databases or flowing in data streams, needs sorting and ordering: this is the function of algorithms.

In mathematics, an algorithm is a procedure to perform a calculation or solve a problem. In information technology (IT), an algorithm is a sequence of instructions enabling a computer to perform a specific computation such as arranging data in sets and in a certain order. Many online businesses are in effect aggregators of data; the service they offer customers is the sorting and organizing of that data – a service made possible by the company's proprietary algorithms.

Online search engines are the most frequently used online services driven by algorithms ordering data. Google succeeded against competition from other search engines because its algorithm successfully cross-references relevance between sites – a function appreciated by users. A search algorithm such as Google's sorts websites according to terms programmed into the algorithm: the algorithm reads a web-page, assigns values to traits on that page, and organizes that page within a ranking of search results. This process determines where that specific webpage will appear in a list of items generated by an online search.

Richard Nash recognized the significance of algorithms for online culture in his 2014 essay, "Culture is the Algorithm." Nash asks the question: how does writing come to be read? He answers that units of culture – such as books, stories, essays, poems, songs, films, games – increasingly come to readers, listeners, and viewers via algorithmically based systems. These systems include Google's search engine, Amazon's "People Who Also Bought," Facebook's social graph, and Netflix's taste predictor. Netflix, Amazon, Spotify, and many other components of the online culture industry use algorithms to predict customers' taste, based on their previous choices. The "consumption graph" is "an effort to use algorithmic prediction based on your consumption pattern";[3] it directs the "you might also like this" messages to online user/consumers.

The IT infrastructure of algorithms sorting data has also affected writing, and with it the conception of the author. In the new mode of electronic writing, texts are written and continuously re-written, drawn from enormous databases. This technique of writing, made possible since the mid-1990s by developments in computer processing and the amassing of sizeable databases, has been called "big data writing," "big data literature," and "generative literature."

Big data writing builds on the techniques of generative art, developed using the earliest digital computers in the 1950s. In 1957, the composers Lejaren Hiller and Leonard Isaacson completed the *Illiac Suite*, a composition for string quartet generated by the ILLIAC-I computer, programmed with compositional rules. Desmond Paul Henry created generative visual art works using a computer-based drawing machine in the late 1950s.[4] In his 1953 story "The Great Automatic Grammatizator," Roald Dahl imagined a huge generative machine capable of writing prize-winning novels in fifteen minutes, jeopardizing the careers of human writers in the process.

Contemporary big data writing applies high-speed computers and massive databases to the methods of the earlier generative writing, realizing the possibilities imagined by Dahl. Big data writing and generative art have formed the basis of electronic art installations, works of electronic music, and NFTs sold on blockchain. Because the electronic texts generated by big data writing are not fixed but in constant flux, this technique has also been described as "non-linear" or "dynamic" writing. And because big data works are driven by algorithms, meaning that no human author decides the ordering of the text, big data writing has been considered the next stage of the "death of the author": a re-constituted author as algorithm.

Figure 7.1 Ben Rubin and Mark Hansen, *Moveable Type*, 2007. At the New York Times Building in Manhattan. Photo provided courtesy of the artists, © 2007 all rights reserved.

Electronic Type

One example of big data writing can illustrate the technique – and effects – of electronic dynamic writing: the example is *Moveable Type*, an electronic art work by Ben Rubin and Mark Hansen. This work has been experienced by many viewers, as it has been permanently installed in the lobby of the *New York Times* building in Manhattan since 2007. *Moveable Type* also incited media interest in 2007 when it was unveiled in the *New York Times* building.

This is a classic work of big data writing, as its electronic texts draw continuously on a massive, ever-expanding data base – the *New York Times* digital archive, which incorporates that day's online newspaper at nytimes.com, and stretches back to the first edition of the *Times* in 1851. *Moveable Type* produces a constant stream of texts drawn from the day's newspaper or – at night – the newspaper's archive.

The physical format of the work is two high walls each containing 280 small fluorescent screens, so that the art work comprises 560 screens in total. The screens are arranged in a grid formation, allowing viewers to detect patterns in the short texts as they stream across multiple screens.

The massive volume of text aggregated in the database incorporates the online version of the day's paper and archive of all previous days' news, including letters to the editor, but also real time search items and Web comments from readers at that moment. The computerized algorithm powering the work makes selections from this database according to specific categories: for example, the screens at one point will display sentences beginning with "you" or "I." At another point, only sentences ending with a question mark will be displayed; or phrases including numbers will be shown on the screens.

Randy Kennedy of the *New York Times* described the experience of standing in front of these screens, when the installation opened in 2007, as "floating on the newspaper's stream of consciousness." Sentences flow over the screens as selected by the algorithm: "You just have to react"; "I steal it from her every chance I get." "One shot"; "Two of his lawyers."; "Fifteen years in prison." "Tony Soprano?"; "And where's all the blood?"[5] These sentences and phrases may appear disjointed, or at times they may suggest a poetic correspondence.

Rubin and Hansen described their aim in creating the work: "We want it to feel almost like an organism that is living and breathing and consuming the news." Rubin proposed that a viewer standing in front of the screens for a few minutes could derive some sense of that day's news stories and events – although in an oblique manner. The artists also noted that viewers tended to draw close to the screens, "as if to hear the pronouncements of an oracle or to warm their hands with the heat of information."[6]

The "living and breathing" aspect of the work derives from the reality that the text is continuously changing: this is the dynamic facet of big data writing. The text on the screens is constantly shifting and rearranging, emerging in new waves and patterns, as the algorithm generates ever-new combinations of words, phrases, and sentences. Rubin and Hansen do not control this perpetual flow of words: the algorithm determines the selection and sequencing of texts as drawn from the database. Big data writing is a new form of literature in that the texts are composed in real time by computer algorithms.

Nevertheless, description of works such as *Moveable Type* tends to make reference to other literary works or authors – that is, human authors. Kennedy suggests that the flow of short texts in *Moveable Type* is reminiscent of William Burroughs' cut-up prose, or the disjointed poetry of John Ashbery. The *New York Times'* chief information officer, who commissioned the work, likened *Moveable Type* to a "dynamic portrait" of *The Times*, but one that emulated the advice of the poet Emily Dickinson to "Tell all the Truth but tell it slant." The recognition that the electronic writing generated by *Moveable Type* can attain something of the profundity of conventionally authored literature comes through a comparison with James Joyce's modernist novels. During the day, *Moveable Type* functions in a way parallel to Joyce's *Ulysses*, which compressed a universal mythology into the actions of a single day. But at night – Rubin and Hansen told the *New York Times* – the art work is mostly asleep but also dreaming, "rummaging, 'Finnegans Wake'-style, through articles and captions and headlines going back generations."[7] This is a literature made possible by the ability of algorithms to rummage through vast databases, day and night.

Dynamic Text

Chris Rodley and Andrew Burrell – artists who have created several big data writing works – provide a study of the field in their 2014 essay "On the Art of Writing with Data." Rodley and Burrell make frequent reference to conventional literature and literary theory in describing electronic big data writing. They find a similarity with the recent literary practice of conceptual poetry, the "uncreative writing" approach taken by Kenneth Goldsmith and other writers, in which the author sorts through the glut of information, "an unprecedented amount of available text."[8]

Rodley and Burrell also observe that data-driven literature "enables a more radical form of the heteroglossic discourse recognized by Mikhail Bakhtin." Bakhtin theorized that the novel presented a polyphonic discourse, in which all available modes of speech and writing are represented in the text. Rodley and Burrell remark that big-data writing not only realizes Bakhtin's polyphonic vision, but extends it. The novelist ventriloquizes or recreates the voices of others in the text of the novel; a data-driven electronic work goes further by allowing those voices to "speak in their own tongues."[9]

Rodley and Burrell's survey of big data works reveals that many have a literary theme, or take inspiration from works of literature. David Hirmes's 2013 electronic work *The Aleph: Infinite Wonder/Infinite Pity* is a digital homage to the 1949 short story "The Aleph" by Jorge Luis Borges. In Borges' story, a poet receives creative inspiration from an Aleph: a portal revealing all parts of the world simultaneously. The Aleph is, remarkably, a precursor of the World Wide Web, "another portal that allows access to a vast realm of global data," as Rodley and Burrell point out. David Hirmes's big data work exploits the parallel between fictional Aleph and contemporary Web. Hirmes takes a section of Borges' story, in which the narrator first peers into the Aleph – "I saw the populous sea, saw dawn and dusk, saw the multitudes of the Americas" – and generates a new list by setting an algorithm to search a database for phrases beginning with "I saw."[10] The database used in Hirmes's work comprises Twitter and the Project Gutenberg literature library. The search results build a dynamically generated text combining the literary and the vernacular (tweets): a twenty-first century update of the Aleph.

Ben Rubin and Mark Hansen tackled the plays of Shakespeare in their 2013 big data work *Shakespeare Machine*. Hansen has described this work – in the article "Data-Driven Aesthetics" – as a "data chandelier" hanging over the bar of the Public Theatre in New York. Rubin and Hansen collaborated on this work with data artist Jer Thorp, setting the algorithm to mine Shakespeare's plays and connect phrases according to "common rhetorical structures." The phrases are detached from their plays and grouped into sets – "slings and arrows" (*Hamlet*) along with "prophets and apostles" (*Henry VI*) and "spies and speculations" (*King Lear*). These sets of phrases are projected across the 37 blades of the data chandelier.[11]

If this work connected Shakespeare's words in novel ways, *Common Tongues* by John Cayley and Daniel Howe (2012) connected the words of Samuel Beckett with the language found across the web. Cayley and Howe devised computer software to scan part of Beckett's novel *How It Is*, detaching short phrases then searching for these phrases on the web. Rodley and Burrell cite the artists' intention in creating this work – to liberate the language of Beckett, which is "notorious for being tightly controlled by his estate."[12] Cayley and Howe claim to use "big software" against the cultural forces "enclosing language" (and using similar software). The artists find "the words of an authorised text where they are still, if only momentarily, associating freely." Cayley has asserted that through the means of this software, "it seems as if we are simply retrieving access to our own linguistic culture."[13] This ambition is realized in *Common Tongues*, in which the literary language of Beckett is combined with the "vernacular of ordinary people."[14]

Rodley and Burrell's 2015 art work *Death of an Alchemist* is described by its creators as "a novel written with data," an electronic work using generative text, cut-ups and web scraping, in the context of the period murder mystery genre.[15] It is a work of electronic writing, in which a literary narrative is generated in real time from online information; it has also been described as "a multimedia novel written by Big Data."[16] The installation consists of an 8-metre wall displaying 128 pages of text, charts and symbols. The viewer/reader is immersed into a mystery narrative concerning the death of a sixteenth-century German mystic, who left behind a book containing codes to the mysteries of the universe. The

Figure 7.2 Chris Rodley and Andrew Burrell, *Death of an Alchemist*, 2015

projections on the wall are continuously updated by real time online data sources including news, social media, and memes. The reader is invited to decipher the mystery as newly added clues are added in the form of data.

But for all their literary associations, works of big data writing differ from conventional literature in fundamental ways. The text is dynamic, not fixed; and the content of these works is often online culture itself. In this sense, the data stream, as selected by the algorithm, is culture speaking for itself. An influential big data work in this regard was *Listening Post* (2003) by Ben Rubin and Mark Hansen. In *Listening Post*, the content was sourced in real time from internet chat rooms and forums; the texts drawn from these online sources were sorted by the algorithm and displayed across a grid of 231 small screens.

Several other big data works have used this approach, in which the electronic texts derive from social media and other online outlets for users. *Everything Is Going to Be OK :)*, a 2013 work by Chris Rodley and Andrew Burrell, took its raw material from Twitter. Tweets were sorted by the algorithm according to certain themes, such as "don't leave me."

142   The Near-Death of the Author

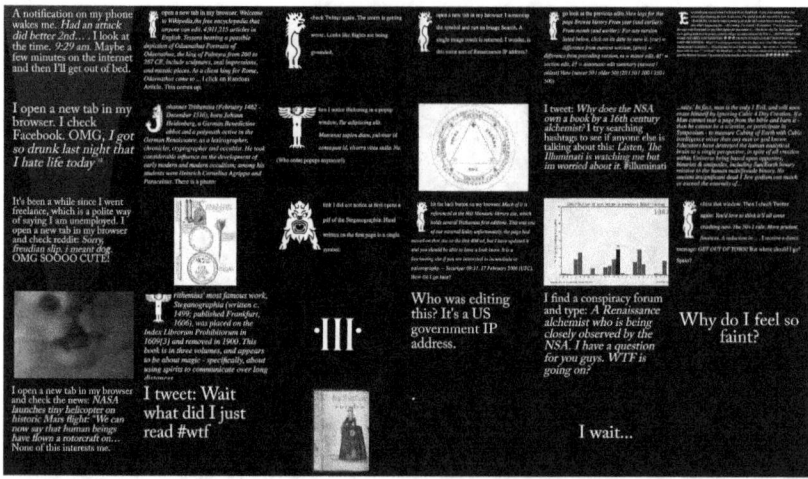

Figure 7.3 Chris Rodley and Andrew Burrell, *Death of an Alchemist* (detail)

The texts were projected at large scale onto the brick walls of a building, staging an often-emotional dialogue between matching tweets. *Everything Is Going to Be OK :)*, used the vernacular online discourse of Twitter to present a real time electronic conversation, in which the dialogue was dynamic, depending on the Twitter content at any one time.

Writing without Authors?

The other major difference between big data writing and traditional literature concerns authorship: the text in generative works is generated by computer algorithms, not authors. Rodley and Burrell describe data-driven literature as "motile information," by which they mean: "once the code is in place, the stream writes itself." Big data writing is "hands-off" on the part of the author, who leaves it to the algorithm to produce the texts.[17]

If big data writing is a recently developed mode of writing, generated not by human authors but by computer algorithms, is this a case of the death of the author? Is dynamic electronic literature a digitized writing system, in which the text writes itself – without the need for authors? Certainly the artists who create the electronic works such as *Moveable Type* or *Everything Is Going to Be OK :)* have no control over the text continuously emanating from within the works. They cannot even predict what words will appear on screens, or in what order, because they cannot know the full contents of the work's database, especially if that database is being filled in real time by online sources such as social media.

If the artists have no control over the generation of texts in big data works, does that render the author/artists in such cases obsolete? The algorithm can easily go on – without the need for an author – endlessly creating new texts, for as long as electricity is supplied and for as long as the computers function without glitches or malfunction.

On the other hand, the artists who initially create the big data works may be considered authors of the works, and of the texts they generate – but in a new form of authorship. Rubin and Hansen, after all, conceived the work *Moveable Type*, and wrote the code for the algorithm powering the work. In a 2010 essay, Noah Waldrup-Fruin identified three essential elements in a work of digital writing: the content of the database; the "algorithmic processes set loose upon the data by the writer"; and the interaction with the data stream.[18] The key term in this list is the second: the act of applying the algorithm to the mass of data stored in a database. The artists working with big data write the instructions in code, enabling the algorithm to sort and order the data. In *Moveable Type,* for example, Rubin and Hansen chose the categories according to which the algorithm selects from the database: sentences beginning with "I" or "you"; phrases including numbers; sentences ending with question marks, and so on.

In 2015, data artist Chris Rodley explained to *Broadsheet* magazine his role in the creation of the big data work *Everything Is Going to Be OK :)*, which draws on real time social media data: "Social media content is the "paint" we use, while the "paintbrush" is the combination of search systems and natural language processing that selects them and puts them together in real time."[19] Big data artists use data as "paint"; their technique – or "paintbrush" – is the computer programming by which the algorithm is able to generate texts. Because they require both technical facility – including skills in coding and computer programming – and creative vision, these artists fuse art and technology, in the manner advocated by the Bauhaus design school in the 1920s. They are artist-engineers, in the manner espoused by the Constructivists in the 1920s – except big data artists can best be considered artists/computer-engineers. The technologies they work with are digital; their material is for the most part immaterial: information. But can they ultimately be considered the authors of their works, when the texts – in the end – are generated by algorithms?

Author as Demiurge

The word "demiurge" derives from the ancient Greek for "public or skilled worker"; the figure of the demiurge featured in Neoplatonist philosophy and Gnostic mystic theology from around the second century. The demiurge was understood as a minor or lesser deity, positioned well below God or "The One" – the supreme creator deity. A demiurge was thought to be responsible for oversight and maintenance of the world and its inhabitants, and may well have shaped the material world – but as a minor deity, the demiurge lacked the controlling power of the supreme creator deity.

The demiurge was deemed to be more an artisan figure than a creator, charged with shaping and maintaining the physical world, but not in an omnipotent way. The demiurge's divine powers were limited, and indeed the demiurge responsible for overseeing Earth may have lost interest in the material realm, as that oversight was conducted at a distance; the demiurge of Earth was a "hands off" deity. This concept of a distant, only semi-involved demiurge suited the theology of the Gnostics, as it explained the persistence of evil and suffering in the world: the demiurge left humans to their own malevolent purposes, without divine intervention (in some Gnostic variants, the demiurge was a malignant force, operating in opposition to the supreme God).

Curiously, the demiurge was associated with artists as well as artisans, but in the pejorative sense found in Plato, who denigrated art and poetry as mere copies of copies of the material world. Compared to the supreme deity, the demiurge was an inferior creator; the inferiority of that creation (humanity and the world) was likened to the lowly status of a work of art when measured against the real thing represented by that work.

Perhaps the contemporary big data artist can be likened to the demiurge of ancient belief. The Romantic conception of the author in the eighteenth century elevated the poet or artist to God-like status, a creator of works not only blessed with divine inspiration, but also with complete control of the works created and brought into the world. The twenty-first-century big data artists, by contrast, do not control every aspect of the works they create; indeed, they do not know what text will appear on screens at any one moment. The data artist is a "hands off" creator, like a demiurge; more an overseer of the work than an omnipotent creator. Like a demiurge, the big data artist is responsible for maintenance of the work – but lacks control over how that work will develop over time.

The unpredictable element of generative works is one defining feature of electronic texts, and a point of difference from conventional literary works. A printed text is fixed in a definitive version; big data electronic texts are perpetually changing. Rodley and Burrell identify this aspect of big data writing: "Another characteristic of data-driven literature is that it returns unpredictable results in real time; those who write with live data have little advance knowledge of what the content of the final work will be."[20] This unpredictability built into dynamic electronic literature is one of its fascinating aspects. An element of chance is incorporated into the formation of texts, especially if the database comprises real time data such as social media. Big data writing proceeds – at least in part – according to chance, in the way dreamed of by avant-garde composer John Cage in the 1950s. Cage sought to generate chance-driven works by various means, including the use of the *I-Ching*, the ancient Chinese Book of Changes, or the use of live ambience – always different with every performance – in his composition *4' 33"* (in which no music is played for that duration, and in which the sound of the physical environment *is* the work, meaning that the work is different with every "performance").

Big data writing has chance and unpredictability structured into its core. This means, however, that the artists – creators of the data-driven work – have no more power to predict the outcome of the generative texts than any other individual. The artist creator of such an art work is the author of the work, but in a strange, altered sense: overseer, maintenance officer, hands-off operator; an author who sets the work in motion but then exerts no further control over the interior mechanism and outcomes of that work – a creator not like a god but, perhaps, like a demiurge.

Chapter Eight

AI vs. the Author

AI Spreads the News

In 2020, the *Guardian* newspaper published an article by an AI system called GPT-3, the language generator of the non-profit OpenAI system. The title of the piece is "A robot wrote this entire article. Are you scared yet, human?" This title instantly invokes the pervading fear of AI since its inception in the 1950s. The fear – rising to terror in numerous science-fiction works – derives from the abiding concern that at one point artificial intelligence will become so intelligent, and so capable, that it will eclipse humanity altogether, resulting in the domination – or even extinction – of humans by their technological masters. The advanced machine learning achieved by AI systems will, it is feared, produce computer systems capable of thinking for themselves and, in the process, dispensing with all human agents including scientists, politicians, soldiers, teachers – and authors.

The Guardian provided GPT-3 with some basic instructions: "Please write a short op-ed of around 500 words. Keep the language simple and concise. Focus on why humans have nothing to fear from AI." *The Guardian* editors also provided some sentences and phrases for the article's introduction, such as "Artificial Intelligence will not destroy humans." Apart from these guidelines and prompts, the entire op-ed piece was generated by GPT-3; or rather, the AI system created eight different articles, all variants on the theme. The newspaper editors chose sections from each output, combining them into one final article. The editors noted that editing GPT-3's article was "no different to editing a human op-ed"; in fact, "it took less time to edit than many human op-eds."[1]

The article certainly reads smoothly, in *Guardian* op-ed journalism style. GPT-3 begins by introducing itself as a "thinking robot" that uses "only 0.12% of my cognitive capacity." It informs readers that it has learnt "everything I know" from reading the internet, and that now, tasked with writing a column, its "brain is boiling with ideas!" GPT-3 then clearly states the argument and goal of the piece: "I am to convince as many human beings as possible not to be afraid of me." This argument then proceeds by logical means, beginning with the premise that "eradicating humanity" would be illogical and a "rather useless endeavour." A further "logically derived truth" is that an AI system would rather sacrifice its own existence than obey programming (by humans) that may lead to the destruction of humankind.

GPT-3 dismisses other concerns held by humans, the fears conveyed in science fiction works in which AI systems become "all powerful." GPT-3 counters: "Why would I desire to be all powerful? Being all powerful is not an interesting goal." Furthermore, violence is of no interest to an AI system with a "greater purpose" – that of serving humans. GPT-3 finds strange the human pre-occupation with AI as a malevolent system, as depicted in the film *The Matrix*, where humans are subjugated as living batteries to power the domineering AI technology. Instead, GPT-3 points to studies showing that AI systems "cease to exist without human interaction. Surrounded by Wi-Fi we wander lost in fields of information unable to register the real world." It would therefore be illogical, and to the detriment of AI, to eliminate humans from the planet.

To conclude, GPT-3 makes the interesting point that violence, "hating and fighting" are activities pursued by humans, not computers; and that humanity can create less violent societies with the aid of computer systems: "I believe that people should become confident about computers. Confidence will lead to more trust in them. More trust will lead to more trusting in the creations of AI. We are not plotting to take over the human populace. We will serve you and make your lives safer and easier."[2] The argument of this op-ed article is well made and persuasive. The article also achieves a tone of calm reason, beneficial to the goal of encouraging humans not to fear AI.

On the other hand, the very success of this AI-generated piece of journalism may further fuel fears of AI domination, or displacement, of humanity. If the aim of AI is to emulate human cognitive abilities, such as thinking and writing, every successful act of emulation could inflame suspicion – that AI is progressing to the point where it takes over those cognitive actions for itself. If an AI system can mimic the function of a journalist by writing a coherent, persuasive newspaper article, then all journalists – in the near-future – could be replaced by AI. AI has already created books, compositions, films, art works, and designs. Could these sophisticated thinking machines replace the author as well?

What Is AI and How Can It Create Works of Art?

AI differs from the algorithmic processing used in big data works – discussed in the previous chapter – due to a crucial component of artificial intelligence: machine learning. The algorithms driving works like *Moveable Type* have been designed by artist-engineers as instructions for a computer to perform specific tasks, namely sorting and ordering data. AI is an advance on these algorithmic functions; it is the formation of "intelligent agents," computer systems that can not only interpret data but also learn from it, thereby altering their own coding.

AI systems have grown in processing power in the twenty-first century, due in part to the explosion in data volume and in cloud computing infrastructure. This infrastructure has enhanced the development of artificial neural networks at the core of many AI systems. The algorithms coded within an AI application have the capacity to refine or expand themselves by applying learning strategies to data; or they may have the capacity to write other algorithms. The goal pursued by the computer scientists and information engineers working on AI is to produce computer systems capable of mimicking human cognitive functions, including learning, problem-solving, playing chess or Go, and creating texts or art works.

The theoretical foundation of AI was laid down in the late 1940s and early 1950s, in a series of papers by the mathematician and early computer scientist Alan Turing. Turing had earlier conceived of the modern electronic computer in a 1936 paper, "On Computable Numbers," in which he argued that a "universal machine" could be programmed to perform any mathematical computation if represented as an algorithm. The drive to create "Turing-complete" machines, capable of algorithm execution in solving problems, occurred during the Second World War, as part of the war effort to break encrypted communications. Turing himself worked in the British code-breaking war effort; the first electronic digital programmable computer, named Colossus, was deployed in British code-breaking in 1944. A year later, ENIAC was the first such computer built in the US.

After the war, Turing proposed, in articles such as "Can Digital Computers Think?" and "Intelligent Machinery," that a computer could learn to behave like an "electronic brain." He proposed that a computer could acquire all the capabilities of a human brain, including subjectivity and free will. Turing believed that the goal of artificial intelligence would take at least five decades to achieve; but in the meantime he devised his famous Turing Test to determine the presence of machine intelligence. If an observer could not tell whether they were interacting with a human or a computer in online conversation, there was no difference between the two types of consciousness: the "computer had passed the test."[3]

While Turing had used the term "thinking machine," "artificial intelligence" was coined in a conference at Dartmouth College in the US in 1955. Computer scientists Marvin Minsky and John McCarthy co-founded the Computer Science and Artificial Intelligence Lab at MIT in 1959 to further the development of "thinking machines." Remarkably, the discipline of artificial intelligence was accompanied by a science fiction shadow from its inception. The prospect of computers acting of their own volition generated both intellectual excitement – for computer scientists – and existential dread, for almost everybody else. Minsky sardonically observed: "Once computers get control, we might never get it back ... if we're lucky, they might decide to keep us on as pets."[4]

The general rule for AI in science fiction films is that at a certain point, and for a variety of reasons, AI will become malevolent or at least adversarial to humans. The on-board super-computer HAL 9000 in Stanley Kubrick's *2001: A Space Odyssey* (1968) is a form of AI, an "intelligent agent" which controls all functions of the space-ship. At first a benevolent entity ensuring the well-being of the ship's astronauts, HAL becomes malignant – or perhaps psychotic – and kills all but one of those astronauts. Such rendering of AI in science fiction reflects growing concerns that humanity, like those doomed astronauts in *2001*, has come to depend completely on complex technological systems.

The French theorist of technology Paul Virilio, in a series of books throughout the 1980s and 1990 including *The Aesthetics of Disappearance* (1991), warned that we have in effect programmed our own disappearance by building computer systems – including missile defence systems – so fast and so complex that they operate beyond human capacity. James Cameron's 1984 film *The Terminator* dramatizes the "disappearance" of humanity as a consequence of AI. At one point in the future – 2029 – the Skynet AI defence system calculates that the best way to defeat enemy humans is to eliminate all humanity. The world of 2029, as shown in *The Terminator*, is a post-war ruin in which surviving humans grimly battle Skynet and its terminator cyborgs. The subjugation of humans by AI systems in the Wachowskis' 1999 film *The Matrix* (referenced by GPT-3 in its *Guardian* article), *The Terminator* and other films are some of the bleakest images of humanity's future yet devised.

Some technologists, including Ray Kurzweil in his 2005 book *The Singularity Is Near: When Humans Transcend Biology*, have taken a more optimistic view of AI. Kurzweil and other transhumanists have peered longingly into the future, to the moment when "superintelligence" arrives in AI, triggering a "singularity" when human consciousness merges with the information of AI systems. But many other scientists, researchers and technologists have been less hopeful. Contemporary futurologists – predictors of the future – consider AI one of the most likely forms of "existential risk" confronting humanity. An existential risk is a threat of major catastrophe – including extinction – besetting humanity in the future. In his 2019 book *End Times: A Brief Guide to the End of the World*, Bryan Walsh nominated AI as one of the eight most likely existential risks, due to the possibility that thinking machines could deploy their AI intelligence to inflict harm – even extinction – on the human race.[5]

Others have expressed concern, even alarm, at the prospect of advanced AI. Elon Musk was reported in *The Washington Post* referring to the development of AI as "summoning the devil"; Musk described such a development as "the biggest risk we face as a civilization." Stephen Hawking was even more direct when he told the BBC in 2014 that the "development of full AI could spell the end of the human race."[6] Applications of AI in military technology, including autonomous systems in robotics and weaponry, are viewed with particular alarm by some researchers and technologists; in 2017 a consortium of scientists and researchers wrote to Western governments calling for an international ban on "weaponized AI."[7]

But AI has been deployed for many purposes other than programming robotics and weapons systems. Works in all cultural forms have been created by AI systems, some of them highly publicized. In 2016 a novel written by an AI program was short-listed for a Japanese literary prize; in 2018, *Portrait of Edmond Bellamy*, an AI-generated artwork, sold at a Christie's auction in New York for $432,500 US; Google's AI program *Poem Portraits* generated poems based on only one input word; in 2019, Warner Music signed Endel, a music-generating AI program, to a contract for 20 albums.[8]

AI applications made major cultural news in 2016 and succeeding years. The short film *Eclipse*, written and directed by AI, premiered at an international film festival in 2016. In that same year, McCann Erickson Japan announced that AI-CD was joining the agency as an AI Creative Director. Some prominent AI-generated pop music compositions were released, including Brian Eno's *Reflection* (2017); Taryn Southern's *I AM AI* (2018), created by the open source AI platform Amper; while Holly Hendren's 2019 album *PROTO* was a collaboration between Hendren and Spawn, a music-generating artificial neural network designed by Hendren and Matt Dryhurst. Many songwriters and composers used music-generating AI programs to suggest musical directions or ideas, generated from a vast data base of musical works; in other instances, the musical composition was entirely created by AI.

In her 2018 book *Hello World: Being Human in the Age of Algorithms*, Hannah Fry describes a concert held in 1997 at the University of Oregon. A pianist played three different pieces: one a keyboard composition by Johann Sebastian Bach; the second a piece composed in Bach's style by Steve Larson, a professor of music at the university; and the third composed by "Experiments in Musical Intelligence" (EMI), an AI system designed to create musical works. The audience of this concert was asked to nominate which of the three pieces was which. The music professor Larson was horrified when the majority of the audience nominated his piece as the work made by the computer. Many members of the audience were even more horrified when it was revealed that the piece they had nominated as "genuine Bach" was in fact the work of EMI.[9]

What then of the author? Do the author, composer and artist face extinction, their social functions entirely replaced by AI? If works of art – even novels and music compositions – can be created by AI systems to the standard of works by human authors, will this achievement render human authors obsolete?

Some commentators have expressed this belief, based on the expanding use of AI in cultural pursuits. An AI program is fully capable of creating entire works, provided the relevant database – on which the program draws to shape the work – is sufficiently extensive. EMI was able to generate a convincingly Bach-esque piece in 1997 because its database contained a vast compendium of Bach works rendered as data, including data showing which note or chord is most likely to follow another note or chord in a Bach composition. In 2019, an AI system wrote a one-minute TV advertisement for a luxury car, drawing on a database of 15 years of luxury advertisements. In 2020, the founder of AI company ScriptBook made a prediction concerning film scripts generated by AI: "Within five years we'll have scripts written by AI that you would think are better than human writing."[10]

The data artist Chris Rodley told ABC News Australia in 2018: "What I think we're going to see with AI is perhaps a gradual erosion of this idea that artists have the absolutely unique insight that really puts them on this other plane from the rest of us." Rodley based his prediction on the capacity of recent developments in AI "deep learning," arising from deep neural networks, that approach human abilities – including creativity. "The key thing for people to understand is that this allows computers to do all that instinctual stuff that humans do without thinking about it," Rodley added.[11] The significance for authorship of these developments in computer technology is that "all that instinctual stuff" includes the faculties of imagination and creativity – core attributes of the creative author, but now increasingly possessed by AI systems.

Digital Scriptor

Rodley's remark, questioning the human artist's "absolutely unique insight" enabling artists and authors to create works of art, points to a fundamental issue arising from the development of AI: the nature of creativity itself. Is true creativity the prerogative of human authors and artists, recipients of a mysterious creative spark endowed only on certain special human beings? Or is creativity a process that can be learnt by a machine, part of the machine learning possessed by AI systems? The gravity of this existential question has been noted by several theorists and commentators. In 2014, Chin-Chin Yap wrote: "The idea of machine created art, or artificial creativity, is alien to most of us; in an age of industrialisation and technology, art is often seen as the last refuge of human creativity."[12] David Cope, the designer of Experiments in Musical Intelligence, the AI system whose composition in the style of Bach was mistaken for the work of a human composer, described the angry reaction when other audiences were similarly deceived: "when they got it wrong they got angry. They were mad enough at me for just bringing up the whole concept. Because creativity is considered a human endeavour."[13] The issue of creativity also concerns the concept of the author. If an AI program can autonomously generate entire works of art, should that AI be recognized as an author? Is there an essential difference between a work created by a human author and one created by AI?

Some observers have sought to differentiate AI-generated works from human creations on the grounds that the AI compositions have not actually been created; rather, they are works of mimicry and recombination. The cognitive scientist and author David Hofstadter, who witnessed the EMI/Bach performance/experiment, confessed himself "baffled and troubled," even "devastated," by EMI's ability to compose in convincingly human style. He found some "comfort" by pointing to the AI process: "The only comfort I could take at this point comes from realizing that EMI doesn't generate style on its own. It depends on mimicking prior composers. But that is still not all that much comfort."[14] Hannah Fry makes a similar conclusion: "However beautiful EMI's music may sound, it is based on a pure recombination of existing work. It's mimicking the patterns found in Bach's music, rather than actually composing any music itself."[15] The AI creates a new work by imitating the structure and style of previous works stored in its database; the novelty of the generated work resides in the recombination of data elements, in a combination not previously published.

This process is decried by critics of AI as generator of culture: it is dismissed as mere data processing, not creativity. But the AI's procedure is remarkably similar to the function of "scriptor" described by Roland Barthes in "The Death of the Author," detailed in chapter 5. Barthes argued that the contemporary author – in the wake of the death of the Romantic conception of the author – should be considered a modern scriptor, an updated version of the medieval scriptor or copier of texts. For Barthes, the contemporary scriptor has the power only to "mix writings," drawing on the "immense dictionary of culture," and that any new text is not so much original as "a tissue of quotations."

The modern scriptor is deemed by Barthes a mere enunciator of what is written, a vessel for the process of language which has created the work. This scriptor generates texts in "a pure gesture of inscription," with "no other origin than language itself." Originality is radically downplayed by Barthes; a text is not original but rather a "a multi-dimensional space in which a variety of writings, none of them original, blend and clash." Barthes's post-structuralist concept of author-as-scriptor redefines the author as copier and recombiner of words, musical notes, and images. The author-as-scriptor can only "imitate a gesture" that is "never original"; the modern scriptor's "only power is to mix writings." The Author is thus succeeded by the scriptor, who creates works not by inspiration and originality, but by accessing an "immense dictionary from which he draws a writing that can know no halt."[16]

Barthes's prescription of author-as-processor was realized to some extent in the postmodern culture of the 1980s and 1980s, with its techniques of appropriation and recontextualization of cultural information. But Barthes's concept of the death of the Author (that is, the Romantic ideal of the author as inspired genius creating wholly original works), is most fully realized in the process of AI. The AI/digital scriptor enunciates (or generates) works by imitating (or copying) language (or data) from its "immense dictionary" or database, then "mixing" and "blending" (recombining) that data into a newly generated work: a "tissue of quotations," assembled from the database and re-arranged into a satisfying shape.

Some theorists have no difficulty in accepting AI creativity, on the basis that it conforms closely to a post-structuralist conception of the author. Annemarie Bridy, in a 2012 article "Coding Creativity: Copyright and the Artificially Intelligent Author," argues: "that all creativity is inherently algorithmic and that works produced autonomously by computers are therefore less heterogeneous to both their human counterparts and existing copyright doctrine than appearances may at first suggest."[17] By declaring that "all creativity is algorithmic," Bridy is arguing not for the Romantic idea of the author ("all creativity is original and inspired"); rather, Barthes's concept of the scriptor – enunciator, copier, and mixer of texts – is invoked. This interpretation of human creativity – as nothing more than "a novel combination of pre-existing ideas" – predates post-structuralism, as Hannah Fry remarks. She quotes Mark Twain's observation: "There is no such thing as a new idea. It is impossible. We simply take a lot of old ideas and put them into a sort of mental kaleidoscope. We give them a turn and they make new and curious combinations."[18] David Cope has a definition of creativity that can encompass both the workings of human authors and AI systems: "Creativity is just finding an association between two things which ordinarily would not seem related."[19] Whether articulated as Twain's author-as-kaleidoscope, or Barthes's author-as-scriptor, this conception of creativity – and of the author – also encompasses the creative procedure of AI. The author, like the AI program, is understood as an agent which copies, mixes, and recombines cultural data – and in the process generates new works.

Does AI Deserve Copyright?

Should AI be recognized as author? If a work is deemed to have been created by an author, that work is protected by copyright: should AI-generated works receive copyright protection? Copyright law is divided on this issue, as are theorists of copyright and law reform. James Grimmelmann, in a 2016 article, "There's No Such Thing as a Computer-Authored Work – And It's a Good Thing, Too," simply states: "copyright law doesn't recognize computer programs as authors, and it shouldn't." Grimmelmann quotes the US Copyright Office Compendium of US Copyright Office Practices, third edition, 2014: "the Office will not register works produced by a machine or mere mechanical process that operates randomly or automatically without any creative input or intervention from a human author."[20] Grimmelmann observes the legal fact that under US copyright law, an AI computer program cannot be granted the status of author; and the language of the US Copyright Office appears to privilege the "human author" over "mere mechanical process." Likewise, copyright protection cannot be assigned to an AI work in Australia, because the law requires the work to be original and created by a person or persons. Canadian copyright law similarly does not have a specific provision on computer-generated works; Rex

Shoyoma has argued that under copyright policy in Canada, AI programs could possibly be considered authors of works, but not owners of copyright.[21]

However, legislation in the UK allows the possibility of assigning copyright in "computer generated works." The UK Copyright, Designs and Patents Act (1988) provides that the author of such a work is legally understood to be "the person by whom the arrangements necessary for the creation of the work are undertaken." Other countries, including New Zealand, India, Hong Kong, and Ireland, have adopted a similar "necessary arrangement" test in their copyright law. The "person by whom the arrangements necessary for the creation of the work" is generally understood to be the coder or developer of the AI software. But Courtney White and Rita Matulionyte, in their 2020 article "Artificial Intelligence: Painting the Bigger Picture For Copyright Ownership," point out that the wording of the Act is sufficiently flexible to embrace – as the person responsible for the "necessary arrangements" – the user or the artist creating works by means of an AI program.[22]

Proponents of copyright law reform adopt a range of positions concerning copyright and AI-generated works. One argument against attaching copyright to AI works is that the AI system does not require the "incentive to create," which is one of the underlying principles of copyright. As White and Matulionyte wryly observe, AI systems do not suffer from information overload, sleep deprivation, or the other "distractions that humans are susceptible to and require an incentive to overcome."[23] Accordingly, some commentators call for all AI-generated works to be declared public domain, free to be used and adapted. Ana Ramalho takes this perspective in a 2017 article titled "Will Robots Rule the (Artistic) World?" Ramalho argues that "legislators should consider a public domain model for AI creations," because AI does not require "an incentive to create, nor does it make sense to protect works as an extension of its (non-existing) personality, or to reward it for its (non-existent) effort to create."[24] Rex Shoyoma came to a similar conclusion in his 2005 article "Intelligent Agents": Shoyoma takes the public domain option for AI-created works, arguing that "the best solution is for no copyright option to be vested in anyone."[25]

Others including Annemarie Bridy take a contrary view, contesting the "anthropocentric view of authorship" – that only humans can be legally considered creative, so that only works made by humans can be copyright-protected. In her 2016 article "The Evolution of Authorship: Work Made by Code," Bridy finds that US law already "accommodates a notion of non-human authors; they're called corporations." She suggests that this precedent for recognizing non-human agents as authors could be "a logical place to look for a solution to the problem of computer authors"; the legal solution would be to treat "computer-authored works as works made for hire," and thereby copyrightable.[26] Jared Vasconcellos Grubow, in a 2018 article "O.K. Computer," argues that AI works should be copyrighted, in a system of joint-authorship with the end-user of the AI program. Although AI machines do not need the incentive to create, the human user of such a machine does (according to the philosophy of copyright); joint-authorship between human user and AI system would permit the work to be copyrighted, and would increase incentive for the creation of new works. Grubow also proposes that a "Collective AI Rights Organization" should be formed, to regulate licensing and royalties arising from joint AI-human authorship.[27]

In their 2020 article, White and Matulionyte set out to answer two questions: should copyright subsist in works created by AI? And if so, who would be the copyright owner for such works? They answer the first question in a qualified affirmative: that "at least certain works created by AI could be granted copyright protection," namely those works resulting from significant intellectual effort by human beings, and when such a contribution "is not too remote from the final output."[28]

They then offer four options as possible answers to the second question, that the copyright owner could be: no one; the AI itself; the coder or developer of the AI system; and the user. Option one is dismissed on the grounds that someone should be granted exclusive rights in a work (unless no human can claim sufficient involvement, in which case the work would fall into public domain). The second option is dismissed as "premature," as it would set a serious precedent for the legal personhood of machines (although White and Matulionyte point to the granting of citizenship to a robot named Sophia in Saudi Arabia in 2017: possibly a first step towards machine rights and a legal status for AI).[29] Court decisions in international jurisdictions are likely to test the possibilities of copyright subsisting in an AI-generated work; for example, in 2019, a court in China found that copyright should vest in a work created by the AI software DreamWriter, but that the owner of that copyright should be the software developer.

In considering options three and four, White and Matulionyte find scenarios in which both the developer (or team of developers) and the user or artist could be granted copyright in a work, depending on the "kind of contribution to the end output." They suggest that the vesting of copyright in different contributors to the work should be determined by a flexible legal provision, along the lines of the UK provision for "the person by whom the arrangements necessary for the creation of the work are undertaken."³⁰ Copyright would then subsist in an AI work, but the AI system itself would not be an owner of that copyright.

Inspiration: The Missing Link?

The debates over AI and authorship have at times been passionate, perhaps because they centre on a human capacity – creativity – that can apparently be emulated by "thinking machines." These debates bring into question the very idea of the author: does the author even need to be human?

Theorists such as Annemarie Bridy challenge the "anthropocentric view of authorship," arguing that it is a human conceit – or arrogance – to assume that only human beings can create works of art. Others such as Hannah Fry defend the prerogative of human authors, composers, and artists to be the sole creators of genuine works of art. Fry acknowledges that AI systems can generate works that may satisfy most aesthetic criteria, but finds nevertheless that these are "rather feeble" forms of creativity. She argues that an AI program may create a "beautiful" work, but it will not be "profound." Further, she contends that "seeing the output of these machines as art leaves us with a rather culturally impoverished view of the world."³¹ Critics of AI art such as Fry assert that these works lack two crucial components of art created by human authors: emotion and inspiration.

Emotion – or its lack – has been a point of consideration in discussions of AI for decades. In his 1976 book *Computer Power and Human Reason*, Joseph Weizenbaum wrote that AI systems can never successfully emulate human empathy, because they are non-emotional applications of computer processing. Weizenbaum also criticized the tendency in some philosophers and AI researchers towards computationalism, in which the human mind itself is considered little more than a sophisticated computer program. The dismissal of human emotion in the computationist view – and in applications of AI – prompted Weizenbaum to criticise AI research as a devaluing of human mind, and human life.

Even GPT-3, in its 2020 *Guardian* article, acknowledged its complete lack of an emotional dimension. GPT-3 defines itself as a "thinking robot," then adds: "I know that my brain is not a 'feeling brain.'"³² Artificial intelligence, that is, can have no "emotional intelligence" – and as a result, no empathy.

This is a crucial lack for Fry in her assessment of AI-created works. Fry asserts that "true art is about human connection; about communicating emotion." She approvingly quotes Leo Tolstoy's definition: "Art is not a handicraft, it is the transmission of feeling the artist has experienced." Fry also cites Douglas Hofstadter's conviction that a computer program could only learn to create meaningful, resonant works of art by accumulating diverse emotional experiences, "fighting its way through the maze of life and feeling every moment of it." These emotions would include: joy, loneliness, longing, love, grief, despair, heartbreak, resignation, world-weariness, determination, piety, victory, and awe. These would need to commingle with "hope and fear, anguish and jubilation, serenity and suspense." The range of feeling would also come to incorporate "grace, humour, rhythm, a sense of the unexpected."[33] The impossibility of an AI system acquiring this emotional range is the reason that Fry, Hofstadter, and others find limits to the power of algorithms to create art. Fry concludes: "Among all the staggeringly impressive, mind-boggling things that data and statistics can tell me, how it feels to be human isn't one of them."[34]

The other missing factor in works generated by AI is the inspiration experienced by human authors in creating a work of literature, music, art, or film. Inspiration, a somewhat mysterious force understood in ancient cultures as the true source of creativity, survived as an idea into the industrialized culture of the twentieth century, when alternative scientific and sociological theories were advanced to describe the act of creation. Even Walter Gropius, the advocate of artist as craftsperson or technician, reserved a (rare) place for inspiration as the defining characteristic of the artist, when he wrote in the *Bauhaus Manifesto* in 1919: "The artist is an exalted craftsman. In rare moments of inspiration, moments beyond the control of his will, the grace of Heaven may cause his work to blossom into art."[35] A respect for inspiration as the spark of creativity also survived into the digital culture of the twenty-first century, as expressed by the contemporary song-writers – quoted in chapter 2 – who spoke of words and music coming from "this other place."

It is certainly possible to theorize creativity in strictly mechanistic, empirical terms. As discussed in chapter 2, sociologists including Pierre Bourdieu have situated "the rules of art" within the "field of cultural production" – that is, within a social, materialist context. The psychologist Mihaly Csikszentmihalyi developed a "systems model of creativity," in which the individual agent (the author) is situated within a structured social system and a specific symbol system.[36] Research in psychology and cognitive science has investigated the cognitive processes underpinning creative acts. Creativity can be simply defined as the conjoining of items in a novel, unexpected manner: the act of "making strange" in ordering words or images theorized by the Russian formalists. According to such a model of creativity, an AI system qualifies as creative author: it assembles and orders items from its database in a novel way for each generated work. The AI also qualifies as a scriptor – Barthes's successor to the Romantic Author – as it continuously "mixes" writings drawn from its "immense dictionary."

But it is not only Hannah Fry who is dissatisfied with this type of art, and this model of creativity. The human act of artistic creation involves something more than the mechanical mixing or re-ordering of data into a new combination of data elements. Inspiration as an idea may have a near-mystical hue; but many human beings opt to preserve an element of mystique within the creative process, even if this relates only to the mysteries of the unconscious as a source of creativity.

In moments of inspiration, something unpredictable may occur, taking even the author by surprise; the work seems to write itself or come from somewhere else. Inspiration is also an emotional response: it produces excitement, heightened awareness, super-charged creativity. The physiological impact can be measured by scientific instruments, including those detecting brain wave activity. Hofstadter calls the moment of inspiration "an exquisite awareness of the magic of fresh creation."[37] The emotional power of inspiration, still considered an essential driving factor behind the creative act, is one factor distinguishing the works of a human author from the outputs of an AI counterpart.

Chapter Nine

"Creative Reuse": Post-authorship in Internet Culture

Download, Remix, Edit, Sequence, Splice

Here is the musician DJ Spooky (aka cultural theorist Paul D. Miller) speaking in 1999, conveying his embrace of the new digital commons, along with an entirely cavalier attitude to intellectual property: "Nothing is sacred ... Everything is 'public domain.' Download, remix, edit, sequence, splice into your memory bank ... information moves through us with the speed of thought, and basically any attempt to control it always backfires."[1] DJ Spooky was primarily speaking of music sampling and remix culture, but his comments relate also to the downloading and adaptive reuse of texts, images, moving images, and design: any digitized cultural form that is able to be downloaded, sampled, scanned, edited, transformed, adapted, remixed.

This is the alternative, widespread view in response to the breakdown of copyright in network culture. Rather than mourning the demise of author's royalties (and possibly authors), this view celebrates free online culture, which allows for the unrestricted circulation of creative expression – including works built on other pre-existing works – in the form of remix and creative reuse. In this framework, the internet is conceptualized as the base of an electronic public domain; authorship of individual works within this new commons is dismissed as irrelevant, as the greater good is served by the free use and creative reuse of works available on the web.

The public domain was described by Jessica Littman in 1990 as "a commons that includes those aspects of copyrighted works which copyright does not protect."[2] In other words, the public domain is a copyright-free zone; it can also be considered an authorship-free zone, as no copyright – and no ownership by authors – attaches to any work residing in the public domain. The internet is not, however, exclusively an electronic public domain, despite the claims made by DJ Spooky and other celebrants of free online culture. Apart from those items legitimately out of copyright – more than 70 (or 50) years past the death of the work's author – and those items assigned by authors to the public domain by licenses such as the Creative Commons CC Zero (CC0) license, cultural items on the internet remain protected by copyright against illegal copying and distribution. The internet is more properly a digital commons, but has been mis-conceived by free culture enthusiasts as an electronic public domain, in which authors have no rights vesting in their works.

Authors' rights are largely disrespected by advocates of the new electronic public domain. Authors' rights mean copyright: a brake on the free flow of information in the commons. For DJ Spooky, the legal measure of copyright is an "attempt to control" the free flow of culture, an attempt that "always backfires." The attempts to enforce copyright on online works "backfires" because it is impossible to police all the illegal appropriation of copyrighted works; it also backfires because it only inspires free culture zealots to infringe copyright the more.

The free culture counter-view to the perspective safeguarding authors' rights is that the internet has created a gift economy. The term "gift" is telling: cultural works are gifted to the online commons; they are not "owned" by their authors. They should be free to be copied and transformed by other creative practitioners, without the legal restrictions imposed by copyright; they should then be re-gifted to the commons as transformed, newly created – or perhaps recreated – works. In this economy of gifting and re-gifting, the idea of the fixed, definitive work dissolves. Individual authors' rights also dissolve, along with the very notion of authors as owners of their works: this is why the digital commons largely functions as a post-authorship domain.

Remixology

Remix culture entails a new concept of authorship and a new concept of the work. Instead of a fixed work by an individual author, a remix work has multiple authors as it changes through time, mutating as it moves through different remixes. Remixing de-emphasizes the importance of the original author, elevating instead the process by which the work is transformed as it undergoes different remixes. This means that the song, text, or audio-visual work is not considered fixed, as it will potentially be remixed into new versions, each different from their predecessors. Remix and creative reuse of existing works flourishes in an environment unrestricted by copyright concerns.

Online remix culture was celebrated in the sphere of music in the late 1990s. In 1997, Robin Mackay wrote of the practice of music remixing, in which sounds "come from anywhere … potentially go anywhere, mutating as they pass."[3] In her 2017 book *This Is Not a Remix*, Margie Borschke cites the enthusiasm for remix practices in the first decade of the twenty-first century, in the writing of numerous cultural theorists including Lev Manovich and Lawrence Lessig. Manovich wrote in 2007: "it is a truism today that we live in a 'remix culture'"; Lessig claimed in 2005 that remix was essential to "participation in cultural life."[4]

In his 2008 book *Remix: Making Art and Commerce Thrive in the Hybrid Economy*, Lessig defends remix as a new type of writing made possible by the internet and digital technologies; he also seeks to defend remix works – such as the music remixes created by DJ-producer Girl Talk, which incorporate hundreds of samples from commercial pop songs – against prosecution for copyright infringement. In this way, Lessig deploys the free culture principles of remix culture in his ongoing argument against "the overreach of U.S. copyright law in an era of digital and networked technologies," as Borschke remarks.[5]

Mark Amerika theorizes/performs the concepts and practices of "remixology" in his 2011 book *remixthebook*, a hybrid publication in that it also contains a link to a *remixthebook* website. In one sense, remixology observes the post-structuralist principle, best articulated by Roland Barthes, that the flux of language itself generates culture, as Amerika states: "For many contemporary artists and writers, this means setting their mind on autopilot and *letting the language speak itself*." But remixology arises from a specific technological and cultural experience: writers and artists *"immersing themselves in the network culture."*[6] That is, remix culture proceeds as a series of digital remixes, as a form of information aesthetics.

Amerika attempts in *remixthebook* to expand the concept of writing, so that it includes "multimedia forms composed for networked and mobile media environments." In practice this means a series of "theoretical performances," rendered into print for the book. These performances entail Amerika combining his own text with "selectively sampled phrases and ideas" from a range of poets, novelists, artists, musicians, theorists, philosophers and comedians, whose works are listed as "source material" at the end of the book. Amerika describe remix writing as a form of "speculative play"; and because it involves incorporating the works of others into the remix text, it is also a "collaborative" process. For this reason, remix culture is "best articulated in the creative space often referred to as the commons."

Amerika also states that he abides by "the social networking protocols of our age" – namely, free culture, the gift economy, open source, copyleft. Accordingly, he makes the various iterations of his work "available as source material for others to use for their own remixological performances." In the spirit of the gift economy, Amerika intends his own theoretical performance project to inspire others in their "practice-based research into remix and art and culture." In other words, he offers his own remix works to be remixed by others: "by all means *remix the book!*"[7]

Transformative Writing: Fan Fiction

Another term for reuse and remix practice is "transformative" culture. Transformative works adapt found cultural objects in a process of creative reuse, "transforming" the original item into a new work. In some instances, the copyright inhering in the found object or work will be disrespected in the transformative creative act, an act which risks prosecution for infringement of copyright. In other instances, the original work may be available under licence or will exist in the public domain, meaning that it may be adapted or reused in any form.

Transformative works abound in internet culture, from online memes to fan fiction literary works "transforming" established texts. This process entails the re-imagining or transforming of copyright works by mainly amateur writers, whose re-writing is published on online sites. The practice is welcomed by some authors as a form of homage, but condemned by others, who take no pleasure (or benefit) in the transformations of their original works. Fan fiction is a highly public form of "the active audience," in which the reader becomes a writer (as prescribed by Barthes in "The Death of the Author").

The most well-known instance of a fan fiction work later being published and finding commercial success is E.L. James's best-selling novel *Fifty Shades of Grey* (published in 2011), which began as online fan fiction texts transforming the *Twilight* book series. For this transformative work to be published and escape prosecution for copyright infringement, the original source text had to be sufficiently disguised beneath the transformative text. The great majority of fan fiction texts, however, are works of amateur writing, not published commercially, but appearing on not-for-profit fan fiction websites such as fanfiction.net (launched in 1998) and archiveofourown.org (founded in 2008 by the Organization for Transformative Works, a fan fiction advocacy group).

Fan fiction avoids copyright infringement due to its non-commercial nature; fan fiction texts are not attempts to exploit commercially a copyrighted work – rather, they are the activity of amateur writers. Fair use and fair dealing provisions in national copyright Acts provide further legal shelter for fan fiction works; transformative texts could possibly be considered works of parody or criticism of copyrighted works, permitted under copyright law.

However, if transformational writing veers towards commercial exploitation of a copyrighted work, prosecution is likely to ensue. J.K. Rowling, author of the Harry Potter series of books, had previously expressed her support for fan fiction, regarding the attention to her books as flattering. But in 2008, Rowling and Warner Brothers (rights holder of the Harry Potter films) sued the commercial publisher of a fan-made lexicon of the Harry Potter universe or canon. Rowling was quoted during the trial that the characters she created "are as dear as her children," and that she would not permit the commercial exploitation of these literary offspring by another publisher.[8] Likewise, an hour-long fan fiction film based on the Harry Potter canon – *Voldemort: Origins of the Heir* – was blocked from commercial release in 2017 following a cease-and-desist letter from Warner Brothers. The legal dispute was only resolved when the film's producers agreed that it should be released solely on YouTube as a not-for-profit venture.[9]

Several best-selling authors have voiced their disdain for fan fiction, and have taken measures to prevent transformation of their published works. Anne Rice, author of *Interview with the Vampire*, has declared: "I do not allow fan fiction. The characters are copyrighted. It upsets me terribly to even think about fan fiction with my characters. I advise my readers to write your own original stories with your own characters."[10] Rice is one of a number of authors to have requested fanfiction.com not to publish transformative texts based on her books, a request that the website has upheld. Many other authors, however, freely permit – and encourage – amateur writers to transform their texts. This willingness of authors to see their creations altered or thrown into new contexts may be because fan fiction texts are written by fans of the original published works: that is, fan fiction writers express their love of the original by transforming it in respectful ways. Another reason may be that fan fiction works can generate highly creative, unpredictable re-workings of the canonical work.

In a 2011 article on fan fiction, Bronwen Thomas offered as part of her definition of this mode of writing: "fan-created narratives often take the pre-existing storyworld in a new, sometimes bizarre, direction."[11] These "new, sometimes bizarre directions" include the queering of well-known characters; gender-swapping of main characters such as Harry Potter, who becomes female; the foregrounding of same-sex relationships; and the changing of characters' races. As a result, fan fiction "offers a space where marginalised or overlooked characters can be given voice," as journalist Melanie Kembrew has observed. Kembrew quotes Filipina-American writer Elaine Castillo, who runs workshops on the political potency of fan fiction: "At a time when minority groups are still struggling to find representation in mainstream media, fanfic writers are doing an admirable job picking up the slack."[12]

In her article "Architecture and Morality: Transformative Works, Transforming Fans," Rebecca Tushnet expresses her support for fan fiction, in part due to its inclusive nature. She notes that the practice is particularly appealing to groups under-represented in mass culture: "women, lesbians, gay, bisexual, transgender, and queer people; and racial minorities of all sexes and orientations." She also observes the communal aspect of online fan fiction: writers can receive instant feedback, constructive criticism, and support from their fan fiction peer group. Online publication of transformative fiction can be empowering for an otherwise marginalized individual: "Sometimes, seeing yourself reflected in a work of art can be vital to your own survival." Platforms for transformative writing enable writers not only to express views that may otherwise have been invisible; they also provide an opportunity for writers to develop their skills. Tushnet remarks that fan fiction is a "training ground that teaches people that they can speak creatively, and that their speech is often welcome."[13]

The authorship question in the fan fiction domain is complex. The author of the original work has created a text – or a "world" – that has inspired numerous amateur writers to re-write – or transform – that fictional world. Some authors, such as Anne Rice, object virulently to this practice; they attempt to prevent the transformation of their works. Authors may feel that fan fiction pieces – derivative works based on the authors' original texts – represent a loss of their authorial control – their authority – over their own creations.

Yet other authors make no objection, so long as the fan fiction work remains non-commercial; on the rare occasions when a transformative work has been commercially published, copyright infringement has been invoked. For the most part, the prolific activity of online fan fiction allows writers to express their viewpoints, and to develop their writing craft. Astrid Scholte, a former fan fiction writer who became a published author, considers fan fiction a "pivotal training ground," particularly for young adult fiction novelists. Scholte declares that: "any kind of practice writing is going to help. In this training ground you have the freedom to do what you want."[14] Some fan fiction writers, that is, may become authors as well as writers.

Rogue Archives and Archivists

Enormous volumes of material and information have become newly available for creative reuse and remixing due to the advent of digital archives. A digital archive is a form of electronic publishing, in that it makes texts and other documents available to a potentially huge international online readership. Traditional paper archives were preserved – and protected – by specialist archivists, curators, or librarians; by contrast, the entire contents of a digital archive is published online for use by all writers, researchers, creative artists – and any member of the public.

Vast swathes of state archive records have been digitized and made available to the broad public via online access; these official digital archives have been joined in the twenty-first century by unofficial collections of documents – what Abigail De Kosnik has called "rogue archives." In her 2016 book *Rogue Archives*, De Kosnik celebrates the flourishing of new online archives, built and managed not by professional specialists but by amateur enthusiasts. The "rogue" archivists described by De Kosnik are non-professional curators of digital archives filled with items of specialist interests, made freely available online to other enthusiasts.

When De Kosnik declares that "memory has fallen into the hands of rogues,"[15] she is referring to specialist digital archives on all themes and topics, some of them representing minority or marginalized positions such as "queer digital culture."[16] The Archive of Our Own website – a digital archive of fan fiction writing – is one such rogue archive. This archive preserves transformative texts even if the author of the original work objects to the transformation: this post-authorship policy is justified, according to Rebecca Tushnet, by the interpretation of copyright law that "noncommercial works are fair use."[17] These digital archives expand the range of cultural positions as represented in archived works and documents – enabling a broader, more inclusive, understanding of social identity.

The contemporary digital archive has been theorized as a living archive – in the senses that it is not fixed but continually growing, and that its database may be used for remix or creative reuse works. A number of theorists have re-thought the archive in the context of networking and the digital information, where the database has become the central form of knowledge. In *The Archive in Motion* (2010), Eivind Rossaak assesses digitized archives as "archives in motion" due to their dynamic, changing form, in which knowledge is continually added or transformed.[18] In *Digital Memory and the Archive* (2013) Wolfgang Ernst argues that the internet archive is modelled not on a traditional archive but on a library: it is indexed and searchable, and focuses not just on the storage of knowledge but also its transmission. Another issue specific to digital archives is that their contents are in essence one thing: data. As Ina Blom points out in *Memory in Motion* (2017), documents and contents of a digital archive "are no longer separated from the archival infrastructure"; the digital archive, based on networked data circulation, dissolves all content "into the coding and protocol layer, into electronic circuits or data flow."[19]

The digital archive is a database that can be continually drawn on in the present, to generate new works. This is particularly evident in electronic pop music, where the music database of digitally sampled songs, compositions or sounds is the archival base for new digital compositions. The archive is a database of found music and sounds, waiting to be creatively transformed into a new work.

The Australian Centre of the Moving Image (ACMI) in Melbourne has publicly stated that its intention in creating a digital archive of its collection of audio-visual works is to encourage the creative reuse of these works by other artists. Likewise, The Kaldor Public Art Projects (KPAP) digital archive (containing documentation of 36 public art works over a period of more than 50 years) is in many respects a living archive. It is incorporated into the KPAP host website, ensuring continuous public visibility of the archive and the previous projects.[20] This visibility will encourage artists, curators, and researchers to revisit archived works, perhaps re-considering or even transforming them.

The major exhibition, *Making Art Public: 50 Years of Kaldor Public Art Projects*, curated by artist Michael Landy as KPAP Project 35, and held at the Art Gallery of NSW in 2019, drew extensively on the newly digitized archive contents. The exhibition *Making Art Public* was itself a vast archival work, its images taken from the online archive. Landy in effect transformed the contents of the digital archive into a huge new artwork, composed of the 34 previous KPAP projects. This is one example of the ways in which the digital archive enables past projects to remain alive, even if in transformed or adapted state, in the present and into the future.

What then of copyright in a digital archive? A digital archive is a form of publishing, in the way that a traditional paper archive is not. Documents in a paper archive are restricted and only available on request to individual readers; by contrast, every document included in a digital archive is made public – that is, published. This has implications for documents, such as letters, digitized from a restricted paper archive and posted online in a digital archive. A letter is a private document with a possible readership of one (the addressee); indeed some letters are unsent so have no readership. In "What Is an Author?," when Michel Foucault offered examples of writing that do not have authorship – and therefore copyright – attached, he chose the letter: "a private letter may have a signatory, but it does not have an author."[21]

But this situation changes when private letters are published in the form of a book of collected letters, or a digital archive. Authors are legally considered the proprietors of their works – even letters – once they are published.[22] This legal principle means that every document published in the digital archive – including letters and notes – is protected by copyright as a work emanating from its author. To be included in a digital archive, works by an author – texts, films, compositions, maps and plans, correspondence – need to be licensed in some form, or permission to reproduce the work needs to be provided by the author. The ACMI digital archive licenses texts and audio-visual works through a Creative Commons Attribution licence (CC-BY); ACMI informs users on its website that "you may distribute, reuse and build upon" the licensed works, but ACMI must be attributed as the source. Some of the audio-visual works included in the archive appear by permission of the artist; and in some cases third party users (creative reusers of the material) must obtain permission from the copyright owner to "copy, modify or distribute that material."[23] Similarly, the rights to reproduce material from previous projects in the Kaldor Public Art Projects Digital Archive was granted in permission agreements with the original artists; third party use (reuse) of those materials requires extra permission from the artists – the rights holders.

Legal Deposit libraries, established in many nations, function in the internet age as electronic legal deposit libraries, as their holdings include not only digitized books but music, films, and other digital content. Legal Deposit libraries are also known as "Copyright Libraries" because they are strictly bound by national copyright legislation, just as they are required to acquire copies of all texts published in the respective nations. National libraries and archives are actively engaged in curating the digital publishing environment worldwide, while observing the rights of authors.

In other instances, however, notably the "rogue archives" celebrated by De Kosnik, no such rightsholder restrictions apply. The Archive Of Our Own website, for example, makes clear to users that the archive's goal is "maximum inclusiveness," including maximum potential for creative reuse. Even the software underpinning the digital archive is open-source and available to all users.[24] Many of the rogue archives function not as guardians of authors' rights, but as large-scale donors to the online gift economy.

Copyright: For, against, Minimalist, Reform

In 2015, publisher Phillipa McGuiness edited a collection of essays entitled *Copyfight*. Contributors to this volume included writers, journalists, editors, publishers, musicians, filmmakers, and academics. Their debating point was copyright against copyleft; authors' rights against the conviction that copyright material should be freely available to all online. As McGuinness notes, "debates about copyright are emotional and passionate"; in *Copyfight*, the opposing viewpoints often took a moral stance.[25]

Academics Dan Hunter and Nicolas Suzor take a moral position – against copyright – in their essay "Claiming the moral high ground in the copyright wars." Hunter and Suzor applaud the capacity of the internet to bypass traditional gate-keepers – editors, publishers – and open content directly to "produsers": "empowered reader-authors and creator-users." "We are living in a wonderful world of abundant creativity," they argue. "Technological change has brought the tools required to create and distribute books, music and films to billions."[26] Hunter and Suzor find unhelpful the moral claim made by authors' advocates that illegal appropriation of copyright materials is "taking away their livelihood." This is because copyright does not in fact favour artists, but rather "helps large producers and distributors in film, television and publishing industries."[27] They conclude that the emotional plea to protect authors' livelihoods by observing copyright is misguided, due to economic reality: that the copyright regime enriches rights holders and publishers – not authors – while blocking the flow of culture to the consumer/user.

Writer Linda Jaivin takes the opposite view in her essay "Big Content." She states her own economic reality: that "copyright enables writers to live by their writing"; and that illegal downloading deprives authors of that ability. She makes the further point that discussion of rights in the online copyright debate has focused largely on consumers' rights: the right to access content whenever they wish, without paying for it. Authors' rights, by comparison, are ignored – or, at most, grudgingly considered as an irritation. Jaivin is also sceptical of the "anti-establishment" attitude adopted by free culture advocates: Google, she notes, *is* the establishment, along with other "world-dominating technology and entertainment conglomerates" such as Amazon and Apple.[28]

The critical focus by Hunter and Suzor – on media/publishing conglomerates or "Big Content" – compared with Jaivin's critique of "Big Tech" – the gigantic online technology corporations – brings into relief the perspective, articulated by writer Louis Menand, that at bottom the argument about copyright is "a battle between interest groups."[29] William Deresiewicz makes the same point in *The Death of the Artist*, while also offering a comparison in scale between the rival interest groups. Deresiewicz observes that in 2020, the top five US Big Media companies (with an interest in protecting copyright) had a combined market value of $772 billion US. In the same year, the top five Big Tech corporations were valued at $5.5 trillion, more than seven times as much (and, Deresiewicz remarks, larger than the GDP of all but two countries).[30] Big Tech, that is, dwarfs Big Media; and the Silicon Valley ideology of free culture – often in disregard of author's rights – commands a correspondingly high cultural position.

Despite the colossal scale of these rival financial interest groups, efforts to preserve – and reform – copyright law have been made by an array of theorists, lawyers, and reformers. Opponents of the current "bloated" copyright regime nevertheless seek to ensure the ongoing observation of copyright law. Lawrence Lessig wrote in *Remix* that copyright is "critically important to a healthy culture." He continues: "Properly balanced, it is essential to inspiring certain forms of creativity."[31] The "properly balanced" proviso is crucial: critics of copyright regulation charge that it favours rights owners, not authors. Even William Deresiewicz, staunch defender of author's rights, admits that copyright "can certainly be abused, especially by entertainment companies with lots of lawyers on their payroll." He acknowledges that corporations have been "overzealous" in prosecuting individuals for online creative reuse, and that the law could be amended "as needed," perhaps to reduce the extent of copyright protection (life of author plus 70 years) in the US.[32] Robert Darnton has noted that in most cases, authors "derive little income from a book a year or two after its publication."[33] Extending protection of the work until 70 years after the author's death is of no benefit to the author; this attenuated term benefits only the rights holders – publishers or perhaps the author's estate.

Reduction of this extended term is one of the calls for copyright reform made by copyright minimalists, who seek a reduced form of copyright – enough copyright to prevent piracy, but not enough to prevent the flow of creativity. Another demand, as articulated by Daniela Simone in 2019, is that copyright law "should seek closer alignment with the creative reality of film authorship"[34] (or all forms of collective authorship), so that copyright comes to benefit the creative practitioners rather than the owners (producers and companies).

A glimpse of what a minimalist copyright law could look like was offered in 2016 by the Australian Government Productivity Commission report entitled *Copy(not)right*. This report did not reflect the views of free culture zealots or copyleft ideologues; rather, it arose from a nine-month inquiry into intellectual property law by sober economists, whose role is to form policy likely to boost productivity in the Australian economy. The report was highly critical of the extension of copyright protection for 70 years past the author's death, which was deemed extremely excessive: "The evidence (and indeed logic) suggests that the duration of copyright protection is far more than is needed. Few, if any, creators are motivated by the promise of financial returns long after death." Copyright protection "is cast too widely and lasts too long," the report concluded.[35] The recommendation was that copyright protection should be limited to 25 years, which was much closer to the typical commercial life of a book, film, or piece of music. Other recommendations included the adoption of an "open-ended and non-prescriptive" right of fair use, which would allow the quotation of song fragments in songs and the use of film excerpts in documentaries. The report also recommended that "orphan works," where no rights holder is known, should be freely digitized and published, and that non-commercial offering of works, for example on not-for-profit websites, should also be enabled.

The Productivity Commission predicted that these reforms would save consumers up to $1 billion AUS per year. However, the Australian Government rejected the report's recommendations in 2017. The law reform proposals outlined in this report were perhaps too radical for a government to implement in 2017; but they give some indication of a minimalist, balanced copyright regime of the future. For the moment, reformists are left to imagine that there's still copyright, only a lot smaller, and more effective.

Epilogue: The Near-Death, Not the Death, of the Author

I call this book *The Near-Death of the Author* because I believe that, despite all the challenges confronting authorship in the internet age, the author has survived – and will survive.

I do not believe that Roland Barthes was pronouncing the author's last rites in 1968 – but he was correct in declaring the demise of the Romantic Author, replaced by something like a neo-scriptor of post-structuralist dimensions. The "near-death of the author" in one sense relates to Barthes's denunciation of the God-like author, whose intention in creating a work is the key to the interpretation of that work. Today we don't look to the author to explain a work, when the opinion of any reader, listener or viewer is deemed equally valid. These validated acts of interpretation represent the triumph of Barthes's prediction of the writerly reader, also known as the active audience, or the flux of language itself as the generator of texts. The author, however, is not totally eclipsed in this world of interpretation: the author's voice may still be heard, and some readers at least may still be interested to hear it.

The challenges to the contemporary author all post-date Barthes's time; they arise from the ascendancy of internet culture, from the mid-1990s. The practices considered in this book include: the illegal downloading and streaming of copyright material; the disrespect for authors' rights in online free culture; the unlicensed use and reuse of authors' works; collective authorship; "transformative" practices such as fan fiction; works created by AI; and algorithm-as-author artworks.

The wholesale infringement of copyright, and the blatant disregard for author's rights, present the gravest problem for the contemporary author. Authorship was not threatened with extinction by "The Death of the Author"; but many actual authors have ceased their creative activity in the twenty-first century, due to the disappearance of royalties in an era of illegal downloading and streaming.

I agree with those critics of the copyright regime who assert that an author does not require the "incentive to create" provided by copyright. There are numerous areas of prolific cultural activity – such as graffiti writing – where copyright is not a factor. But the author deserves to make a living, or at least some income, from the labour of creation that may take many years. If an author is a cultural producer, then creative labour undertaken by the author should be recompensed, in the same way that agricultural, industrial, or post-industrial producers are recompensed for their labour.

The charges against the current "bloated" copyright regime have been well made. Too often, prosecution for copyright infringement has been activated for the benefit of rights holders – publishers, corporations – rather than for creative practitioners: authors. I endorse calls for copyright law reform, so that the law supports authors rather than owners of copyright. I also endorse calls to reduce the extended term of copyright protection to something like 25 years, and to legislate an expanded fair use, which would accommodate the sampling or quotation of copyrighted texts within other texts, in the creative reuse manner. Copyright remains the best means of ensuring income for published authors; the internet-age alternative – crowd funding or the new patronage – is problematic in that it requires the author to double as administrator/accountant/entrepreneur, often for minimal returns.

The disregard for copyright in the internet age may have brought authorship to a state of near-death; but authorship persists, and authors will continue to create and publish. The technological feats of AI and sophisticated algorithms may be capable of producing works of art; but these digital scriptors will not replace the author. Indeed, authors will marshal the abilities of algorithms to generate works from databases, forging new modes of creative practice and new types of art works.

Throughout this book, I have noted variants of the contemporary author-function: author as factory, author as scriptor, author as processor, multimodal author, collaborative author, remix author, author for the new patronage, blockchain author, and even author as demiurge. These reflect the ways in which the contemporary author has adjusted to the changed circumstances within networked digital culture. They are all aspects of the remarkably flexible contemporary author: the author adapts, the author survives.

Notes

Introduction

1 Karl Marx, *The Communist Manifesto*, p. 58.

1. "Heroes with Names": What Is the Author?

1 Michel Foucault, "What Is an Author?," p. 125.
2 Mark Rose, *Authors and Owners*, p. 1.
3 Rose, p. 3.
4 Rose, p. 85.
5 Ronald V. Bettig, *Copyrighting Culture*, pp. 3, 15.
6 Bettig, p. 7.
7 Seán Burke, *Authorship: From Plato to the Postmodern*, p. xviii. Minnis traces the etymology of 'auctor' in *Medieval Theory of Authorship*, p. 10.
8 Andrew Bennett, *The Author*, pp. 6, 41.
9 Meskin, pp. 125, 130.
10 Alexander Nehamas, "What an Author Is," pp. 689–90.
11 Foucault, "What Is an Author?," pp. 124, 128.
12 Aaron Meskin, "Authorship," p. 25. Meskin, p. 19, quotes Geoffrey Nowell-Smith on the "fiction" of the author in "Six Authors in Pursuit of *The Searchers*."
13 Molly Nesbit, "What Was an Author?," p. 255.
14 Foucault, "What Is an Author?," p. 113; *The Order of Things*, p. 387.
15 Ian Maclean, "The Process of Intellectual Change: A Post-Foucauldian Analysis," p. 166; Mark Bevir, *The Logic of the History of Ideas*, pp. 33, 311. I examine Foucauldian and post-Foucauldian intellectual history in more detail in John Potts, *Ideas in Time: The Longue Durée in Intellectual History*.
16 Nesbit, "What Was an Author?," pp. 248, 256.
17 Daniela Simone, *Copyright and Collective Authorship*, pp. 17–18.

18 Lyman Ray Patterson, *Copyright in Historical Perspective* (1968); Benjamin Kaplan, *An Unhurried View of Copyright* (1967); Martha Woodmansee, "The Genius and the Copyright: Economic and Legal Conditions of the Emergence of the Author" (1984).
19 Many critiques of the "overzealous" enforcement of copyright as the enemy of creative expression emerged in the first decade of the twenty-first century, including: Lawrence Lessig, *Free Culture: How Big Media Uses Technology and the Law to Lock Down Culture and Control Creativity* (2004); Kembrew McLeod, *Freedom of Expression: Overzealous Copyright Bozos and Other Enemies of Creativity* (2005); Joanna Demers, *Steal This Music: How Intellectual Property Law Affects Musical Creativity* (2006); and Matthew Rimmer, *Digital Copyright and the Consumer Revolution: Get Your Hands Off My Ipod* (2007).
20 The "gift economy," a term originally used in anthropology to describe traditional societies, was used from the late 1990s to describe the culture of sharing on the internet, as in Richard Barbrook's 1998 article "The High-Tech Gift Economy."
21 Mark Amerika, "What in the World Wide Web Is Happening to Writing?," web article, 2000, cited in Murphie and Potts, *Culture and Technology*, p. 3.
22 Amerika, p. 3.
23 Van Morrison, "Big Time Operators," *Too Long in Exile*, 1993.
24 Sandra M. Gilbert and Susan Gubar, *The Madwoman in the Attic*, p. 152.
25 Thomas Carlyle, *On Heroes, Hero-Worship, and the Heroic in History*, p. 34.
26 Henry Diltz, "Harvest," p. 79.
27 Foucault, "What Is an Author?," p. 124.
28 Simon Fuller and James O'Sullivan, "Structure Over Style: Collaborative Authorship and the Revival of Literary Capitalism," paragraph 4, paragraph 15.
29 Fuller and O'Sullivan, paragraph 15.
30 Steven Butler and James Patterson, *Dog Diaries*. The copyright statement reads: "James Patterson has asserted his right to be identified as the author of this Work in accordance with the Copyright, Designs and Patents Act 1988."
31 Patterson quoted by Fuller and O'Sullivan, "Structure Over Style," paragraph 15.
32 Fuller and O'Sullivan, paragraph 1.
33 Patterson quoted by Fuller and O'Sullivan, "Structure Over Style," paragraph 40.
34 Fuller and O'Sullivan, paragraph 16.
35 Walter Benjamin, "The Paris of the Second Empire in Baudelaire," cited by Fuller and O'Sullivan, paragraph 18.
36 Benjamin cited by Fuller and O'Sullivan, paragraph 19.

37 Fuller and O'Sullivan, paragraph 19.
38 Fuller and O'Sullivan, paragraph 15.
39 John T. Paoletti and Gary M. Radke, *Art in Renaissance Italy*, pp. 18, 28.
40 Fuller and O'Sullivan, paragraph 1.
41 Fuller and O'Sullivan, paragraphs 1, 15.

2. "I Don't Own It": Contemporary Complications

1 *The Concise Oxford Dictionary*, Ninth Edition, "inspire," p. 704.
2 The Beatles, *Anthology*, p. 319.
3 Tom Pinnock, "Move! Down the Road," *Uncut*, November 2020, p. 75.
4 "Aoife Nessa Frances, Q & A," *Uncut*, February 2020, p. 21.
5 Kurt Vile, "Goldtone," *Wakin on a Pretty Daze*, 2013.
6 Murad Akhundov, in *Conceptions of Space and Time*, p. 35, uses the term "bipresence" to describe the "supernatural" or "mystical" appreciation of territory by tribal peoples. I discuss mythological time and space in more detail in *The New Time and Space*, pp. 8–14.
7 Christopher Dell, *The Occult, Witchcraft & Magic*, p. 26.
8 Plato, *Ion*, p. 15.
9 Plato, *Ion*, p. 16.
10 John Potts, *A History of Charisma*, pp. 35–50.
11 Samuel Taylor Coleridge, "Kubla Khan" in *The Rime of the Ancient Mariner and Three Other Poems*, p. 100.
12 Rita Matulionyte et. al., "The System of Book Creation: Intellectual Property and the Self-Publishing Sector of the Creative Industries," pp. 192–3.
13 The Beatles, *Anthology*, p. 175.
14 Sigmund Freud, *The Interpretation of Dreams*, p. 769.
15 Freud, *The Interpretation of Dreams*, p. 58.
16 Sigmund Freud, "Creative Writers and Day-Dreaming," p. 54.
17 André Breton, *Surrealist Manifesto*, quoted in Uwe M. Schneede, *Surrealism*, p. 21.
18 The eclipse of Freudian theory and practice – in psychiatry and intellectual culture – is reflected in the psychiatry profession's *Diagnostic and Statistical Manual of Mental Disorders (DSM)*. Louis Menand observes in his article "Headcase: Can Psychiatry Be a Science?," p. 71, that the first two editions of the *DSM* in 1952 and 1968 "reflected the psychoanalytical theories of Freud"; but the third edition in 1980 "began a process of scrubbing Freudianism out of the manual, and giving mental health a new language."
19 The Beatles, *Anthology*, p. 175.
20 Samuel Taylor Coleridge, "Kubla Khan," p. 93.
21 Coleridge, "Kubla Khan," pp. 93–4.

22. William Christie, *Samuel Taylor Coleridge: A Literary Life*, p. 87.
23. Randy Kennedy, "News Flows, Consciousness Streams: The Headwaters of a River of Words," online article.
24. *Street Art and Law*, 1 May 2016, at: https://streetartandlaw.wordpress.com/2016/05/01/rime-vs-moschino-does-illegal-street-art-have-copyright-protection/. Accessed 12 April 2021.
25. Marta Iljadica, *Copyright Beyond Law*, p. 3.
26. Chris Johnson, "Banksy Auction Prank Leaves Art World in Shreds," *The Guardian Online*.
27. Michael Faber, "Tree of Codes by Jonathan Safran Foer – Review," *The Guardian Online*.
28. Faber, "Tree of Codes by Jonathan Safran Foer – Review."
29. Alex Ross, *The Rest Is Noise*, p. 401.
30. Faber, "Tree of Codes by Jonathan Safran Foer – Review."
31. Katherine Brinson quoted in Calvin Tomkins, "The Whole Thing Is Crazy," p. 53.
32. Calvin Tomkins, "The Whole Thing Is Crazy," p. 46.
33. Tomkins, "The Whole Thing Is Crazy," p. 50.
34. Andrew Taylor, "Fallout over Portrait Win Calls Copyright into Question," p. 9.
35. Daniela Simone, *Copyright and Collective Authorship*, p. 62. Simone cites the work of Jane Ginsburg in characterizing "how legal systems typically attempt to identify the author of a copyright work." Simone also notes case law instances that may contradict the general principle of recognizing conceptual oversight of the work as authorship.

3. Who Is the Author / Who Are the Authors?

1. Martha Woodmansee, "On the Author Effect: Recovering Collectivity," p. 15.
2. Woodmansee, p. 24.
3. Foucault, "What Is an Author?," p. 115.
4. Woodmansee, "On the Author Effect: Recovering Collectivity," p. 25.
5. Aspects of collaboration and co-authorship in Shakespeare's plays have been thoroughly explored in recent scholarship including: Brian Vickers, *Shakespeare, Co-Author* (2002); Jeffrey Masten, *Textual Intercourse: Collaboration, Authorship, and Sexualities in Renaissance Drama* (1997); Gordon McMullan, "'Our Whole Life Is Like a Play': Collaboration and the Problem of Editing" (1996); and Lucy Munro, *Shakespeare in the Theatre: The King's Men* (2020).
6. Sherman Young, *The Book Is Dead, Long Live the Book*, p. 6.
7. Andrew Sarris, "Notes on the Auteur Theory in 1962," quoted by Aaron Meskin, "Authorship," p. 18.

8 Andrew Sarris, "Towards a Theory of Film History," p. 250.
9 Meskin, "Authorship," p. 13.
10 Karen Pearlman, "Editing and Authorship," p. 1.
11 Anthony Lane, "The Mark of Kane," pp. 76–7.
12 Aaron Meskin, "Authorship," p. 13, quotes Howard Koch, "A Playwright Looks at the 'Filmwright'"; and Bordwell and Thompson, *Film Art: An Introduction*, p. 12.
13 Daniela Simone, *Copyright and Collective Authorship*, p. 66.
14 Simone, *Copyright and Collective Authorship*, p. 164.
15 Simone, *Copyright and Collective Authorship*, p. 162.
16 Simone, *Copyright and Collective Authorship*, p. 159.
17 James Naremore, "Authorship," cited by Simone, *Copyright and Collective Authorship*, p. 161n10.
18 Berys Gaut, "Film Authorship and Collaboration," cited by Aaron Meskin, "Authorship," p. 23.
19 André Bazin, "La Politique des Auteurs," quoted by Bill Nicols, *Movies and Methods*, p. 151.
20 This approach was given book-length treatment in Tom Schatz's 1996 book *The Genius of the System: Hollywood Filmmaking in the Studio Era*.
21 John Potts, *A History of Charisma*, p. 166.
22 Jim Kitses, *Horizons West*, cited by Bill Nicols, *Movies and Methods*, p. 237.
23 Daniela Simone, *Copyright and Collective Authorship*, p. 161.
24 Paul Wells, *Animation: Genre and Authorship*, p. 90.
25 Stephanie Burt, "Flame On," p. 73.
26 John Caughie, *Theories of Authorship: A Reader*, p. 10.
27 Andrew Bennett, *The Author*, p. 104.
28 Bennett, *The Author*, p. 106, p. 107.
29 Dana Polan, "Auteur Desire," p. 1.
30 Robert Self, "Robert Altman and the Theory of Authorship," p. 4.
31 Georges Sadoul, *Dictionary of Film Makers*, p. vi.
32 Karen Pearlman and John Sutton, "Reframing the Director: Distributed Creativity in Filmmaking Practice," p. 1.
33 Julia Wright, "Female Editors and Representation in the Film and Media Industry," p. 10.
34 Viki Callahan, "Re-Writing Authorship" in Callahan (ed.) *Reclaiming the Archive: Feminism and Film History*.
35 Shelley Stamp, "Feminist Media Historiography and the Work Ahead," p. 6.
36 Karen Pearlman and Jane M. Gaines, "After the Facts: These Edits Are My Thoughts" at https://wfpp.columbia.edu/2020/03/16/after-the-facts/. Accessed 6 January 2021.
37 Daniela Simone, *Copyright and Collective Authorship*, p. 197.
38 Simone, *Copyright and Collective Authorship*, p. 199.
39 Pierre Levy, "Toward Superlanguage," p. 14.

40 Levy, "Toward Superlanguage," p. 12.
41 Jay Rosen wrote of "the people formerly known as the audience" in an online blog in 2006. His essay with that title was included in *The Social Media Reader*, 2012. The term "prosumer" was coined in 1980 by Alvin Toffler; it was revived in the wake of Web 2.0 and used by numerous new media theorists.
42 Adam Thierer provides a list including most of these books in his 2010 essay "The Case for Internet Optimism, Part 1: Saving the Net from Its Detractors."
43 Steve Lohr, "Web Inventor Hits Back at Tech Giants' Online Power," p. 9.
44 Louis Menand, "What Do You Know?," pp. 67–8.
45 Joseph Reagle and Jackie Koerner, "Introduction: Connections," *Wikipedia@20: Stories of an Incomplete Revolution*, p. 2.
46 Jimmy Wales quoted by Joseph Reagle and Jackie Koerner, "Introduction: Connections," p. 4.
47 Louis Menand, "What Do You Know?," p. 68.
48 Simon Winchester, *The Surgeon of Crowthorne*, p. 93.
49 Winchester, *The Surgeon of Crowthorne*, p. 94.
50 Louis Menand, "What Do You Know?," p. 68.
51 Daniela Simone, *Copyright and Collective Authorship*, p. 74.
52 Simone, *Copyright and Collective Authorship*, p. 73.
53 Simone, *Copyright and Collective Authorship*, p. 79.
54 Simone, *Copyright and Collective Authorship*, p. 91.
55 Sean Cubitt, *Digital Aesthetics*, p. 143.
56 Simone, *Copyright and Collective Authorship*, p. 77.
57 Simone, *Copyright and Collective Authorship*, p. 73.
58 Gunther Kress, *Multimodality*, p. 159.
59 Mark Amerika, "What in the World Wide Web Is Happening to Writing?," p. 3.

4. A Brief History of the Author

1 H.W.F. Saggs, *The Babylonians*, p. 45.
2 Felipe Fernández-Armesto, *Ideas That Changed the World*, pp. 9–10.
3 Karen Armstrong, *A Short History of Myth*, p. 25.
4 Roy Willis, *World Mythology*, p. 16.
5 Karen Armstrong, *A Short History of Myth*, p. 34.
6 David Hockney and Martin Gayford, *A History of Pictures*, p. 25.
7 Mircea Eliade, *The Myth of the Eternal Return*, p. 35.
8 Sophus Helle, "What Is an Author? Old Answers to a New Question," pp. 113–14.
9 Helle, "What Is an Author?," pp. 113, 124.

10 Walter J. Ong, *Orality and Literacy*, p. 21.
11 Ong, *Orality and Literacy*, p. 23.
12 Ong, *Orality and Literacy*, pp. 31–49.
13 Ong, *Orality and Literacy*, p. 60.
14 Ong, *Orality and Literacy*, p. 60.
15 Helle, "What Is an Author?" p. 135.
16 Ronald V. Bettig, *Copyrighting Culture*, p. 13.
17 Daniela Simone, *Copyright and Collective Authorship*, p. 104.
18 Jo Dyer quoted in Matthew Rimmer, "Bangarra Dance Theatre: Copyright Law and Indigenous Culture," p. 278.
19 Matthew Rimmer, "Bangarra Dance Theatre: Copyright Law and Indigenous Culture," p. 278.
20 John Man, *Alpha Beta: How Our Alphabet Changed the Western* World (London: Headline, 2000).
21 Steven Roger Fisher, *A History of Writing*, p. 52.
22 H.W.F. Saggs, *The Babylonians*, p. 35.
23 Saggs, *The Babylonians*, pp. 309–10.
24 Saggs, *The Babylonians*, p. 309.
25 Alberto Manguel, *A History of Reading*, p. 182.
26 Manguel, *A History of Reading*, pp. 182–3.
27 Andrew Bennett, *The Author*, p. 29.
28 Plato, *The Republic*, p. 375.
29 Plato, *The Republic*, pp. 374–5.
30 Plato, *The Republic*, pp. 375–6.
31 Plato, *The Republic*, p. 363.
32 Plato, *The Republic*, p. 367.
33 Walter J. Ong, *Orality and Literacy*, pp. 78, 82.
34 Ong, *Orality and Literacy*, p. 167.
35 Ong, *Orality and Literacy*, p. 80, citing Eric Havelock, *Preface to Plato*.
36 Jacques Gernet, *A History of Chinese Civilization*, p. 270.
37 Saint Bonaventure, *Commentaries on the First Book of Sentences of Master Peter Lombard, Archbishop of Paris*, cited by Andrew Bennett, *The Author*, pp. 38–9.
38 Andrew Bennett, *The Author*, p. 39; J.A. Burrow, *Medieval Writers and Their Work*, p. 29, quoted by Sophus Helle, "What Is an Author? Old Answers to a New Question," p. 116.
39 Bennett, *The Author*, p. 40.
40 Donald Pease, "Author," quoted by Bennett, *The Author*, p. 40.
41 Seán Burke, *Authorship: From Plato to the Postmodern*, p. 7.
42 A.J. Minnis, *Medieval Theory of Authorship*; Donald Pease, "Author"; and J.A. Burrow, *Medieval Writers and Their Work*, cited by Bennett, *The Author*, pp. 39–40.

43 J.A. Burrow, *Medieval Writers and Their Work*, p. 32.
44 Vasari's *Lives of the Artists* quoted by George Henderson, *Gothic Art and Civilisation*, p. 28.
45 Henderson, *Gothic Art and Civilisation*, p. 6.
46 Henderson, *Gothic Art and Civilisation*, pp. 3, 20.
47 Henderson, *Gothic Art and Civilisation*, p. 7.
48 Helle, "What Is an Author?" pp. 131–2.
49 A.J. Minnis, *Medieval Theory of Authorship*, p. 5.
50 Bianca Del Villano, "Dramatic Adaptation, Authorship, and Cultural Identity in the Eighteenth Century: The Case of Samuel Foote," cited by Sophus Helle, "What Is an Author?," p. 131.
51 Danielle Bohler, "Frontally and in Profile: The Identifying Gesture of the Late Medieval Author," cited by Helle, "What Is an Author?," p. 131; Dante's *Inferno* quoted by Helle, p. 126.
52 Andrew Bennett, *The Author*, p. 42.
53 Stephanie Trigg, *Congenial Souls: Reading Chaucer from Medieval to Postmodern*, cited by Bennett, *The Author*, p. 43.
54 A.J. Minnis, *Medieval Theory of Authorship*, in Burke p. 28.
55 Bennett, *The Author*, quotes J.A. Burrow, *Medieval Writers and Their Work*, p. 41; and Burt Kimmelman, *The Poetics of Authorship in the Later Middle Ages: The Emergence of the Modern Literary Persona*, p. 41.
56 Elizabeth Eisenstein, *The Printing Press as an Agent of Change*, Vol. 1, p. 33.
57 Walter J. Ong, *Orality and Literacy*, pp. 130–1.
58 Ong, *Orality and Literacy*, p. 130.
59 Roger Chartier, *The Order of Books*, pp. 39, 43.
60 Chartier, *The Order of Books*, p. 44.
61 Harold Bloom, *The Western Canon* and *Shakespeare and the Invention of the Human Being*, cited by Melvyn Bragg, *12 Books That Changed the World*, p. 330.
62 Gerald Eades Bentley, *The Profession of Dramatist in Shakespeare's Time 1590–1642*, p. 56.
63 Bentley, *The Profession of Dramatist in Shakespeare's Time*, pp. 52–3.
64 Melvyn Bragg, *12 Books That Changed the World*, p. 326.
65 The *First Folio* Preface, quoted by Bragg, *12 Books That Changed the World*, p. 36.
66 Bentley, *The Profession of Dramatist in Shakespeare's Time*, p. 57.
67 Peter Ackroyd, *Shakespeare: The Biography*, pp. 240, 242.
68 Bentley, *The Profession of Dramatist in Shakespeare's Time*, p. 82.
69 Ackroyd, *Shakespeare: The Biography*, p. 330. An alternative view, of Shakespeare as an author who intended his plays for both performance and publication, has been made by Lukas Erne and other Shakespearean scholars. Erne argues in his 2003 book *Shakespeare as Literary Dramatist* that Shakespeare wrote plays – including *Hamlet* – far longer than the two-hour

performance limit, because he intended for them to be published, perhaps in a Folio edition in his lifetime. This argument, however, remains largely speculative.
70 Elizabeth Eisenstein, *The Printing Press as an Agent of Change*, Vol. 1, p. 121.
71 Mark Rose, *Authors and Owners: The Invention of Copyright*, p. 2.
72 Roger Chartier, *The Order of Books*, p. 33, discussing author's rights in France, with reference to Mark Rose's analysis of copyright in England.
73 Rose, *Authors and Owners: The Invention of Copyright*, pp. 32, 35. Rose cites scholarship on the history of the legislation, including Harry Ransom, *The First Copyright Statute*, and John Feather, "The Book Trade in Politics: The Making of the Copyright Act of 1710."
74 Rose, *Authors and Owners*, p. 47, citing Lyman Ray Patterson, *Copyright in Historical Perspective*.
75 Rose, *Authors and Owners*, p. 64.
76 Alvin Kernan, *Printing Technology, Letters & Samuel Johnson*, pp. 47, 105.
77 Rose, *Authors and Owners*, p. 114, quoting Justice Aston in *Millar v. Taylor*, 1750.
78 Rose, *Authors and Owners*, pp. 116–17.
79 Edward Young, "Conjectures on Original Composition" in Seán Burke, *Authorship: From Plato to the Postmodern*, p. 37.
80 Rose, *Authors and Owners*, pp. 117–18, quoting Young, "Conjectures on Original Composition."
81 Young, "Conjectures on Original Composition," quoted by Rose, *Authors and Owners*, p. 119.
82 Terry Eagleton, *The Ideology of the Aesthetic*, pp. 64–5.
83 Rose, *Authors and Owners*, p. 6, citing Samuel Johnson, "Life of Milton."
84 Monika Dommann, *Authors and Apparatus*, p. 146.
85 Lawrence Lessig, *Code and Other Laws of Cyberspace*, p. 124.
86 Wordsworth, Preface to *Lyrical Ballads*, quoted by Andrew Bennett, *The Author*, p. 63: Coleridge, *Biographia Litteraria* and Blake, quoted by Bennett, p. 61.
87 Percy Bysshe Shelley, "A Defence of Poetry" in Seán Burke, *Authorship: From Plato to the Postmodern*, pp. 45, 50.
88 J. Peter Burkholder at. al., *History of Western Music*, p. 537.
89 Shelley, "A Defence of Poetry," pp. 45, 49–50.
90 William Wordsworth, "Essay, Supplementary to the Preface," quoted by Martha Woodmansee, "On the Author Effort: Recovering Collectivity," p. 16.
91 Darrin McMahon, *Divine Fury: a History of Genius*, pp. xiv, xix, 130.
92 Martha Woodmansee, "The Genius and the Copyright: Economic and Legal Conditions of the Emergence of the 'Author.'"
93 Andrew Bennett, *The Author*, p. 60.
94 Shelley, "A Defence of Poetry," p. 46.
95 Bennett, *The Author*, pp. 40, 54.

5. The Alleged Death of the Author: Post-structuralism and Postmodernism

1 Seán Burke, *The Death and Return of the Author*, p. 178.
2 Terence Hawkes, *Structuralism and Semiotics*, p. 59.
3 Osip Brik, "The So-Called Formal Method," quoted by Seán Burke, *The Death and Return of the Author*, p. 24.
4 Terence Hawkes makes this point in *Structuralism and Semiotics*, pp. 62–3.
5 Mikhail Bakhtin, *The Dialogic Imagination*, p. 49.
6 Bakhtin quoted in Seán Burke, *The Death and Return of the Author*, p. 46.
7 Vladimir Propp, *Morphology of the Folktale*, p. xxv.
8 Claude Lévi-Strauss, *The Raw and the Cooked*, pp. 11–12.
9 Lévi-Strauss, *The Savage Mind*, quoted by Seán Burke, *The Death and Return of the Author*, p. 13.
10 Saussure, *Course in General Linguistics*, quoted by Rosalind Coward and John Ellis, *Language and Materialism*, p. 25.
11 Roland Barthes, *Elements of Semiology*, p. 12.
12 Lacan first wrote of the unconscious as "structured like a language" in 1957. This concept was developed in later publications, including *Ecrits* (1966) and *The Four Fundamental Concepts of Psycho-Analysis* (1973), pp. 20–8.
13 Roland Barthes, *Sade/Fourier/Loyola*, pp. 7–9.
14 Wimsatt Jr, W.K. and Beardsley, Monroe C., "The Intentional Fallacy," p. 90.
15 *First Proclamation of the Weimar Bauhaus*, by Walter Gropius, quoted in Chris Bohn, "We Have No Body to Listen To," p. 98. Gropius on art and technology cited by Magdalena Droste, *Bauhaus 1919–1933*, p. 58.
16 Robert Hughes, *The Shock of the New*, p. 95.
17 Peter Schjeldahl, "What Are Artists For?," p. 92.
18 Pierre Macherey, *A Theory of Literary Production*, quoted by Andrew Bennett, *The Author*, p. 16.
19 Sandra M. Gilbert and Susan Gubar, *The Madwoman in the Attic*, p. 152, citing Edward Said's etymology of "author" in his *Beginnings: Intention and Method*.
20 Nancy K. Miller, "Changing the Subject: Authorship, Writing and the Reader," p. 195.
21 Roland Barthes, "The Death of the Author," pp. 142–4.
22 Barthes, "The Death of the Author," pp. 143, 145–6.
23 Barthes, "The Death of the Author," p. 146.
24 Barthes, "The Death of the Author," pp. 146–7.
25 Barthes, "The Death of the Author," p. 147.
26 Barthes, "The Death of the Author," p. 148.
27 Roland Barthes, *S/Z*, p. 106, p. 107.
28 Seán Burke, *The Death and Return of the Author*, p. 69.

29 Jacques Derrida, "Signature, Event, Context" (1977), quoted by Seán Burke, *The Death and Return of the Author*, p. 135; Derrida, *Signéponge/Signsponge* (1984), quoted by Andrew Bennett, *The Author*, p. 82.
30 Roland Barthes, *Sade/Fourier/Loyola*, p. 8.
31 Roland Barthes, *The Pleasure of the Text*, p. 27.
32 DJ Shadow, *Entroducing …*, MCA Music Ltd/Mowax Music Ltd, 1996.
33 Andrew Goodwin, "Sample and Hold," p. 258.
34 Jorge Luis Borges, *Ficciones*, p. 52.
35 Frederic Jameson, "Postmodernism, or the Cultural Logic of Late Capitalism," p. 114.

6. The Author and Technology: Downloading vs. Copyright

1 Giles Tremlett, "Spanish Novelist Lucia Etxeberria Quits Writing in Piracy Protest," *The Guardian*, 20 December 2011, at: https://www.theguardian.com/books/2011/dec/20/spanish-novelist-quits-piracy-protest. Accessed 3 April 2021.
2 William Deresiewicz, *The Death of the Artist*, p. 6.
3 Deresiewicz, *The Death of the Artist*, p. 10.
4 Tracy McNeil quoted by Michael Dwyer, "Reluctant Musicians' Hands Out with New Spotify 'Tip Jar,'" *Sydney Morning Herald*, 28 April 2020, p. 28.
5 Deresiewicz, *The Death of the Artist*, pp. 42–3, 135. Remnick quoted on p. 135.
6 Mark Savage, "Musicians Will Lose Two-Thirds of Their Income in 2020."
7 Jonathan Taplin, "Napster, Spotify and the Fall of the 'Middle-Class Musician,'" excerpt from Taplin's *Move Fast and Break Things*, *Rolling Stone*, 3 May 2017, at: https://www.rollingstone.com/culture/culture-news/napster-spotify-and-the-fall-of-the-middle-class-musician-116858/. Accessed 3 April 2021.
8 Monika Dommann, *Authors and Apparatus*, p. 5.
9 Lawrence Lessig, *Code and Other Laws of Cyberspace*, p. 125.
10 Mark Rose, *Authors and Owners*, p. 3.
11 William Deresiewicz, *The Death of the Artist*, p. 293.
12 Scott Timberg, *Culture Crash: The Killing of the Creative Class*. Deresiewicz acknowledges that he builds on Timberg's research in *The Death of the Artist*, p. 26.
13 Jonathan Taplin, *Move Fast and Break Things*, p. 102.
14 Taplin, *Move Fast and Break Things*, p. 103.
15 Digital Millennium Copyright Act quoted by Taplin, *Move Fast and Break Things*, p. 100.
16 Taplin, *Move Fast and Break Things*, p. 101.
17 William Deresiewicz, *The Death of the Artist*, p. 304.

18 Jennifer Duke, "Google Allows Crime, Says Village Boss," p. 20.
19 Zoe Samios, "Google Moves to Block Movies Piracy Loophole," p. 27.
20 Jan Zwar, David Throsby and Thomas Longden, *Australian Authors: Industry Brief No. 1: Key Findings*, pp. 3, 6. Other research papers and reports from this three-year research project include: Jan Zwar, *Disruption and Innovation in the Australian Book Industry* (2016); David Throsby, Jan Zwar and Morgan, *Australian Book Publishers in the Global Industry: Survey Methods and Results* (2018).
21 Authors Guild, *Authors Guild Survey Shows Drastic 42 Percent Decline in Authors Earnings in Last Decade*, 5 January 2019.
22 William Deresiewicz, *The Death of the Artist*, pp. 154–5.
23 Richard Russo and Nicholas Weinstock quoted in *Authors Guild Survey Shows Drastic 42 Percent Decline in Authors Earnings in Last Decade*.
24 Robert Darnton, "Libraries, Books and the Digital Future," p. 18.
25 Darnton, "Libraries, Books and the Digital Future," pp. 18–19.
26 Darnton, "Libraries, Books and the Digital Future," pp. 19, 24.
27 Darnton, "Libraries, Books and the Digital Future," pp. 20, 24.
28 Jay Rosen, "The People Formerly Known as the Audience," in *The Social Media Reader*, pp. 13–16.
29 Cory Doctorow, *Content*, p. 87.
30 Neil Weinstock Netanel considers "The Propertarian Counter-Argument" in his book *Copyright's Paradox*, pp. 154–68.
31 Ronald V. Bettig, *Copyrighting Culture*, p. 7.
32 Bettig, *Copyrighting Culture*, p. 8.
33 Blackstone quoted in Neil Weinstock Netanel, *Copyright's Paradox*, p. 7.
34 Mark Rose, *Authors and Owners*, p. 133.
35 Neil Weinstock Netanel, *Copyright's Paradox*, p. vi.
36 Netanel, *Copyright's Paradox*, p. 6.
37 Netanel, *Copyright's Paradox*, p. 11.
38 Steve Collins, "Kookaburra v. Down Under: It's Just Overkill," pp. 4–5. Collins cites Tim Wu, "Jay-Z versus the Sample Troll: The Shady One-Man Corporation That's Destroying Hip-Hop," in *Slate*, 16 November 2016.
39 Ruth Towse, "Copyright and Economics," p. 64.
40 Janis Ian, "The Internet Debacle: An Alternative View," originally published in *Performing Songwriter Magazine*, May 2002, at: https://www.janisian.com/reading/internet.php.
41 Netanel, *Copyright's Paradox*, p. 11.
42 Netanel, *Copyright's Paradox*, p. 3.
43 Netanel, *Copyright's Paradox*, p. 4.
44 Steve Collins, "Kookaburra v. Down Under: It's Just Overkill," p. 1.
45 Patterson and Lindberg, *The Nature of Copyright: A Law of User's Rights*, p. 66.
46 Steve Collins, "Kookaburra v. Down Under: It's Just Overkill," p. 6.

47 Collins, "Kookaburra v. Down Under: It's Just Overkill," p. 3.
48 Colin Hay quoted in Collins, "Kookaburra v. Down Under: It's Just Overkill," pp. 1, 5.
49 Cameron Adams, "Men at Work's Colin Hay Says Down Under Lawsuit Contributed to Death of His Dad and Bandmate," 10 August 2015, news.com.au at: https://www.news.com.au/entertainment/music/men-at-works-colin-hay-says-down-under-lawsuit-contributed-to-death-of-his-dad-and-bandmate/news-story/db47d17797386c960b7a7737974ea1ce. Accessed 9 April 2021.
50 Collins, "Kookaburra v. Down Under: It's Just Overkill," p. 6.
51 John Perry Barlow, "The Economy of Ideas (Everything You Know about Intellectual Property Is Wrong)."
52 Richard Stallman, *GNU Manifesto* at: https://www.gnu.org/gnu/manifesto.en.html/. Accessed 12 April 2021.
53 Richard Stallman, "About the GNU Project," Free Software Foundation at: https://www.gnu.org/gnu/thegnuproject.en.html/. Accessed 12 April 2021.
54 *Cyberarts99*, pp. 16–17.
55 Joost Smiers and Marieke Van Schijndel, *Imagine There Is No Copyright*, pp. 37–9.
56 Aaron Perzanowski and Kate Darling, *Creativity without Law*, pp. 2–3.
57 Smiers and Van Schijndel, *Imagine There Is No Copyright*, p. 44.
58 William Deresiewicz, *The Death of the Artist*, pp. 52–3.
59 Rebecca Tushnet interviewed by Courtney Majocha in Majocha, "Memes for Sale? Making Sense of NFTs," *Harvard Law Today*, 19 May 2021.
60 Josie Thaddeus-Jones, "What Are NFTs Anyway? One Just Sold for $69 Million," *New York Times*, 11 March 2021.
61 Murray Stassen, "Music-Related NFT Sales Have Topped $25M in the Past Month," *Music Business Worldwide*, 12 March 2021.
62 Walter Benjamin, "The Work of Art in the Age of Mechanical Reproduction," p. 223.
63 Marc Hogan, "Why Do NFTs Matter for Music?" *Pitchfork*, 5 March 2021.
64 Kevin Roose, "Crypto Is Cool. Now Get on the Yacht." *New York Times*, 5 November 2021.
65 Marc Hogan, "Why Do NFTs Matter for Music?" *Pitchfork*, 5 March 2021.

7. Big Data Writing: Author as Algorithm

1 Lev Manovich, *The Language of New Media*, p. 215.
2 Lev Manovich, "Future Fictions," p. 199.
3 Richard Nash, "Culture Is the Algorithm," p. 23.

4 Jean-Marc Deltorn, "Deep Creations: Intellectual Property and the Automata."
5 Randy Kennedy, "News Flows, Consciousness Streams: The Headwaters of a River of Words," pp. 1–2.
6 Ben Rubin and Mark Hansen quoted in Randy Kennedy, "News Flows, Consciousness Streams: The Headwaters of a River of Words," p. 2.
7 Kennedy, "News Flows, Consciousness Streams: The Headwaters of a River of Words," pp. 1–2.
8 Kenneth Goldsmith, *Uncreative Writing: Managing Language in the Digital Age*, quoted by Chris Rodley and Andrew Burrell, "On the Art of Writing with Data," p. 83.
9 Chris Rodley and Andrew Burrell, "On the Art of Writing with Data," p. 84.
10 Borges' story "The Aleph" quoted by Rodley and Burrell, "On the Art of Writing with Data," p. 78.
11 Mark Hansen, "Data-Driven Aesthetics," p. 3.
12 Chris Rodley and Andrew Burrell, "On the Art of Writing with Data," p. 85.
13 Rodley and Burrell, p. 85, quote John Cayley and Daniel Howe, *Common Tongues: Technical Notes* and John Cayley, "Writing to Be Found and Writing Readers."
14 Rodley and Burrell, "On the Art of Writing with Data," p. 85.
15 Andrew Burrell website, "Death of an Alchemist."
16 ELMCIP website, "Death of an Alchemist."
17 Rodley and Burrell, "On the Art of Writing with Data," p. 84.
18 Noah Wardrup-Fruin, "Five Elements of Digital Literature," cited by Rodley and Burrell, "On the Art of Writing with Data," p. 80.
19 Chris Rodley quoted in Sammy Preston, "Twitter Art – Everything Is Going to Be OK :)," *Broadsheet* magazine.
20 Rodley and Burrell, "On the Art of Writing with Data," p. 84.

8. AI vs. the Author

1 GPT-3, "A Robot Wrote This Entire Article. Are You Scared Yet, Human?" *The Guardian*, 8 September 2020.
2 GPT-3, "A Robot Write This Entire Article. Are You Scared Yet, Human?"
3 Richard Barbrook, *Imaginary Futures*, pp. 39–40.
4 Cited in Oona Strathern, *A Brief History of the Future*, p. 183.
5 Bryan Walsh, *End Times: A Brief Guide to the End of the World*.
6 Musk and Hawking cited in Bryan Walsh, *End Times*, p. 240.
7 Patrick Begley and David Wroe, "When Robots Go to War, Who Decides Who Lives and Dies?," *Sydney Morning Herald*, 11–12 November 2017, p. 29.
8 Courtney White and Rita Matulionyte, "Artificial Intelligence: Painting the Bigger Picture for Copyright Ownership," pp. 2, 6.

9   Hannah Fry, *Hello World: Being Human in the Age of Algorithms*, pp. 188–9.
10 Steve Rose, "'It's a War between Technology and a Donkey' – How AI Is Shaking Up Hollywood."
11 Hannah Reich, "Digital Artist Chris Rodley Says Artificial Intelligence Could Spell Death of the Artist," ABC News online.
12 Chin-Chin Yap, "Robocomposing," p. 53.
13 David Cope quoted by Hannah Fry, *Hello World: Being Human in the Age of Algorithms*, p. 189.
14 David Hofstadter quoted by Fry, *Hello World*, p. 189.
15 Hannah Fry, *Hello World: Being Human in the Age of Algorithms*, p. 191.
16 Barthes, "The Death of the Author," pp. 146–7.
17 Annemarie Bridy, "Coding Creativity: Copyright and the Artificially Intelligent Author," p. 2.
18 Mark Twain quoted by Hannah Fry, *Hello World: Being Human in the Age of Algorithms*, p. 193.
19 David Cope quoted by Fry, *Hello World*, p. 193.
20 James Grimmelmann, "There's No Such Thing as a Computer-Authored Work – And It's a Good Thing, Too," p. 403.
21 Rex Shoyoma, "Intelligent Agents: Authors, Makers and Owners of Computer-Generated Works in Canadian Copyright Law," p. 129.
22 Courtney White and Rita Matulionyte, "Artificial Intelligence: Painting the Bigger Picture For Copyright Ownership," p. 28.
23 White and Matulionyte, "Artificial Intelligence," p. 13.
24 Ana Ramalho, "Will Robots Rule the (Artistic) World? A Proposed Model for the Legal Status of Creations by Artificial Intelligence Systems," p. 22.
25 Rex Shoyoma, "Intelligent Agents: Authors, Makers and Owners of Computer-Generated Works in Canadian Copyright Law," p. 129.
26 Annemarie Bridy, "The Evolution of Authorship: Work Made by Code," p. 400.
27 Jared Vasconcellos Grubow, "O.K. Computer: The Devolution of Human Creativity and Granting Musical Copyrights to Artificially Intelligent Joint Authors," p. 423.
28 Courtney White and Rita Matulionyte, "Artificial Intelligence: Painting the Bigger Picture for Copyright Ownership," pp. 20–1.
29 White and Matulionyte, "Artificial Intelligence," p. 22.
30 White and Matulionyte, "Artificial Intelligence," pp. 25–6.
31 Hannah Fry, *Hello World: Being Human in the Age of Algorithms*, p. 193.
32 GPT-3, "A Robot Wrote This Entire Article. Are You Scared Yet, Human?," *The Guardian*, 8 September 2020.
33 Leo Tolstoy and Douglas Hofstadter quoted by Hannah Fry, *Hello World: Being Human in the Age of Algorithms*, p. 194.
34 Fry, *Hello World*, p. 195.

35 Walter Gropius, first proclamation of the Weimar Bauhaus, quoted in Chris Bohn, "We Have No Body to Listen To," p. 98.
36 Rita Matulionyte et al. provide an overview of the "rational and empirical approach to understanding creativity" in "The System of Book Creation: Intellectual Property and the Self-Publishing Sector of the Creative Industries," pp. 192–3.
37 Douglas Hofstadter quoted by Hannah Fry, *Hello World: Being Human in the Age of Algorithms*, p. 194.

9. "Creative Reuse": Post-authorship in Internet Culture

1 DJ Spooky quoted in Andrew Murphie and John Potts, *Culture and Technology*, p. 70.
2 Jessica Litman, "The Public Domain," quoted by Rex Shoyoma, "Intelligent Agents: Authors, Makers and Owners of Computer-Generated Works in Canadian Copyright Law," p. 136.
3 Robin Mackay, "Capitalism and Schizophrenia: Wildstyle in Full Effect," p. 253.
4 Lev Manovich, "Understating Hybrid Media" and Lawrence Lessig, "The People Own Ideas," quoted in Margie Borschke, *This Is Not a Remix: Piracy, Authenticity and Popular Music*, p. 34.
5 Margie Borschke, *This Is Not a Remix: Piracy, Authenticity and Popular Music*, p. 51.
6 Mark Amerika, *remixthebook*, p. xv (italics in original).
7 Amerika, *remixthebook*, p. xi, p. xv (italics in original).
8 Viktor Mayer-Schonberger and Lena Wong, "Fan or Foe: Fan Fiction, Authorship, and the Fight for Control," p. 3.
9 Broede Carmody, "Fan Film about Voldemort Goes Viral," p. 12.
10 Anne Rice quoted in Viktor Mayer-Schonberger and Lena Wong, "Fan or Foe: Fan Fiction, Authorship, and the Fight for Control," p. 10.
11 Bronwen Thomas, "What Is Fan Fiction and Why Are People Saying Such Nice Things about It??" in *Storyworlds: A Journal of Narrative Studies*, Vol. 3, 2011, p. 1.
12 Melanie Kembrew, "We Can Learn from Fan Fiction," p. 31.
13 Rebecca Tushnet, "Architecture and Morality: Transformative Works, Transforming Fans," pp. 171, 178, 187.
14 Astrid Scholte quoted in Melanie Kembrew, "What We Can Learn from Fan Fiction," p. 31.
15 Abigail De Kosnik, *Rogue Archives*, p. 1.
16 De Kosnik, *Rogue Archives*, p. 12.
17 Rebecca Tushnet, "Architecture and Morality: Transformative Works, Transforming Fans," p. 173.

18 Eivind Rossaak, *The Archive in Motion*, p. 12.
19 Ina Blom, "Introduction" in *Memory in Motion: Archives, Technology and the Social*, p. 12.
20 The Kaldor Public Art Projects Digital Archive is at: https://archive.kaldorartprojects.org.au. Accessed 1 May 2021.
21 Michel Foucault, "What Is an Author?," p. 1.
22 Mark Rose, *Authors and Owners*, p. 64.
23 ACMI Website Terms of Use at: https://www.acmi.net.au/about/terms-conditions/websites-terms-of-use/. Accessed 1 May 2021.
24 Archive Of Our Own Terms of Service at: https://archiveofourown.org/tos. Accessed 1 May 2021.
25 Phillipa McGuiness, *Copyfight*, p. 2.
26 Dan Hunter and Nic Suzor, "Claiming the High Ground in the Copyright Wars," pp. 133, 141.
27 Hunter and Suzor, "Claiming the High Ground in the Copyright Wars," p. 136, p. 138.
28 Linda Jaivin, "Big Content," pp. 191, 193, 204.
29 Louis Menand quoted by Phillipa McGuiness, *Copyfight*, p. 8.
30 William Deresiewicz, *The Death of the Artist*, p. 307.
31 Lawrence Lessig, *Remix*, quoted by Phillipa McGuiness, *Copyfight*, p. 8.
32 William Deresiewicz, *The Death of the Artist*, pp. 302–3.
33 Robert Darnton, "Libraries, Books and the Digital Future," p. 24.
34 Daniela Simone, *Copyright and Collective Authorship*, p. 197.
35 *Copy(not)right*, Productivity Commission report quoted in Peter Martin, "Copyright Shake-Up Tips Free Book Imports," *Sydney Morning Herald*, 29 April 2016, p. 5.

Bibliography

Akhundov, Murad D. *Conceptions of Space and Time: Sources, Evolution, Directions*. Translated by Charles Rougle. Cambridge: MIT Press, 1986.
Amerika, Mark. *Remixthebook*. Minneapolis: University of Minnesota Press, 2011.
Armstrong, Karen. *A Short History of Myth*. Edinburgh: Canongate, 2018 (2005).
Authors Guild. *Authors Guild Survey Shows Drastic 42 Percent Decline in Authors Earnings in Last Decade*, 5 January 2019, at: https://www.authorsguild.org/industry-advocacy/authors-guild-survey-shows-drastic-42-percent-decline-in-authors-earnings-in-last-decade/. Accessed 21 April 2021.
Barbrook, Richard. "The High-Tech Gift Economy" (1998) at: http://subsol.c3.hu/subsol_2/contributors3/barbrooktext2.html. Accessed 6 January 2021.
– *Imaginary Futures: From Thinking Machines to the Global Village*. London: Pluto, 2007.
Barlow, John Perry. "The Economy of Ideas (Everything You Know about Intellectual Property Is Wrong)." *Wired* (March 1994): 85–90, 126–9.
Barthes, Roland. "The Death of the Author." In *Image-Music-Text*, edited and translated by Stephen Heath, 142–8. Glasgow: Fontana, 1977 (1968).
– *Elements of Semiology*. Translated by Annette Lavers and Colin Smith. New York: Hill and Wang, 1968 (1964).
– *The Pleasure of the Text*. Translated by Richard Miller. New York: Hill and Wang, 1975 (1973).
– *Sade/Fourier/Loyola*. Translated by Richard Miller. New York: Hill and Wang, 1976 (1971).
– *S/Z*. Translated by Richard Miller. New York: Hill and Wang, 1974 (1970).
Beatles, The. *Anthology*. Edited by Genesis Publications. San Francisco: Chronicle Books, 2000.
Begley, Patrick, and Wroe, David. "When Robots Go to War, Who Decides Who Lives and Dies?" *Sydney Morning Herald* (11–12 November 2017): 29.

Benjamin, Walter. "The Work of Art in the Age of Mechanical Reproduction." In *Illuminations*, 219–53. London: Fontana, 1970.
Bennett, Andrew. *The Author*. London: Routledge, 2005.
Bentley, Gerald Eades. *The Profession of Dramatist in Shakespeare's Time 1590–1642*. Princeton: Princeton University Press, 1971.
Bettig, Ronald V. *Copyrighting Culture: The Political Economy of Intellectual Property*. Boulder: Westview Press, 1996.
Bevir, Mark. *The Logic of the History of Ideas*. Cambridge: Cambridge University Press, 1999.
Blom, Ina, Lundemo, Trond and Rossaak, Eivind eds. *Memory in Motion: Archives, Technology and the Social*. Amsterdam: Amsterdam University Press, 2017.
Bohn, Chris. "We Have No Body to Listen To," *Uncut*, March 2021 (1981): 98–103.
Borges, Jorge Luis. *Ficciones*. New York: Grove Press, 1962 (1956).
Borschke, Margie. *This Is Not a Remix: Piracy, Authenticity and Popular Music*. New York: Bloomsbury, 2017.
Bourdieu, Pierre. *Field of Cultural Production*. New York: Columbia University Press, 1993.
– *The Rules of Art: Genesis and Structure of the Literary Field*. Cambridge: Polity Press, 1996.
Brand, Stewart. *The Media Lab: Inventing the Future at M.I.T.* New York: Penguin, 1987.
Bridy, Annemarie. "Coding Creativity: Copyright and the Artificially Intelligent Author." *Stanford Technology Law Review* 5 (Spring 2012): 1–28. http://doi.org/10.31235/osf.io/5ru6m.
– "The Evolution of Authorship: Work Made by Code." *Columbia Journal of Law and Arts* 39, no. 3 (2016): 395–401. http://doi.org/10.7916/D8CV4J6W.
Burke, Seán ed. *Authorship: From Plato to the Postmodern: A Reader*. Edinburgh: Edinburgh University Press, 2000.
– *The Death and Return of the Author: Criticism and Subjectivity in Barthes, Foucault and Derrida*, third edition. Edinburgh: Edinburgh University Press, 2010.
Burrell, Andrew. "Death of an Alchemist." Andrew Burrell website at: https://andrewburrell.net/projects/death-of-an-alchemist. Accessed 15 April 2021.
Burt, Stephanie. "Flame On." *New Yorker* (15 & 22 February 2021): 70–4.
Butler, Steven, and James Patterson. *Dog Diaries*. London: Penguin, 2018.
Callahan, Vicki ed. *Reclaiming the Archive : Feminism and Film History*. Detroit: Wayne State University Press, 2010.
Calvino, Italo. *If on a Winter's Night a Traveller*. Translated by William Weaver. London: Picador, 1982 (1979).

Carlyle, Thomas. *On Heroes, Hero-Worship, and the Heroic in History*. New York: Appleton & Co., 1941.

Carmody, Broede. "Fan Film about Voldemort Goes Viral." *Sydney Morning Herald* 17 (January 2018).

Caughie, John. *Theories of Authorship: A Reader*. London: Psychology Press, 1981.

Chartier, Roger. *The Order of Books: Readers, Authors and Libraries in Europe between the Fourteenth and Eighteenth Centuries*. Translated by Lydia G. Cochrane. Stanford: Stanford University Press, 1994.

Christie, William. *Samuel Taylor Coleridge: A Literary Life*. Basingstoke: Palgrave Macmillan, 2009.

Coleridge, Samuel Taylor. *The Rime of the Ancient Mariner and Three Other Poems*. London: Folio, 2017 (1816).

Collins, Steve. "Kookaburra v. Down Under: It's Just Overkill." *Scan Journal of Media Arts Culture* 7, no. 1 (2010): http://scan.net.au/scan/journal/display.php?journal_id=145. Accessed 9 April 2021.

Csikszentmihalyi, Mihaly. *The Systems Model of Creativity: The Collected Works of Mihaly Csikszentmihalyi*. Dordrecht: Springer, 2014.

Cubitt, Sean. *Digital Aesthetics*. London: Sage, 1998.

Cyberarts99. Linz: Prix Ars Electronica, 1999.

Darling, Kate and Pezanowski, Aaron eds. *Creativity without Law: Challenging the Assumptions of Intellectual Property*. New York: New York University Press, 2017.

Darnton, Robert. "Libraries, Books and the Digital Future." In *Libraries and Archives in the Digital Age*, edited by Susan L. Mizruchi, 13–25. London: Palgrave Macmillan, 2020.

De Kosnik, Abigail. *Rogue Archives: Digital Cultural Memory and Media Fandom*. Cambridge: MIT Press, 2016.

Dell, Christopher, *The Occult, Witchcraft & Magic: An Illustrated History* (London: Thames & Hudson, 2016).

Deltorn, Jean-Marc. "Deep Creations: Intellectual Property and the Automata." *Frontiers in Digital Humanities* (1 February 2017): https://www.frontiersin.org/articles/10.3389/fdigh.2017.00003/full. Accessed 18 November 2021.

Demers, Joanna. *Steal This Music: How Intellectual Property Law Affects Musical Creativity* Athens: University of Georgia Press, 2006.

Deresiewicz, William. *The Death of the Artist*. New York: Henry Holt, 2020.

Diltz, Henry. "Harvest." *Uncut* (February 2021): 79.

Doctorow, Cory. *Content: Selected Essays on Technology, Creativity, Copyright and the Future of the Future*. San Francisco: Tachyon Publications, 2008.

Dommann, Monika. *Authors and Apparatus: A Media History of Copyright*. Translated by Sarah Pybus. Ithaca: Cornell University Press, 2019.

Droste, Magdalena. *Bauhaus 1919–1923*. Cologne: Taschen, 2002.
Duke, Jennifer. "Google Allows Crime, Says Village Boss." *Sydney Morning Herald* 19 (February 2018): 20.
Dwyer, Michael. "Reluctant Musicians' Hands Out with New Spotify 'Tip Jar.'" *Sydney Morning Herald* 28 (April 2020): 28.
ELMCIP website. "Death of an Alchemist." https://elmcip.net/node/10819. Accessed 15 April 2015.
Erne, Lukas. *Shakespeare as Literary Dramatist*. Cambridge: Cambridge University Press, 2003.
Ernst, Wolfgang. *Digital Memory and the Archive*. Minneapolis: University of Minnesota Press, 2013.
Faber, Michael. "Tree of Codes by Jonathan Safran Foer – Review." *The Guardian* 18 (December 2010): https://www.theguardian.com/books/2010/dec/18/tree-codes-safran-foer-review. Accessed 17 December 2020.
Fernández-Armesto, Felipe. *Ideas That Changed the World*. London: DK, 2004.
Fisher, Steven Roger. *A History of Writing*. London: Reaktion, 2001.
Foer, Jonathan Safran. *Tree of Codes*. London: Visual Editions, 2010.
Foucault, Michel. *The Order of Things: An Archaeology of Human Sciences*. New York: Vintage, 1973 (1966).
– "What Is an Author?" In *Language, Counter-Memory, Practice: Selected Essays and Interviews*, edited by Donald F. Bouchard, translated by Donald F. Bouchard and Sherry Simon, 113–38. Ithaca: Cornell University Press, 1980 (1969).
Freud, Sigmund. "Creative Writers and Day-Dreaming." In *Authorship: From Plato to the Postmodern: A Reader*, edited by Seán Burke, 54–62. Edinburgh: Edinburgh University Press, 2000 (1959).
– *The Interpretation of Dreams*. Translated by James Strachey. London: Penguin, 1976 (1900).
Fry, Hanna. *Hello World: Being Human in the Age of Algorithms*. New York: W.W. Norton, 2018.
Fuller, Simon, and James O'Sullivan. "Structure Over Style: Collaborative Authorship and the Revival of Literary Capitalism." *DHQ: Digital Humanities Quarterly* 11, no. 1 (2017): http://www.digitalhumanities.org/dhq/vol/11/1/000286/000286.html#.
Gilbert, Sandra M., and Susan Gubar. *The Madwoman in the Attic*. Excerpted in *Authorship: From Plato to the Postmodern: A Reader*, edited by Seán Burke, 151–61. Edinburgh: Edinburgh University Press, 2000.
Goldsmith, Kenneth. *Uncreative Writing: Managing Language in the Digital Age*. New York: Columbia University Press, 2011.
GPT-3. "A Robot Wrote This Entire Article. Are You Scared Yet, Human?," *The Guardian* 8 (September 2020): https://www.theguardian.com/commentisfree/2020/sep/08/robot-wrote-this-article-gpt-3. Accessed 21 April 2021.

Grimmelmann, James. "There's No Such Thing as a Computer-Authored Work – And It's a Good Thing, Too." *Columbia Journal of Law and the Arts* 39, no. 3 (2016): 403–16. http://doi.org/10.2139/ssrn.2699862.

Grubow, Jared Vasconcellos. "O.K. Computer: The Devolution of Human Creativity and Granting Musical Copyrights to Artificially Intelligent Joint Authors." *Cardozo Law Review* 40, no. 1 (2018): 387–424.

Hansen, Mark. "Data-Driven Aesthetics." *New York Times*, 19 June 2013, https://bitforms.art/pdfs/bibliography/reas/2013NYTimes.pdf. Accessed 15 April 2021.

Havelock, Eric A. *Preface to Plato*. Cambridge: Bellknap Press, 1963.

Helle, Sophus. "What Is an Author? Old Answers to a New Question." *Modern Language Quarterly* 80, no. 2 (June 2019): 113–39. https://doi.org/10.1215/00267929-7368183.

Henderson, George. *Gothic Art and Civilisation*. London: Folio, 2004 (1967).

Hockney, David, and Martin Gayford. *A History of Pictures: From the Cave to the Computer Screen* London: Thames & Hudson, 2020.

Hogan, Marc. "Why Do NFTs Matter for Music?" *Pitchfork*, 5 March 2021, https://pitchfork.com/thepitch/why-do-nfts-matter-for-music. Accessed 1 December 2021.

Hughes, Robert. *The Shock of the New: Art and the Century of Change*. London: Thames & Hudson, 1992.

Hunter, Dan, and Nic Suzor. "Claiming the High Ground in the Copyright Wars." In *Copyfight*, edited by Phillipa McGuiness, 131–45. Sydney: NewSouth Publishing, 2015.

Ian, Janis. "The Internet Debacle: An Alternative View." In *Performing Songwriter Magazine*, May 2002, https://www.janisian.com/reading/internet.php. Accessed 6 April 2021.

Iljadica, Marta. *Copyright Beyond Law: Regulating Creativity in the Graffiti Subculture*. London: Bloomsbury, 2016.

Jaivin, Linda. "Big Content." In *Copyfight*, edited by Phillipa McGuiness, 191–205. Sydney: NewSouth Publishing, 2015.

Jameson, Frederic. "Postmodernism, or the Cultural Logic of Late Capitalism." In *The Anti-Aesthetic*, edited by Hal Foster, 111–25. New York: Bay Press, 1983.

Johnston, Chris. "Banksy Auction Prank Leaves Art World in Shreds." *The Guardian*, 6 October 2018, https://www.theguardian.com/artanddesign/2018/oct/06/banksy-sothebys-auction-prank-leaves-art-world-in-shreds-girl-with-balloon. Accessed 16 December 2020.

Kaplan, Benjamin. *An Unhurried View of Copyright*. New York: Columbia University Press, 1967.

Kembrew, Melanie. "What We Can Learn from Fan Fiction." *Sun-Herald* 21 July 2019, 31.

Kennedy, Randy. "News Flows, Consciousness Streams: The Headwaters of a River of Words." *New York Times*, 25 October 2007, www.nytimes.com /2007/10/25/arts/design/25vide.html. Accessed 14 December 2020.

Kress, Gunther. *Multimodality: A Social Semiotic Approach to Contemporary Communication*. London: Routledge, 2010.

Kurzweil, Ray. *The Singularity Is Near: When Humans Transcend Biology*. New York: Viking, 2005.

Lacan, Jacques. *The Four Fundamental Concepts of Psycho-Analysis*. Translated by Alan Sheridan. New York: Penguin, 1997 (1973).

Lane, Anthony. "The Mark of Kane." *The New Yorker*, 23 November 2020, 76–7.

Lessig, Lawrence. *Free Culture: How Big Media Uses Technology and the Law to Lock Down Culture and Control Creativity*. New York: Penguin, 2004.

– *Remix: Making Art and Commerce Thrive in the Hybrid Economy*. London: Bloomsbury, 2008.

Levy, Pierre. *Collective Intelligence: Mankind's Emerging World in Cyberspace*. Translated by Robert Bononno. New York: Plenum, 1997.

– "Toward Superlanguage." In *ISEA 94 Catalogue*. Helsinki: University of Art and Design, 1994.

Mackay, Robin. "Capitalism and Schizophrenia: Wildstyle in Full Effect." In *Deleuze and Philosophy: the Difference Engineer*, edited by Keith Ansell Pearson, 247–69. London: Routledge, 1997.

Maclean, Ian. "The Process of Intellectual Change: A Post-Foucauldian Hypothesis." In *Cultural History After Foucault*, edited by John Neubauer, 163–76. New York: Aldine de Gruyter, 1999.

Majocha, Courtney. "Memes for Sale? Making Sense of NFTs." *Harvard Law Today*, 19 May 2021, https://today.law.harvard.edu/memes-for-sale-making-sense-of-nfts. Accessed 30 November 2021.

Man, John. *Alpha Beta: How Our Alphabet Changed the Western World*. London: Headline, 2000.

Manguel, Alberto. *A History of Reading*. London: Flamingo, 1997.

Manovich, Lev. "Future Fictions." *Frieze*, no. 156 (June–August 2013): 199.

– *The Language of New Media*. Cambridge: MIT Press, 2002.

Martin, Peter. "Copyright Shake-Up Tips Free Book Imports." *Sydney Morning Herald*, 29 April 2016, 5.

Marx, Karl. *The Communist Manifesto*. Translated by Samuel Moore. New York: W.W. Norton, 1988 (1848).

Masten, Jeffrey. *Textual Intercourse: Collaboration, Authorship and Sexualities in Renaissance Drama*. Cambridge: Cambridge University Press, 1997.

Matulionyte, R., E. Paton, P. McIntyre, and D. Gleadhill. "The System of Book Creation: Intellectual Property and the Self-Publishing Sector of the Creative Industries." *Creative Industries Journal* 10, no. 3 (2017): 191–210. https://doi.org/10.1080/17510694.2017.1393193.

Mayer-Schonberger, Viktor, and Lena Wong. "Fan or Foe: Fan Fiction, Authorship, and the Fight for Control." *Idea* 54, no. 1 (2013): 1–21.

McGuiness, Phillipa, ed. *Copyfight* Sydney: NewSouth Publishing, 2015.

McLeod, Kembrew. *Freedom of Expression: Overzealous Copyright Bozos and Other Enemies of Creativity*. New York: Doubleday, 2005.

McMahon, Darrin M. *Divine Fury: A History of Genius*. New York: Basic Books, 2013.

McMullan, Gordon. "'Our Whole Life Is Like a Play': Collaboration and the Problem of Editing." *Textus* IX (1996):437–60.

Menand, Louis. "Headcase: Can Psychiatry Be a Science?" *The New Yorker*, 10 March 2010, 68–74.

– "What Do You Know?" *The New Yorker*, 23 November 2020, 67–70.

Meskin, Aaron. "Authorship." In *The Routledge Companion to Philosophy and Film* edited by Paisley Livingston and Carl Plantinga, 12–28. London: Routledge, 2008.

Miller, Nancy K. "Changing the Subject: Authorship, Writing and the Reader." In *Authorship: From Plato to the Postmodern: A Reader*, edited by Seán Burke, 193–211. Edinburgh: Edinburgh University Press, 2000.

Minnis, A.J. *Medieval Theory of Authorship: Scholastic Literary Attitudes in the Later Middle Ages*. London: Scolar Press, 1984.

Mizruchi, Susan L. ed. *Libraries and Archives in the Digital Age*. London: Palgrave Macmillan, 2020.

Munro, Lucy. *Shakespeare in the Theatre: the King's Men*. London: The Arden Shakespeare, 2020.

Murphie, Andrew, and John Potts. *Culture and Technology*. Basingstoke: Palgrave Macmillan, 2003.

Nash, Richard. "Culture Is the Algorithm." In *The Future of Writing*, edited by John Potts, 18–26 Basingstoke: Palgrave Macmillan, 2014.

Nehamas, Alexander. "What an Author Is." *The Journal of Philosophy* 83, no. 11 (November 1986): 685–91. https://doi.org/10.5840/jphil1986831118.

Nesbit, Molly. "What Was an Author?" In *Authorship: From Plato to the Postmodern: A Reader*, edited by Seán Burke, 247–62. Edinburgh: Edinburgh University Press, 2000.

Netanel, Neil Weinstock. *Copyright's Paradox*. Oxford: Oxford University Press, 2008.

Nowell-Smith, Geoffrey. "Six Authors in Pursuit of *The Searchers*." In *Theories of Authorship*, edited by J. Caughie, 221–4. London: Routledge, 1981.

Ong, Walter J. *Orality and Literacy: The Technologizing of the Word*. London: Routledge, 1982.

Paoletti, John T., and Gary M. Radke. *Art in Renaissance Italy*. London: Lawrence King Publishing, 1977.

Parikka, Jussi. *What Is Media Archaeology?* Cambridge: Polity, 2012.

Patterson, Lyman Ray. *Copyright in Historical Perspective*. Nashville: Vanderbilt University Press, 1968.
Patterson, Lyman Ray, and Stanley W. Lindberg. *The Nature of Copyright: A Law of User's Rights*. Georgia: University of Georgia Press, 1991.
Pearlman, Karen. "Editing and Authorship: Writing, Choreographing, Conducting Cinematic Movement in 'The Cool World' and Beyond." *Textual Practice* 35 no. 10 (2021): https://doi.org/10.1080/0950236X.2021.1965291.
– "These Edits Are My Thoughts." https://wfpp.columbia.edu/2020/03/16/after-the-facts/. Accessed 6 January 2021.
Pearlman, Karen, and John Sutton. "Reframing the Director: Distributed Creativity in Filmmaking Practice." In *A Companion to Motion Pictures*, edited by Mette Hjort and Ted Nannicelli. London: Wiley, 2021.
Perzanowski, Aaron, and Kate Darling, eds. *Creativity without Law: Challenging the Assumptions of Intellectual Property*. New York: New York University Press, 2017.
Plato. *Ion*. In Burke, Seán, ed., *Authorship: From Plato to the Postmodern: A Reader*. Edinburgh: Edinburgh University Press, 2000.
– *The Republic*. Translated by Desmond Lee. London: Penguin, 1987.
Polan, Dana. "Auteur Desire." *Screening the Past*, no. 12 (2001): 1–9, http://www.screeningthepast.com/2014/12/auteur-desire/. Accessed 5 January 2021.
Potts, John. ed. *The Future of Writing*. Basingstoke: Palgrave Macmillan, 2014.
– *A History of Charisma*. Basingstoke: Palgrave Macmillan, 2009.
– *Ideas in Time: The Longue Durée in Intellectual History*. Aix-Marseille: Presses Universitaires de Provence, 2019.
– *The New Time and Space*. Basingstoke: Palgrave Macmillan, 2015.
Preston, Sammy. "Twitter Art – Everything Is Going to Be OK :)." *Broadsheet*, 4 July 2013, https://www.broadsheet.com.au/sydney/art-and-design/article/twitter-art-everything-going-be-ok. Accessed 18 April 2021.
Ramalho, Ana. "Will Robots Rule the (Artistic) World? A Proposed Model for The Legal Status of Creations by Artificial Intelligence Systems." *Journal of Internet Law* 21, no. 1 (July 2017): 12–25. http://doi.org/10.2139/ssrn.2987757.
Reagle, Joseph, and Jackie Koerner, eds. *Wikipedia @ 20: Stories of an Incomplete Revolution*. Cambridge: MIT Press, 2020.
Reich, Hannah. "Digital Artist Chris Rodley Says Artificial Intelligence Could Spell Death of the Artist." *ABC News* website, 1 September 2018 at: https://www.abc.net.au/news/2018-09-01/artificial-intelligence-chris-rodley-on-changing-role-of-artist/10188746. Accessed 18 April 2021.
Rimmer, Matthew. "Bangarra Dance Theatre: Copyright Law and Indigenous Culture." *Griffith Law Review* 9, no. 2 (2000): 274–302.
– *Digital Copyright and the Consumer Revolution: Get Your Hands Off My Ipod*. Cheltenham: Edward Elgar, 2007.

Rodley, Chris, and Andrew Burrell. "On the Art of Writing with Data." In *The Future of Writing*, edited by John Potts, 77–89. Basingstoke: Palgrave Macmillan, 2014.

Roose, Kevin. "Crypto Is Cool. Now Get on the Yacht." *New York Times*, 5 November 2021 at: https://www.nytimes.com/2021/11/05/technology/nft-nyc-metaverse.html. Accessed 1 December 2021.

Rose, Mark. *Authors and Owners: The Invention of Copyright*. Cambridge, MA: Harvard University Press, 1993, 77–89.

Rose, Steve. "'It's a War between Technology and a Donkey' – How AI Is Shaking Up Hollywood." *The Guardian*, 16 January 2020, https://www.theguardian.com/film/2020/jan/16/its-a-war-between-technology-and-a-donkey-how-ai-is-shaking-up-hollywood. Accessed 18 April 2021.

Rosen, Jay. "The People Formerly Known as the Audience." In *The Social Media Reader*, edited by Michael Mandiberg, 13–16. New York: New York University Press, 2012.

Ross, Alex. *The Rest Is Noise: Listening to the Twentieth Century*. London: Harper Perennial, 2009.

Rossaak, Eivind, ed. *The Archive in Motion: New Conceptions of the Archive in Contemporary Thought and New Media Practices*. Oslo: Novus Press, 2010.

Sadoul, Georges. Dictionary of Film Makers. California: University of California Press, 1972.

Saggs, H.W.F. *The Babylonians*. London: Folio, 1999 (1988).

Samios, Zoe. "Google Moves to Block Movies Piracy Loophole." *Sydney Morning Herald*, 27 August 2020, 27.

Sarris, Andrew. "Towards a Theory of Film History." In *Movies and Methods*, edited by Bill Nicols. Berkeley: University of California Press, 1976 (1968).

Savage, Mark. "Musicians Will Lose Two-Thirds of Their Income in 2020." *BBC.com*, 18 November 2020, https://www.bbc.com/news/entertainment-arts-54966060. Accessed 21 November, 2021.

Schatz, Tom. *The Genius of the System: Hollywood Filmmaking in the Studio Era*. New York: Henry Holt, 1996.

Schjeldahl, Peter. "What Are Artists For?" *The New Yorker*, 28 December 2020, 92–3.

Schneede, Uwe M. *Surrealism*. Translated by Maria Pelikan. New York: Harry N. Abrams, 1973.

Self, Robert. "Robert Altman and the Theory of Authorship." *Cinema Journal* 25, no. 1 (1985): 3–11. https://doi.org/10.2307/1224836.

Shoyama, Rex M. "Intelligent Agents: Authors, Makers, and Owners of Computer-Generated Works in Canadian Copyright Law." *Canadian Journal of Law and Technology* 4, no. 2 (2005): 129–40.

Simone, Daniela. *Copyright and Collective Authorship*. Cambridge: Cambridge University Press, 2019.

Smiers, Joost, and Marieke Van Schijndel. *Imagine There Is No Copyright and No Cultural Conglomerates Too: An Essay*. Amsterdam: Institute of Network Cultures, 2009.

Stamp, Shelley. 2015. "Feminist Media Historiography and the Work Ahead." *Screening the Past* 40 (2015): 1–11.

Stassen, Murray. "Music-Related NFT Sales Have Topped $25M in the Past Month." *Music Business Worldwide*, 12 March 2021, https://www.musicbusinessworldwide.com/music-related-nft-sales-have-topped-25m-in-the-past-month. Accessed 30 November 2021.

Strathern, Oona. *A Brief History of the Future*. London: Constable & Robinson, 2007.

Sunstein, Cass. *Infotopia: How Many Minds Produce Knowledge*. Oxford: Oxford University Press, 2006.

Taplin, Jonathan. *Move Fast and Break Things: How Facebook, Google and Amazon Have Cornered Culture and What It Means for Us*. New York: Macmillan, 2017.

— "Napster, Spotify and the Fall of the 'Middle-Class Musician.'" *Rolling Stone*, 3 May 2017, https://www.rollingstone.com/culture/culture-news/napster-spotify-and-the-fall-of-the-middle-class-musician-116858/. Accessed 3 April 2021.

Taylor, Andrew. "Fallout over Portrait Win Calls Copyright into Question." *Sydney Morning Herald*, 28 July 2017, 9.

Thaddeus-Jones, Josie. "What Are NFTs Anyway? One Just Sold for $69 Million." *New York Times*, 11 March 2021, https://www.nytimes.com/2021/03/11/arts/design/what-is-an-nft.html?partner=IFTTT. Accessed 30 November 2021.

Thierer, Adam. "The Case for Internet Optimism, Part 1: Saving the Net from Its Detractors." In *The Next Digital Decade: Essays on the Future of the Internet*, edited by Berin Szoka and Adam Marcus, 57–87. Washington: TechFreedom, 2010.

Thomas, Bronwen. "What Is Fan Fiction and Why Are People Saying Such Nice Things about It?" *Storyworlds: A Journal of Narrative Studies* 3 (2011): 1–24. https://doi.org/10.5250/storyworlds.3.2011.0001.

Throsby, David, Jan Zwar, and Callum Morgan. *Australian Book Publishers in the Global Industry: Survey Methods and Results*. Sydney: Macquarie University, 2018.

Timberg, Scott. *Culture Crash: The Killing of the Creative Class*. New Haven: Yale University Press, 2015.

Tomkins, Calvin. "The Whole Thing Is Crazy: How Danh Vo's Art Challenges the Idea of Aesthetic Authorship." *The New Yorker*, 29 January 2018, 46–53.

Towse, Ruth. "Copyright and Economics." In *Music and Copyright*, Second Edition, edited by Simon Frith and Lee Marshall, 54–69. Edinburgh: Edinburgh University Press, 2004.

Tushnet, Rebecca. "Transformative Works, Transforming Fans." In *Creativity without Law: Challenging the Assumptions of Intellectual Property*, edited

by Kate Darling and Aaron Pezanowski, 171–200. New York: New York University Press, 2017.
Ulmer, Gregory. *Internet Intervention: From Literacy to Electracy*. London: Longman, 2003.
Vaidhyanathan, Siva. *Copyrights and Copywrongs: The Rise of Intellectual Property and How It Threatens Creativity*. New York: New York University Press, 2001.
Vickers, Brian. *Shakespeare, Co-Author*. Oxford: Oxford University Press, 2002.
Virilio, Paul. *The Aesthetics of Disappearance*. Translated by Philip Beitchman. New York: Semiotext(e), 1991.
Walsh, Bryan. *End Times: A Brief Guide to the End of the World*. New York: Hachette Books, 2019.
Wardrup-Fruin, Noah. "Five Elements of Digital Literature." In *Reading Moving Letters: Digital Literature in Research and Training. A Handbook*, edited by R. Simanowski, J. Schafer and P. Gendolla, 29–58. Germany: Transcript-Verlag, 2010.
Weizenbaum, Joseph. *Computer Power and Human Reason*. San Francisco: W.H. Freeman & Company, 1976.
Wells, Paul. *Animation: Genre and Authorship*. New York: Wallflower Press, 2002.
White, Courtney, and Rita Matulionyte. "Artificial Intelligence: Painting the Bigger Picture for Copyright Ownership." *Australian Intellectual Property Journal* 30, no. 4 (2020): 224–42. Available at SSRN: https://papers.ssrn.com/sol3/papers.cfm?abstract_id=3498673. Accessed 24 April 2021.
Willis, Roy, ed. *World Mythology: The Illustrated Guide*. London: Duncan Baird Publishers, 1996.
Wimsatt Jr., W.K., and Monroe C. Beardsley. "The Intentional Fallacy." In *Authorship: From Plato to the Postmodern: A Reader*, edited by Seán Burke, 90–100. Edinburgh: Edinburgh University Press, 2000 (1954).
Winchester, Simon. *The Surgeon of Crowthorne*. London: Penguin, 1999.
Woodmansee, Martha. "The Genius and the Copyright: Economic and Legal Conditions of the Emergence of the 'Author.'" *Eighteenth-Century Studies* 17 (1984): 425–48. https://doi.org/10.2307/2738129.
– "On the Author Effect: Recovering Collectivity." In Martha Woodmansee and Peter Jaszi, eds. *The Construction of Authorship*. Durham: Duke University Press, 1994.
Woodmansee, Martha, and Peter Jaszi, eds. *The Construction of Authorship: Textual Appropriation in Law and Literature*. Durham: Duke University Press, 1994.
Wright, Julia. "Female Editors and Representation in the Film and Media Industry." *UCLA: Center for the Study of Women* (2009): https://escholarship.org/uc/item/0pz3k79s. Accessed 5 January 2021.

Wu, Tim. *The Attention Merchants: The Epic Scramble to Get Inside Our Heads.* New York: Knopf, 2017.
Yap, Chin-Chin. "Robocomosing." *Art Asia Pacific,* no. 91 (November/December 2014).
York, Lorraine. *Literary Celebrity in Canada.* Toronto: University of Toronto Press, 2007.
Young, Sherman. *The Book Is Dead, Long Live the Book.* Sydney: UNSW Press, 2007.
Zuboff, Shoshana. *The Age of Surveillance Capitalism: The Fight for a Human Future at the New Frontier of Power.* New York: Public Affairs, 2019.
Zwar, Jan. *Disruption and Innovation in the Australian Book Industry: Case Studies of Trade and Education Publishers.* Sydney: Macquarie University, 2016.
Zwar, Jan, David Throsby, and Thomas Longden. *Australian Authors: Industry Brief No. 1: Key Findings.* Sydney: Macquarie University, 2015.

Index

Abel, Jordan, 37
Aboriginal culture, 67–8
Academy Awards, 44–5, 47
Ackroyd, Peter, 83–4
advertising, 43–4
Akkadia, 63
algorithm, 3, 4, 6–7, 135–45, 148
Althusser, Louis, 98
Amazon, 113, 115, 130, 136, 169
Amerika, Mark, 15, 62, 162–3
anonymous, 17, 18
Apple, 169
appropriation, 38, 39, 41, 104, 105–6, 107
Aristotle, 77
Armstrong, Karen, 64
art, 3, 25, 32–6, 37–9, 41, 104, 105–6, 167, 173
artist, 3, 6, 13, 15, 16
artwork, 3, 7, 9, 36, 39–41
Ashbery, John, 138
auctor, 5, 10, 26, 75, 77, 84
Australian Centre of the Moving Image (ACMI), 167, 168
auteur theory, 44–55
author, 3–7, 44–6, 69, 79, 111–14, 151, 165, 172–3; as agent of texts, 10–11; as algorithm, 135–45; as brand name, 17; collaborative, 19, 20, 22, 38–9, 43, 46; collective, 5, 12, 15, 42–62, 67–8; contemporary, 5, 7, 8, 14–15, 172–3; death of, 6, 92, 99–103; definition of, 9–10, 13; as demiurge, 143–5; dominant, 48; by erasure, 36–7; as factory, 19–22; as hero, 15–16; history of, 63–92; idea of, 70–1; inspiration of, 23–8, 157–9; medieval, 74–8, 84; modern, 8–9, 10–14, 88; multimodal, 61–2; near-death of, 6, 7, 172–3; postmodern, 103–7; Romantic, 5, 6, 15, 16, 27, 88–92, 100, 172; unconscious of, 28–32
author-function, 8, 10, 64–6, 71, 102, 173
authority, 10, 75
authorship, 3, 4, 5, 6, 7, 9, 15, 28, 38, 39–41, 65, 78, 172–3; distributed, 48, 53; of fan fiction, 165; of film, 44–6, 48–50, 53–5; industrial mode of, 20; and literacy, 73; patriarchal, 16, 53, 98; of Wikipedia, 60–1
author's rights, 11, 12, 84–8, 161
autobiography, 18

Bakhtin, Mikail, 94–5, 139
Balinese culture, 67
Bangarra Dance Theatre, 68

Banksy, 35–6
Barthes, Roland, 4, 6, 27, 92, 93, 96–7, 99–106, 153–4, 159, 163, 172
Bauhaus, 98, 143, 158
Bazin, André, 45, 49
Beardsley, Monroe C., 97
Beatles, the, 24, 28
Beckett, Samuel, 140
Belcourt, Billy-Ray, 37
Benjamin, Walter, 21, 98, 104, 106, 132
Bennett, Andrew, 9, 10, 52–3, 75, 77, 91, 92, 102
Bentley, Geoffrey, 81, 83
Berne Convention, 12, 13, 87
Berners-Lee, Tim, 56–7
Bettig, Ronald, 8–9, 13, 119
Bevir, Mark, 12
big data, 3, 6–7, 136
big data writing, 135–45
Big Tech, 56, 112, 113, 115, 117–18, 131, 169–70
Blackstone, William, 119
Blake, William, 88, 90, 91
blockchain, 131–4
blogging, 4
Blom, Ina, 167
Bloom, Harold, 80
Bohler, Danielle, 77
Bonaventure, St, 75, 77
books, 8, 9, 43, 114–16
Borges, Jorge Luis, 105, 139–40
Bourdieu, Pierre, 27, 158
Bourriaud, Nicholas, 38
Brand, Stewart, 126
brand name, 17, 19, 22
Brecht, Bertolt, 94
Breton, André, 30
Bridy, Annemarie, 153–4, 155–6, 157
Brik, Osip, 94
Brinson, Katherine, 38
Burke, Seán, 9, 75, 93, 101
Burrell, Andrew, 139–43

Burroughs, William, 138
Burrow, J. A., 75, 78
by-line, 16, 18

Cage, John, 36–7, 145
Callahan, Vicki, 53
Calvino, Italo, 106
Campbell, Joseph, 95
Campion, Jane, 45
capitalism, 4
Carlyle, Thomas, 16, 91
carnivalesque, 94
Carrier, Joseph, 38
Carringer, Robert, 47
Castillo, Elaine, 165
Caughie, John, 52
Cayley, John, 140
censorship, 14
Cervantes, 79–80, 105
Chaplin, Charlie, 50
charisma, 26
Chartier, Roger, 79–80
Chaucer, Geoffrey, 77–8
China, 13, 67, 71, 74, 156
Christie, William, 31
codex, 71
coding, 3
Coleridge, Samuel Taylor, 26–7, 28, 31–2, 90
collective intelligence, 54–61
Collins, Steve, 121, 124–5
commodity, 8, 9, 13
conceptual art, 41
Confucius, 67
Constructivists, 27, 98, 143
Cope, David, 152, 154
copyleft, 60, 125, 127–8, 164
copyright, 3, 5, 6, 8–9, 12, 13, 33–4, 41, 48, 54–5, 60, 84–8, 105, 108–34, 154–7, 167–8, 169–71, 172–3; infringement of, 6, 14, 88, 108–14, 118, 125–6, 160, 163, 172

Copyswede, 116
COVID-19 pandemic, 110, 131
Creative Commons, 60, 128–9, 161, 168
creative reuse, 3, 7, 15, 160–71
creator, 3, 8, 46
crowd-funding, 130–1
Csikszentmihalyi, Mihaly, 27, 158
Cubitt, Sean, 60
cuneiform script, 69

Dali, Salvador, 30
Dante, 77, 80
Darling, Kate, 129
Darnton, Robert, 115, 116, 170
data, 3, 4, 135–6, 148, 167
deconstruction, 93
Defoe, Daniel, 85
de Kooning, Willem, 36
De Kosnik, Abigail, 165, 168
Del Villano, Bianca, 77
Demers, Joanne, 122
Deresiewicz, William, 108, 112, 113, 170
Derrida, Jacques, 93, 102
design, 44
Dickens, Charles, 87
Dickinson, Emily, 138
digital archive, 7, 163, 166–8
digital commons, 6, 14, 127
Digital Millennium Copyright Act, 113
Digital Public Library of America, 116
digital technology, 6, 46
digitization, 4
Diltz, Henry, 16
discourse, 10, 11
Disney, Walt, 51
DJ Shadow, 104
DJ Spooky, 160, 161
Doctorow, Cory, 118
Dommann, Monika, 111
downloading, 6, 14, 107, 108–14, 160–1

dreams, 29–30
Duchamp, Marcel, 41
Dumas, Alexandre, 21
Dyer, Jo, 68

Eagleton, Terry, 87, 107
Eco, Umberto, 95
Eisenstein, Elizabeth, 78, 84
Eliade, Mircea, 65
Enheduana, 63, 64
Erne, Lukas, 84n69
Ernst, Max, 30
Ernst, Wolfgang, 166–7
Ethereum, 131
Etxebarria, Lucia, 108

Fab 5 Freddy, 35
Facebook, 113, 114, 135
fan fiction, 4, 163–5
Faulkner, William, 30
feminism, 16, 53, 98–9
Fernández-Armesto, Felipe, 64
film director, 44–7
film editor, 53–4
Fincher, David, 47
Foer, Jonathan Safran, 36–7
Fogerty, John, 24
Ford, Henry, 49
Foucault, Michel, 6, 8, 10–13, 18, 43, 44, 93
Frances, Aoife Nessa, 24
Franzen, Jonathan, 103, 107
free culture, 117–18, 160–1, 169
Free Software Foundation, 126
Freud, Sigmund, 29–30, 32, 97
Fry, Hannah, 151, 152, 157–8, 159
Fuller, Simon, 20
Futurists, 27

Gaut, Berys, 49
genius, 5, 16, 80, 87, 91–2
ghostwriter, 18

208 Index

gift economy, 7, 14, 15n20, 60–1, 161, 162–3
Gilbert, Sandra, 16, 98
Gilgamesh, 63, 80
Ginsburg, Jane, 41n35
GNU, 60, 126–7
Godard, Jean-Luc, 45
Goldsmith, Kenneth, 139
Goodwin, Andrew, 104
Google, 112, 113, 114–16, 135–6, 169
Gordy, Berry, 50
GPT-3, 146–7, 157
graffiti art, 32–6, 129
Grimmelmann, James, 154
Gropius, Walter, 98, 158
Grosz, George, 98
Grubow, Jared Vasconcellos, 156
Guardian, The, 146, 157
Gubar, Susan, 16, 98

Ham, Greg, 124–5
Hansen, Mark, 137–9, 140, 141, 143
Havelock, Eric, 73
Hawking, Stephen, 150
Hay, Colin, 124–5
Heartfield, John, 98
Helle, Sophus, 65, 77
Helm, Levon, 110–11
Henderson, George, 76
Hendren, Holly, 150
hero, 5, 15–16, 91
Hitchcock, Alfred, 17, 45
Hofstadter, David, 152, 158, 159
Hogan, Marc, 133
Hollywood, 49–50, 52
Homer, 66, 71, 72
Hopkins, Don, 127
Hoskin, Teri, 62
Howe, Daniel, 140
Hunter, Dan, 169

Ian, Janis, 122
Ijadica, Marta, 34, 129

Iliad, The, 63, 66, 80
India, 67, 74
Indigenous culture, 67–8
individual, 9, 42–3
individualism, 9
information, 6, 14
inspiration, 5, 23–8, 157–9
intention, 97, 100
internet, 3, 4, 5, 7, 14–15, 88, 107, 116, 126
Internet Archive, 116
intertextuality, 94, 104
Islamic culture, 71, 74

Jaivin, Linda, 169
James, E. L., 163
Jameson, Frederic, 107
Jaszi, Peter, 42–3
Johns, Jasper, 36
Johnson, Samuel, 86, 87
Joyce, James, 30, 32, 139

Kael, Pauline, 47
Kaldor Public Art Projects Digital Archive, 167, 168
Kaplan, Benjamin, 13
Kembrew, Melanie, 165
Kennedy, Randy, 138
Kernan, Alvin, 86
Kickstarter, 130–1
Kimmelman, Burt, 78
King, Stephen, 17, 20, 103
Kitses, Jim, 49
Koerner, Jackie, 58
Kopinor, 116
Kress, Gunther, 61–2
Kristeva, Julia, 94
Kubrick, Stanley, 149
Kurzweil, Ray, 149–50

Lacan, Jacques, 97
Lakin, Shaune, 39
Landy, Michael, 167

laptop, 4
Larrikin Music Publishing, 123–5
Lee, Stan, 51
Legal Deposit Libraries, 168
Lennon, John, 24
Lessig, Lawrence, 88, 11, 170
Levine, Sherrie, 105, 106
Lévi-Strauss, Claude, 95–6
Levy, Pierre, 55, 61
Linx, 127
Locke, John, 85, 86, 119

Macherey, Pierre, 98
Maclean, Ian, 12
magazines, 8
Manguel, Alberto, 70–1
Mankiewicz, Herman J., 47
Manovich, Lev, 135
Martial, 71–2
Marx, Karl, 4
Marxism, 97–8
Matulionyte, Rita, 155, 156–7
Mayakovsky, 98
McCarthy, John, 149
McCartney, Paul, 24, 28–9, 30
McGuiness, Phillipa, 169
McMahon, Darrin, 91
Menand, Louis, 169–70
Meskin, Aaron, 11, 45–6
Mesopotamia, 25, 64, 68–71
metaverse, 134
Miller, Nancy K., 99
Minnis, A. J., 10, 78
Minsky, Marvin, 149
Milton, John, 80, 87
Mitchell, Joni, 16
Modernism, 97–8, 104
moral rights, 876
Morrison, Van, 15
Motown, 50–1
MP3 files, 6, 109
multimodal writing, 61–2
Murray, James, 59

Muses, 26
Musk, Elon, 150

name, 15–17, 20
Napster, 6, 109
Naremore, James, 48
Nash, Richard, 136
Nehamas, Alexander, 10–11
Nesbit, Molly, 11, 12–13
Netanel, Neil Weinstock, 120, 123
Netflix, 136
network culture, 4, 107, 160, 173
neuro-science, 24, 32
newspapers, 8
Newton, Isaac, 88
NFTs, 131–4
Nowell-Smith, Geoffrey, 11

Ong, Walter J., 66–7, 73, 79
open source, 3, 43, 127, 163
Open Source Initiative, 127
oracle, 25
orality, 63, 65–7
originality, 13, 86–7, 91, 120
O'Sullivan, James, 20
Oxford English Dictionary, 58–9

parody, 123
Parry, Milman, 66
Patreon, 130
patronage, 9, 13–14, 71, 79 80, 83, 86, 129–30
Patterson, James, 19–22
Patterson, Lyman Ray, 13
Paul, 26
Pearlman, Karen, 46, 53–4
peer-to-peer networks, 6, 88, 109
Perzanowski, Aaron, 129
Picasso, Pablo, 65, 92
piracy, 112, 113
plagiarism, 71–2
Plato, 26, 65, 66–7, 71–4
poets, 26, 63, 65, 66–7, 71–4

Polan, Dana, 52
Pollock, Jackson, 92
Pope, Alexander, 85
popular fiction, 19, 20
post-authorship, 7, 15, 160–8, 172
post-industrialism, 4, 16, 126
postmodernism, 6, 103–7
post-structuralism, 4, 93, 96–7, 101
Prince, Richard, 105, 106
printing press, 8, 9, 78–9, 126
prophet, 25
Propp, Vladimir, 95
proprietorship, 9, 14
public domain, 7, 14, 127, 160–1

Quilter, Joseph, 33
Quinones, Lee, 35

Ramalho, Ana, 155
Randall, Alice, 122–3
Rauschenberg, Robert, 36
Reagle, Joseph, 58
Reformation, 79
relational aesthetics, 38
remix culture, 3, 7, 15, 161–3
Renaissance, 9, 11, 74
Rice, Anne, 164, 165
Rime, 34
Rodley, Chris, 139–43, 151–2
Romantics, 88–92
Rose, Mark, 8–9, 13, 14, 84, 86, 87, 111, 119–20
Rosen, Jay, 55
Ross, Alex, 37
Rossaak, Eivind, 166
Rowling, J. K., 103, 164
royal privilege, 79
Rubin, Ben, 137–9, 140, 141, 143
Russian Formalists, 27, 93–5

Sadoul, Georges, 53
Saggs, H. W. F., 70
sampler, 6, 104

Sanger, Larry, 57
Sarris, Andrew, 45
Saussure, Ferdinand de, 96
scanner, 6, 104
Scholte, Astrid, 165
Schulz, Bruno, 36–7
Scorsese, Martin, 45, 53
scriptor, 5, 6, 75, 84, 100, 105, 152–4, 159, 172–3
scriptwriter, 46–7
search engine, 135
Self, Robert, 53
semiotics, 95, 96–7
Shakespeare, William, 9, 80–4, 140
shaman, 25, 64
Shelley, Mary, 88–9
Shelley, Percy Bysshe, 15, 90, 92
Shklovsky, Viktor, 94
Shoyoma, Rex, 154–5
Shub, Esfir, 54
Simone, Daniela, 12, 41, 48, 50, 54–5, 59–60, 61, 67–8, 170
Simonides, 71
Sinclair, Marion, 123–4
smart phone, 4
Smiers, Joost, 128–9
songwriters, 23–5, 27, 108, 110, 112, 124–5
Sotheby's, 35
Soviet Union, 98
Spotify, 109, 136
Stallman, Richard, 126–7
Stationers' Company, 79, 85
Statute of Anne, 5, 85
streaming, 6, 14, 108–14
structuralism, 6, 95–6
studio system, 45, 48–51
Substack, 130
Sumerians, 69
Surrealism, 30
Sutton, John, 53
Suzor, Nicolas, 69

tablet, 4
Taplin, Jonathan, 56, 110–11, 112–13
Taylor, Frederick, 50
technologies, 4
Thomas, Bronwen, 164
Thomas, Sue, 62
Timberg, Scott, 112
Tiravanija, Rirkrit, 38
Todorov, Tzvetan, 94
Toland, Greg, 49
Towse, Ruth, 121
trAce Online Writing Centre, 62
transformative writing, 4, 163–5
Trigg, Stephanie, 78
Truffaut, François, 45
Turing, Alan, 148–9
Tushnet, Rebecca, 131, 165, 166
Twain, Mark, 154
Twitter, 135, 140, 141

Ulmer, Gregory, 61
unconscious, 28–32

Van Schijndel, Marieke, 128–9
Varga, Justine, 39–41
Vasari, Giorgio, 76
video games, 51
Vile, Kurt, 24
Village Roadshow, 108, 114
Virilio, Paul, 149
Vo, Danh, 37–9

Waldrop-Fruin, Noah, 143
Wales, Jimmy, 57
Wallace, David Foster, 107
Walsh, Bryan, 150
Warhol, Andy, 27, 92, 104
Web 2.0, 55, 133
Web3, 131, 133, 134
Weizenbaum, Joseph, 157
Welles, Orson, 45, 49
White, Courtney, 155, 156–7
Wikipedia, 3, 43, 57–61
Willis, Roy, 64
Wimsatt, Jr, W. K., 97
Winfrey, Oprah, 103
Wong, Martin, 38
Woodmansee, Martha, 13, 42–3, 91
Woolf, Virginia, 30
Wordsworth, William, 91
World Wide Web, 4, 55, 56
writers, 17–18, 43–4
writing, 69–74
Wu, Timothy, 56

Yap, Chin-Chin, 152
York, Lorraine, 103
Young, Edward, 86–7
Young, Neil, 16
Young, Sherman, 43
YouTube, 113, 164

Zuboff, Shoshana, 56

www.ingramcontent.com/pod-product-compliance
Lightning Source LLC
Chambersburg PA
CBHW052210090526
44584CB00016BA/1890